MASTERING
the ART *of*
FRENCH
EATING

Ann Mah

MASTERING
the ART *of*
FRENCH
EATING

*Lessons
in Food and Love
from a Year
in Paris*

PAMELA DORMAN BOOKS
VIKING

VIKING

Published by the Penguin Group
Penguin Group (USA) LLC
375 Hudson Street
New York, New York 10014

USA | Canada | UK | Ireland | Australia | New Zealand | India | South Africa | China
penguin.com
A Penguin Random House Company

First published by Viking Penguin, a member of Penguin Group (USA) LLC, 2013

Copyright © 2013 by Ann Mah

A Pamela Dorman Book / Viking

LIBRARY OF CONGRESS CATALOGING-IN-PUBLICATION DATA
Mah, Ann.
Mastering the art of French eating : lessons in food and love from a year in Paris / Ann Mah.
pages cm
Includes index.
ISBN 978-0-670-02599-2
1. Mah, Ann.—Travels—France. 2. Gastronomy—France. 3. Cooking, French—Anecdotes. 4. Diplomats' spouses—United States—Biography. 5. Chinese Americans—France—Paris—Biography. 6. Paris (France)—Social life and customs—21st century.
I. Title. II. Title: Lessons in food and love from a year in Paris.
TX637.M34 2013
641.5944—dc23
2013016794

Printed in the United States of America
1   3   5   7   9   10   8   6   4   2

Set in Fournier MT Std
Designed by Francesca Belanger

*Penguin is committed to publishing works of quality and integrity.
In that spirit, we are proud to offer this book to our readers;
however, the story, the experiences, and the words
are the author's alone.*

To *la belle France*,
and her home cooks, *fromagers, charcutiers, boulangers,* chefs,
and other food artisans who continue to preserve a fine art.

And to my husband, who took me there.

France was my spiritual homeland: it had become a part of me, and I a part of it, and so it has remained ever since.

—*My Life in France,* Julia Child with Alex Prud'homme

The pleasures of the table belong to all times and all ages, to every country and every day; they go hand in hand with all our other pleasures, outlast them, and remain to console us for their loss.

—*The Physiology of Taste,* Jean-Anthelme Brillat-Savarin

Acknowledgments

My thanks to Deborah Schneider, fellow food lover and Francophile, for her constant encouragement and enthusiasm. Pamela Dorman, whose brilliant editing pushed and inspired me. Kiki Koroshetz, for her keen edits and cheerful efficiency. My friends and former colleagues at Pamela Dorman Books/Viking and Penguin, who worked so hard on this book and welcomed me home with such warmth: Clare Ferraro, Kathryn Court, Francesca Belanger, Carolyn Coleburn, Maureen Donnelly, Bruce Giffords, Kristin Matzen, Patrick Nolan, Roseanne Serra, Maureen Sugden, Nancy Sheppard, John Fagan, Hal Fessenden, Leigh Butler, and the rights team; Dick Heffernan, Norman Lidofsky, and their sales teams. Thanks also to Cathy Gleason, Michael Lin, Geoff Martin, and Katie McGowan. My heartfelt gratitude to Susan Hans O'Connor for her astute editorial suggestions and friendship.

Excerpts from *As Always Julia: The Letters of Julia Child and Avis DeVoto*, edited by Joan Reardon. Copyright © 2010 by Joan Reardon. Used by permission of Houghton Mifflin Harcourt Publishing Company. All rights reserved.

In France, I am grateful to Jérôme Avenas; Lucette Baudin and her late husband, André Baudin; Solange Brihat; Katia Grimmer-Laversanne; Sylvain Laversanne; Kim Lê Minh; Camille Malmquist; Jennifer Mayle; Alain Miquel; Didier Miquel; Ann Morrison; Judith Pillsbury; Erin Reeser; Steve Rhinds; Arnaud Rohmer; Charlie Trueheart; Anna Tunick; Lucy Vanel; René Vogel; my colleagues at the American Library in Paris—and all the friends who shared their knowledge and helped make Paris feel like home.

Contents

ACKNOWLEDGMENTS

ix

Introduction

1

Chapter 1

Paris / Steak Frites

7

Chapter 2

Troyes / Andouillette

29

Chapter 3

Brittany / Crêpes

55

Chapter 4

Lyon / Salade Lyonnaise

75

Chapter 5

Provence / Soupe au Pistou

99

Chapter 6

Toulouse, Castelnaudary, Carcassonne / Cassoulet

129

Chapter 7

Alsace / Choucroute

157

Chapter 8

Savoie & Haute-Savoie / Fondue

181

Chapter 9

Burgundy / Boeuf Bourguignon

203

Chapter 10

Aveyron / Aligot

231

Epilogue—Rue de Loo

261

INDEX

267

MASTERING
the ART *of*
FRENCH
EATING

Introduction

Before we moved to Paris, in the summer of 2008, my husband, Calvin, and I used to pore over the atlas of France. I would stand in the kitchen cooking dinner, and he would lean on the counter, keep my wineglass filled, and turn the book's wide pages. He'd read the names of regions out loud—Alsace, Bretagne, Champagne, Provence, Normandie—and we would dream about renting a car and circling the country, a road trip to the regions with the food we wanted to eat. Of course, this being France, that narrowed down the list to almost everywhere.

We talked about the road trip a lot as we crunched toast on Sunday mornings. We listened to the Charles Trenet song "Route Nationale 7" and dreamed about the *route des vacances,* about the highway that makes a recipe. We read books set in hilltop Provençal villages and bourgeois Left Bank apartments. And yet I don't think either one of us ever really thought we would take the trip. At the time we were living in New York, then Beijing, then Washington, D.C., moving every three years or so, blown hither and yon by Calvin's job as a diplomat. "Maybe when we're retired," we said. "We'll rent a car and drive everywhere in France. . . ." And so the fantasy began anew. But retirement was decades away.

In the fall of 2007, Paris couldn't have been further from our minds. We had just moved to Washington, D.C., after four years in China. Calvin was traveling to Asia for work almost two weeks out of every month. And at thirty-two years old, I was struggling to ignite a career as a freelance food writer in a town whose favorite dish was power. But the wonderful, terrible thing about foreign-service life is that you move all the time. Our stint in Washington was for only a year, and by October, Calvin was already bidding on his next assignment. He put France on the list with lots of hope but very little expectation. Yet somehow, against all odds, we found out we were going to Paris.

In the months before the move, I could barely talk about it. I was petrified that any discussion, any expression of joy, any speculation about *supermarchés* or métro stops, would jinx everything. It just seemed too good to be true—a three-year sojourn in Paris with my favorite person, a chance to try the 246 varieties of cheese that de Gaulle had joked about, an opportunity to discover the cuisine of *la belle France*, to taste things that I had both read and dreamed about for half my life. And—the crowning flourish of shaved truffles— we would finally get to take the road trip. So I held my breath as we packed boxes, bought towels and sheets, and ticked off the days one by one. I held it throughout seven weeks of French immersion at a language school in rural Vermont. I held it as I stepped onto the plane in Washington and off it at Roissy, on the RER commuter rail, all the way to the Left Bank. And there, inside our new apartment, my mind dizzy with jet lag and happiness, I lay down on the bare parquet floor, stared up at the ornate crown molding, and sighed.

Perhaps I exhaled too soon. For we had scarcely unpacked our boxes and picked a favorite local *boulangerie* when Calvin got called away. To Baghdad. For a year. I stayed in Paris because Iraq was one of the few places in the world where we couldn't be together. Instead of the shared adventure I had anticipated, I found myself navigating a new country, a new language, and a new culture alone while trying to keep the worry and loneliness at bay. Paris was still its elegant, gold-tipped, gleaming, curlicued self—as heartbreakingly lovely up close as when I'd dreamed about it from afar—but my dream of living there had changed.

At first I wasn't sure how to maneuver myself *toute seule*. I missed my husband like an internal organ, and the city, which had seemed so quaintly formal when we were together—with its *bonjours* and *bonsoirs*, and four-course-dinner parties, and cheek kisses instead of hugs—felt a little cold now that I was alone. I wandered with trepidation, conscious of my American accent and Asian face and unsure grasp of French verbs. How could I find a place in this city that was so elegant and so uninviting? It felt like a herculean challenge, which I realized afresh every time I bought vegetables in the market and the *vendeur* corrected my French. (Me: *Un botte de carottes, s'il vous plaît?* Him: *UNE botte. UNE! UNE!*)

And then, somewhere in the midst of navigating new markets and memorizing new vocabulary, I remembered the wife of another American diplomat, a woman who had lived here sixty years earlier, another trailing spouse who needed a push to find her way: Julia Child.

Julia Child came to Paris because of the career of her husband, Paul Child. At first she was just another embassy spouse—albeit one who loved to eat—but when she started taking cooking classes at the Cordon Bleu, her path unfurled in a clear direction, one guided by food. Living in France and studying French cuisine changed her life. Food gave her a structure, a reason to ask questions, read history, explore, learn. It gave her a voice.

As I leafed through the butter-spattered pages of my copy of *Mastering the Art of French Cooking*, it occurred to me that the book could provide a basic itinerary for the road trip that Calvin and I had talked about for so many years. The recipes spanned the country—

from Burgundy's beef stew to Provence's vegetable soup to the cassoulet of the southwest. But although each one offered practical head notes and precise instructions, I found myself wanting more information, itching for the story behind the dishes. Did people from Burgundy *really* eat boeuf bourguignon? Why was the wild and rocky coast of Brittany famous for buckwheat crêpes? How did pistou—which sounded an awful lot like "pesto"—end up in Provence?

And then there were the French dishes Julia and her coauthors *hadn't* included. Was cheese fondue Swiss or French? Was choucroute garnie French or German? Was there a penchant in Troyes for tripe before the city started producing that most divisive of French sausages, andouillette? (And why was it always labeled AAAAA, as if it were trying to appear first in the phone book?)

The longer I lived in France, the more I ate. And the more I ate, the more questions I had. I yearned to discover French regional cuisine, and, I soon realized, the only way to truly understand it was to visit the regions themselves, to be curious, explore, taste, learn. In France dining is meant to be a special, pleasurable part of the day; food offers not only fuel for the body but also a connection—between the people who have joined you at the table, between the generations who have shared a recipe, between the *terroir* (the earth) and the culture and cuisine that have sprung from it. Separate from cooking, the very act of *eating* is in itself an art to master.

The story I tell here is of ten different regions of France and their signature dishes, of the link between history and place, culture and cuisine. I chose these ten dishes and regions because of their significance in the United States or, as is the case with Aveyron, because of its significance to me. But the list is not meant to be comprehensive—I could, for example, write an entire second volume on the ten *least*-known dishes of French cuisine—and there are many regions and foods of France that I still look forward to discovering. This book is also the story of one American woman who was lucky enough to live in Paris for a while, of a solitary year mixed with loneliness and discovery, of creating a home when you move every few years, of building a life that balances work and personal ambition with love and family—and food.

"People who love to eat are always the best people," said Julia Child. During my sojourn in France, I met many of these best people, and all of them—from chefs to *charcutiers* to home cooks to representatives of local *offices du tourisme* and so many others—touched me with their generosity and kindness, their infectious enthusiasm for their region. I hope this book honors their stories and work and recipes. For various reasons, I have compressed time in some instances, condensing the events of two years into one; I've also changed the names and identifying details of some friends and family; the names of the food professionals I interviewed, however, are all real.

I've always felt there are two states of existence: being in Paris and being out of it. This is the story of my time in the first state, before I returned to the second. The four years I spent in Paris felt like the shortest of my life, except for one—the year Calvin was in Baghdad—which was the longest. It changed me, of course, living in France—Julia Child could have told me that it would—even though, like a lot of big things, the change crept up on me little by little. Bite by bite. Which, I suppose, is the only way to savor life.

As they say in French, *bonne continuation*.

Chapter 1

Paris / Steak Frites

I'm not a voracious carnivore, but there's something about being in Paris that makes me want to sink my teeth into a bloody piece of beef. Perhaps it's the French paradox, the seductive theory that a diet rich in cheese, meat, and red wine actually lowers cholesterol. Perhaps it's watching all those sexy French women purse their lipsticked mouths while slicing through a juicy chop.

Steak frites is a relatively easy thing to order if, like me, you're still struggling to master those nasal French vowels. The words fly off the tongue, without any hidden surprises—unlike, say, asking the waiter about preservatives only to find out you've interrogated him on condoms. But, as I found out during one of my first meals in a classic Paris bistro, ordering a steak leads to more questions.

"Quel cuisson désirez-vous?" said the waiter in an offhand way, like asking my date of birth or my hair color. He wore round glasses, a white shirt with a black bow tie, and a long black apron that reached past his knees. It was difficult to discern who was older: him or the desiccated leg of ham hanging from the ceiling in the middle of the room.

Thus far I had tricked the waiter into thinking I spoke French, but now, I realized, the jig was up. Medium, I thought, and tried a quick, desperate translation. "Uh . . . *moyen?*"

A look of weary disappointment crossed his face. But he'd been around enough American tourists to know what I meant. *"À point,"* he corrected me.

Later I would memorize all my steak vocabulary—the hot sear and chilled interior of *bleu*, the rosy glow of *à point*, the tough brown gnaw of *bien cuit*. I would learn how to enjoy a steak the French way—*saignant*—with a magenta center and juices that ran red. But at that moment I just repeated the words after him and washed them down with a gulp of wine.

I've wanted to live in Paris since I was six, when my family and I took a summer vacation to Europe. We went to London first, gray and proper, where we spent a week shivering into our teacups, even though it was mid-July, and I stared in terrified fascination at the Mohawked punks in Piccadilly Circus. Then we arrived in Paris, which was ablaze in a high-summer heat wave. It seemed alive, Paris, alive with warmth, and days that never ended, and beautiful people on the streets wearing beautiful clothes and speaking a beautiful, strange language. Every aspect of the city assailed my senses: the grand buildings in pale limestone, the parks teeming with half-naked sunbathers, the taste of baguette dipped in chocolat chaud, the seesawing sound of the sirens, the imprint of wicker café chairs against my sticky thighs, the Coca-Cola poured from chilled glass bottles that turned tepid without ice cubes, the smell of fresh croissants and ripe cheese and human sweat. It was all so new and different from the only place I really knew, our home in the sterile suburbs of Southern California. I didn't like everything, but it all gripped me, holding me in an embrace that I would come to know was Francophilia.

The trip has gone down in Mah family lore as the nadir (or zenith, depending on who you're talking to) of my brother's rebellious teenage years. He spent a lot of time plugged into his Walkman while my parents coped by drinking red wine. As our voyage continued, they—my parents and brother—seemed to grow more and more matted and worn, more impatient to return home to their own routines and clothes and space. In contrast, I became more energetic as the days passed.

"I want to learn French," I proclaimed. It felt like my destiny. After all, hadn't my parents given me a French name, Ann Marie? They responded with wan enthusiasm, dampened even further by the sticky oppression of our hotel room. We'd had a long week of sightseeing, my parents juggling the manic highs of their nursery-rhyme-chanting young daughter with the manic lows of their adolescent son. My mother considered French impractical, a pastel bonbon of a language, the linguistic equivalent of empty calories, unlike her native tongue, the useful, fibrous Mandarin Chinese. If you have any experience at all with Chinese mothers, I'm sure it will come as no surprise that I ended up studying Mandarin.

By the time I made another trip to Paris, twenty-two years had passed. The second visit was with my husband, Calvin, who had lived there for a few years during and after college. He showed me two sides of the city—his old haunts in Belleville, a scruffy neighborhood in the twentieth arrondissement, contrasted by the sweeping grandeur of Haussmann's boulevards. Unlike so many childhood memories revisited, Paris didn't disappoint. The city was on its best behavior during that vacation, all bright, clear June skies, a profusion of flowers in the Luxembourg Gardens, and unusually patient waiters who refrained from speaking English when I tried to order in French. They say you're supposed to be in love in Paris, and I was, headily—with my husband, with the beautiful city, with the slim flutes of Champagne we drank while gazing at the rushing fountain on place Saint-Sulpice.

Is Paris addictive? Maybe. After that trip I abandoned all other holiday dreams. Every penny saved, every vacation week earned, was earmarked for France. We visited in the winter to shiver under covered skies that never brightened; we went in the summer to bask in the sizzle of light that stretched until eleven o'clock at night. And each time I left, I craved more. More crusty baguettes split lengthwise and spread with butter and jam. More wrought-iron balconies adorned with window-box geraniums. More Art Nouveau métro stations, more walks along the Seine, more surprise glimpses of Notre Dame caught from the bus.

When I wasn't in Paris, I sometimes dreamed of living there, of making a home in one of the ornate stone buildings that give the city such elegant propriety. What would it be like, I wondered, to become part of a neighborhood, to be greeted at the café with a handshake, to have the woman at the *boulangerie* prepare my baguette without asking, to commute home by crossing the Seine? I wanted to know bus routes, to have secret shortcuts, to greet neighbors with a murmured *"Bonjour."* Most of all I wanted to watch the seasons change in the market, to consume and contribute to my own small patch of French *terroir*, to participate—if only for a short window of time—in the small, prosaic, unbroken traditions of French cuisine. I wanted to buy a galette des rois on Epiphany and chocolate bells on Easter and foie gras at Christmas. I wanted those traditions to be mine, however temporarily, even though I knew that was a dream both impractical and abstract. We had American passports, not European ones. How could we navigate France's notoriously Sisyphean bureaucracy? How would we support ourselves without working papers? How on earth would we ever convince one of its wooden-faced civil servants to allow us to stay?

There *was* one possibility but I didn't believe it would ever happen. Calvin's career as a diplomat meant we moved often between overseas assignments—he'd already served in Turkmenistan, New York, Beijing, and D.C. Why not Paris? And yet it seemed far-fetched to hope for such a plum assignment, even though Calvin spoke fluent French and followed French politics as avidly as he did the National League baseball standings. The American embassy in Paris was one of the most desired posts in the world, often considered a reward after hardship tours in places like Africa or Haiti, or unaccompanied stints in war zones. But now the unbelievable had happened.

We were in rural Pennsylvania, on our way to visit Calvin's grandparents in State College, when we stopped for gas at a rest stop, Calvin checked his e-mail, and we discovered the good news. Later, in our motel room, I didn't sleep the whole night, my mind dancing with images of picnic lunches in the Luxembourg Gardens, and casual glimpses of the Eiffel Tower, and late-night ice cream cones licked while crossing the Seine. It seemed impossible to believe— too good to be true—that we would live in Paris, together, each with our own work that we loved. The frustration I'd felt over the challenges of trailing-spousehood—lack of a steady job, lack of a steady home, distance from friends and family, loss of independence and identity—melted away with the promise of three years in Paris. Some lucky confluence of fate and aligning stars had brought us to the City of Light. Or, for me, the City of Dreams.

Before I moved to Paris, back when I was an American who fantasized about living there, I had an image of the perfect café. It had mirrored columns and a zinc bar, rattan chairs and sidewalk tables where I would nurse a glass of red wine while watching the world pass by. Grumpy waiters would serve up succulent steaks, charred on the outside, rosy within, tender enough for a knife to slip through, paired with a pile of crisp frites to mop up all the juices.

Once I got to Paris, I found out that plenty of cafés fulfilled different parts of my fantasy—some had historic charm oozing out of the coffee machine, others were modern with square plates and a list of overly sweet cocktails, still others had sun-drenched *terrasses* where I could indulge in a *citron pressé* on a summer afternoon. The café nearest to our apartment had rattan chairs and sidewalk tables; its owner, Amar, came from Tunisia, and I loved his couscous. But despite their differences, there were a few elements that tied all these cafés together: the coffee, the wine, and the steak.

The more meals I ate in Paris, the more I wanted to know: What makes the perfect steak frites? And how did it become the town's favorite plat du jour?

The meal's basic ingredients—beef, potatoes—don't point back to Paris. Cattle are not traditionally raised in the surrounding area, and *frites*—or French fries—come, arguably, from Belgium. Perhaps its popularity lies in the dearth of options on a typical café menu, so few choices that most French people know what they're going to order before they even sit down. Or perhaps—as William Bernet, a former butcher and owner of the lauded Paris steak bistro Le Severo, told me—it's because of the rush of city life. "A piece of seasoned meat, it cooks in an instant—and it's fast to eat," he said.

Steak was brought to France by occupying English forces, sometime after the Battle of Waterloo in 1815. Even the word comes from the other side of the Channel, derived from the Old Norse *steikjo*, which means "to roast." In fifteenth-century England, cooks dished up their meat sizzling, sprinkled with cinnamon, but by the time of Napoleon's defeat it was eaten plain, without sauce. As is true today, steaks were originally cut from the sirloin, rump, or fillet—that is, the animal's loin—though modern butchering techniques vary among countries and cultures. Talk to any butcher and he'll convince you that his method produces the best, most bountiful and tender pieces of meat.

Steak is a relatively easy thing to prepare—season it, slap it into a hot pan, don't overcook—but while talking to meat aficionados, I quickly learned about the skill and patience required for a superior version of the dish. When I arrived in Paris, a food-loving American friend sent me to the southern edge of the city to the fourteenth arrondissement, to visit William Bernet at Le Severo. Who better could explain the intricacies of a hunk of beef and a few fried potatoes?

Bernet is a thickset man with the observant eyes of an experienced waiter and professorial-style glasses that slide down his nose. He grew up in the Vosges, in northeastern France, where he trained as a butcher, eventually moving to Paris and working, among other places, at the famed Boucheries Nivernaises. In 2005 he opened Le Severo, a shoe box of a restaurant with a handful of dark wooden tables, a series of scrawled chalkboard menus covering the room's longest wall, and a short zinc bar overlooking a kitchen big enough for one. Bernet fulfilled front-of-the-house duties—taking orders, delivering food, and recommending wine from the two hundred bottles on offer—while the cook presided over this tiny kitchen. I heard the fresh sizzle of meat hitting a hot saucepan, the crack and bubble of freshly cut Bintje potatoes twice bathed in hot oil, first an initial dip of 140°F and then a second one at 350°F.

Steak's true magic, Bernet explained, happens before the meat ever hits the heat—it's found in the aging process. He hangs whole cuts of well-marbled beef in a dry, chilled space for weeks, sometimes months, a process that concentrates the meat's flavor and breaks down its connective tissues, resulting in richly beefy, butter-tender fillets. In French, dry-aged meat is called *rassis,* a term that can also refer to stale bread or to a stick-in-the-mud.

Aside from a few first-course salads; side dishes of green beans, fries, or potato puree; and classic desserts like crème brûlée, I spotted only meat on the menu: beef or veal, served plain, without sauce. That's it. "If you write about my restaurant," Bernet said to me with a pleading note in his voice, "please say that I would prefer it if vegetarians came here as little as possible. I just don't have anything to offer them."

One flight down from the dining room was Bernet's lair, a tiny, brightly lit basement workshop where he butchered sides of beef into individual portions like the bavette (skirt steak), faux-filet (strip steak), or entrecôte (rib eye). In a corner of the room was a walk-in refrigerator, cooled to 35°F, where he hung his oversize cuts to dry and age. Inside, the racks of meat gleamed dully, like unpolished jewels, ruby red against a startlingly white layer of fat. Bernet held up two pieces of beef, one aged, one not. "Before it's *rassis* it still smells like the slaughterhouse," he said. I dutifully sniffed both pieces. They smelled exactly the same to me—a faint, raw, damp whiff of aging animal. Some of the older pieces of beef had developed a dark, furry mold on their surface, a crust that Bernet would trim off when portioning the meat for service. (When I asked if I could take a photo of the meat locker, he gave me a horrified look. "I would never allow a picture of this to be published!" he said. "It's too unappetizing—no one would ever come to eat in my restaurant again.")

Today, under the constraints of time and profit, the practice of aging beef in France is disappearing. A well-aged slice of beef has lost at least 30 percent of its original volume in evaporation—a considerable amount if your product is sold by weight. It's next to impossible to find a Parisian butcher or steak bistro offering *boeuf rassis*, Bernet told me. He checked the refrigerator's meat, rewrapping some pieces in muslin, turning others, handling them as if he were an artist and these hunks of flesh his oeuvres. He showed me a côte de boeuf, a prized cut that sells in the restaurant for eighty euros for two people, turning it from one side to the other. "It takes at least thirty days—minimum—to age a côte de boeuf properly," he said. "If only I could double that. Sixty days . . . now, that would be exceptional," he added dreamily.

I ate steak the very first week we moved to Paris, before we even had a chance to unpack a box of kitchenware. Calvin and I hopped on the métro and headed across town to the twentieth arrondissement, to the café that he thinks of as his own—as a loyal customer, a friend, and a former neighbor. Le Mistral was the place he used to frequent when he was studying in Paris. We'd come for the steak and red wine, of course, but we'd also come to see our friend Alain, who, along with his brother Didier, owns Le Mistral.

Twenty years ago, when Calvin was an exchange student living in Belleville, he'd wandered into the café, armed only with basic French. He met one of the brothers, serving behind the counter, and, after a few days of morning coffee and evening beer the three became friends. Didier and Alain helped Calvin find a job and an apartment. They invited him on visits to Aveyron, their region of France. They offered him hot meals in exchange for writing out the daily specials on the chalkboard menu. And their daily conversations—on politics, history, and the Doobie Brothers—left Calvin speaking fluent, almost unaccented French. Despite the constraints of time and distance, the three never lost touch.

They owed their friendship partly to Le Mistral itself, a neighborhood institution opened by Didier and Alain's father in 1954. It sits on the corner outside métro Pyrénées, a grande dame of the neighborhood with a welcoming golden glow. Inside, there's the smell—a mix of fresh coffee and toasting cheese, a hint of damp from the cellar below—and the noise—the bustle of voices, the call of the servers ordering *un café allongé* or *un quart de vin rouge*. There are round columns covered in tiny rectangles of mirrored tile, red pleather banquettes, wall sconces emitting warm light, checkered paper place mats, blackboard menus propped up on chairs, the requisite zinc bar.

On that late-summer evening, we stood at the counter drinking red wine produced by the brothers at a cooperative in Aveyron and chatted with Alain as he constructed elaborate salads. The twentieth, with its shop signs in a mix of Arabic, Vietnamese, and Chinese, felt very different from the hushed polish of the Left Bank, not a gleaming tourist attraction but a *quartier populaire*, a working-class neighborhood. Next to us two young men stirred sugar into their coffee while chatting in a combination of Arabic and French. Across the bar an older man sipped a magenta-colored drink from a long, cool glass. *"C'est un monaco,"* said Alain, following my gaze—beer with a splash of grenadine syrup, he explained. A woman with white hair and a dark green waxed raincoat, whom Calvin recognized from 1988, moved a lone stool to a secluded corner of the bar to sip a *demi* of beer and read the newspaper.

The last time I'd seen Alain, three years earlier, my French had been limited to a vocabulary of about ten words. But I had just finished a French-immersion program at Middlebury College in Vermont—seven weeks of grammar exercises, drama classes, poetry recitals, and essays on the Nouvelle Vague. I had lived in a dorm with college freshmen fifteen years my junior, written letters to a fictional pen pal named Innocence, and memorized lines for a play that would be forever embedded in my subconscious. It had been an experience worthy of a book itself, one that had quite literally turned my hair white, and aside from the shared bathrooms and cafeteria grub, I'd loved every second.

During my Chinese American childhood, studying French had been discouraged. My mother had never shaken her terror and dislike for her cruel, half-French stepmother, and as a result she had dissuaded me from learning French; though she didn't exactly declare the language verboten, she definitely disapproved of it. "Why would you want to learn French?" she asked me when I started high school. "No one speaks French." And so I took Spanish, and in college I switched to the language she considered truly useful, Mandarin. At age twenty I spent a summer on that same verdant Vermont campus in a nine-week Chinese-immersion program, gazing jealously at the French students as they smoked hand-rolled cigarettes while I stuffed another five hundred Chinese characters into my brain.

My mother, I'm forced at gunpoint to admit, was right about studying Chinese. When I moved to Beijing with my husband almost ten years after that summer of Mandarin immersion, my rusty language skills proved very useful indeed. But she had underestimated the most important factor in language study: love. I respected Chinese, but I didn't love it. I loved French, and it fueled me to memorize extra vocabulary, to read Georges Simenon novels before bed, to practice phonetics exercises over and over again. It had been a dream come true to immerse myself in the language of diplomacy, of romance and poetry. Now I was eager to show off my progress.

"*Tout le monde va bien? Christine? Les enfants? Didier?*" I asked, exchanging cheek kisses with Alain.

"*Ça va, ça va. Tout le monde va bien, ouais.*" He tore up some red-leaf lettuce and scattered a handful of canned corn on top.

The conversation continued as I described our new apartment, the weekend we'd spent on a dairy farm in northern Vermont, and asked about his kids' favorite subjects at school. Alain chatted away without even a flicker of acknowledgment at my improved language skills. I started to wonder if he'd even noticed that I was speaking French.

Finally Calvin, who had been watching me struggle to contain my frustration, broke in. "Hasn't Ann's French improved?"

Alain grinned, a smile that spread across his wide features. *"C'est pas mal!"*

Pas mal? Not bad? At the time I didn't know that those lukewarm words were actually a great compliment for the French, who seem reluctant ever to express too much enthusiasm.

"Tu as vraiment fait des progrès!" Alain added kindly, perhaps sensing my disappointment.

"Oh, non . . . Je fais des efforts, c'est tout." I tried to be modest, but I couldn't stop beaming from ear to ear. After so many years of longing to speak French, I could actually communicate! I was participating in a conversation with a real live French person! I felt like breaking into song.

Alain launched into a long anecdote about one of the café's former clients . . . an American musician? a drummer? a member of the Doobie Brothers? who he ran into at the airport? I have to admit, I was lost from the first sentence. It was a feeling I remembered from living in Beijing, of trying to stay afloat in a foreign language, clutching desperately at familiar words as they drifted by, hoping they could save me from drowning. I'd managed to pick up quite a bit of French in a short period of time, helped along by many English cognates. But as I watched Calvin absorb every nuance of Alain's story without a flicker of effort, I quietly despaired of achieving complete fluency. Would I ever be able to interview someone for an article, recount a story, or even tell a joke?

Eventually we made our way to the back of the café, past the teeny kitchen, really a small box just big enough for the lone chef, to a dining room converted from an old garage after Calvin's student days. Murals adorned the walls, bucolic scenes of Aveyron. Though Didier and Alain were both born in Paris, they consider this isolated region in south-central France their *pays*, their native land.

Over fifty-five years ago, Didier and Alain's father, Monsieur Alex, gathered his savings and moved from Aveyron to Paris to seek his fortune. Part entrepreneur, part *charbonnier*, or coal seller, he hoped to open a neighborhood café that would offer drinks and simple meals and also sell coal. Thus Le Mistral was born. Though the idea of a combination coal shop and café seems rather eccentric from a modern perspective, at the time it was quite common. In fact, there is even a French word—*bougnat*—that is defined as a coal seller–turned–café owner from Aveyron. Today many Parisian cafés honor this tradition with names like Le Petit Bougnat, L'Aveyronnais, or Le Charbon.

Cafés have existed in Paris since 1686, when an Italian named Francesco Procopio dei Coltelli opened Le Procope on the rue des Fossés Saint-Germain on the Left Bank. The self-proclaimed "oldest café in the world" still stands in the same spot, though the street has been renamed rue de l'Ancienne Comédie. Inside, the scarlet dining room is lined with portraits of its former patrons, including French artists and revolutionaries like Voltaire, Rousseau, and Napoleon (whose three-cornered hat hangs in the entry). Today the sprawling café has become a tourist hub serving some dubious-looking meals. But if you stop by in the hush of late afternoon, you can sit at a corner table, sip coffee, and imagine the debates launched within these red walls, the impassioned speeches, the laughter and rebellion.

Over the centuries, as the popularity of coffee waxed and waned, cafés evolved from informal social clubs to centers of political debate to the smoke-filled lairs of artists, writers, and musicians. But the Parisian institutions we know today—with their tiny cups of coffee and balloon glasses of wine—weren't firmly established until the nineteenth century, when the Aveyronnais began to migrate to Paris from their mountainous region.

Poverty brought them to the capital, and in the beginning, like most immigrants, they worked menial jobs, delivering hot water and hauling buckets of coal to private homes. This gave way to coal shops, warm places where regular customers could indulge in a glass of wine while placing an order for delivery, which eventually turned into cafés. By the end of the twentieth century, the region of Aveyron was synonymous with a Parisian café empire that at one point numbered over six thousand and included some of the most storied establishments in Paris history: Brasserie Lipp, La Coupole, Les Deux Magots, Café de Flore. At 320,000 strong, the Aveyronnais form the largest French community in Paris—greater even than the population of Aveyron itself. These days, despite improved roads and rail service, the region remains known as *la France profonde*, a remote and rough part of the country that still leans on Paris for survival.

"What's the signature meal of Paris?" I asked Alain one evening. Calvin and I had joined him for dinner at a café in Montmartre, a cozy neighborhood place with yellow walls owned by a friend of Alain and Didier's—yet another Aveyronnais—named Jean-Louis.

The sandwich, he said without hesitation. He called it *le casse-*

croûte, an old-fashioned term meaning "snack" or "fast lunch." "My mother used to make piles of them for the café."

Every morning Madame Odette would slice an armload of baguettes lengthwise and fill them with butter and ham, or sticky slices of Camembert, or pâté and cornichons. She'd stack the sandwiches like logs in a woodpile and sell them throughout the day to *ouvriers,* workmen or factory hands, who formed the base of Le Mistral's clientele. "In the 1950s," Alain said, "most cafés were *pure limonade*"— they sold only beverages and lacked kitchens and, often, refrigerators. *Ouvriers* transported meals from home in a *gamelle,* or lunch box, and cafés reheated the food over simple camp stoves. (These were also the days when every cup of coffee was accompanied by a shot of liquor, no matter the hour. Alain's father once told him, "If someone asks for a coffee without the booze, that means the guy is sick.")

"Do you still make a stack of sandwiches every morning at Le Mistral?" I asked.

"*Oh, non.* It's rare to eat a sandwich at a café these days."

"Why?"

Alain took a sip of wine. "There used to be a lot of factories in Paris, especially in our neighborhood, but they're closed now," he said. "Replaced by offices. And bureaucrats like a hot meal more than *ouvriers.* Customers kept asking for a plat du jour"—a hot lunch—"and cafés needed something quick to eat and easy to prepare. *Et voilà, le steak frites est arrivé!* It's in the same spirit as the sandwich." He paused. "Except it's hot."

In the nineteenth arrondissement, in the northeast reaches of the city, sits a large swath of green: Le Parc de la Villette. I had come here in search of Paris's carnivorous roots. For over a hundred years, from 1864 to 1970, La Villette was known as the "Cité du

Sang," the bloody center of the French wholesale-meat industry. In the 1980s an urban-renewal project turned the area into a postmodern park, designed by architect Bernard Tschumi. But as I wandered through the verdant space, I tried to catch a whiff of its gruesome origins as a cattle market and abattoir. A pack of young boys passed me on their kick scooters racing toward a futuristic playground.

In its heyday La Villette was like another country, a sprawling complex with more than twelve thousand employees speaking a special slang and operating under a complex secret code of warring families, fierce loyalties, honor, and alliances. Cattle farmers and merchants from all over France brought beasts here to be sold and slaughtered. *Chevillards,* wholesale butchers who killed the animals, bargained with retail shopkeepers who traveled there to stock their boutiques, transacting business over glasses of wine in the café or heavy, meaty lunches in neighborhood restaurants.

At the southern edge of the park, I found a relic of the era: a grande dame of Parisian steak bistros, Au Boeuf Couronné, which opened in 1865. Stepping through the restaurant's revolving wooden doors, I tried to imagine the dining room as it was a century ago, when men wore hats and La Villette diners used to provide their own meat for the chef to cook. White tablecoths covered the tables, Art Deco light fixtures suffused the room with a golden glow, and old photographs lined the walls—a child with a steer, men clad in long black smocks—memories of La Villette washed clean and sweet. I watched black-and-white-clad waiters deliver steaks to diners who leaned toward each other, speaking in hushed voices. Could this bustling bistro, which has specialized in beefy business lunches for almost 150 years, be the cradle of steak frites?

These days Au Boeuf Couronné is part of the restaurant group Gérard Joulie, a vast chain of bistros that is in fact owned by an

Aveyronnais. But I found the menu old-fashioned, with things like marrow bones, different cuts of steak, frites, and the occasional piece of salmon. I ate my lunch while skimming the restaurant section of *Le Figaroscope*, occasionally setting down my fork to turn the newsprint pages. My knife sliced through my *pavé*—so named because it resembles a cobblestone—to release a pool of rosy juices. The fries were hand-cut, hot enough to sting my fingers, a glass of red wine was cheaper than bottled water, a pile of nondescript steamed green beans turned oddly addictive when dipped into the tarragon-scented béarnaise sauce. I pursed my mouth and sawed at my steak, took a bite and chewed, put down my fork to circle an address in a restaurant review. I felt almost Parisian.

About five years ago, Alain and Didier decided to take an early retirement. They left Le Mistral in the hands of a cousin and moved down to Aveyron. Though only in their forties, after more than twenty years behind the counter they were ready for a quiet life among the cows. Alain wanted to raise his kids, and Didier began a series of construction projects, renovating old farmhouses. They both bought a few hectares of vineyard and started cultivating grapes, joining a wine cooperative in the local village.

But back in Paris things weren't going well. Business at the café had dropped off, who knew why? Maybe the cousin in charge was too much of an introvert. Maybe it was the new smoking ban, which outlawed cigarettes in cafés, restaurants, and offices. Whatever the case, something had to be done. Didier and Alain returned to Le Mistral, commuting between Paris and Aveyron, swapping shifts that each lasted a couple of weeks.

That first night at Le Mistral, I watched Alain behind the counter, smiling, shaking hands, and greeting customers eager to welcome him back after his long absence. *"Oui, je suis revenu!"* Alain said as a mustached man pumped his arm up and down. He joked with a family as they settled their bill, poured another beer for the white-haired woman at the end of the counter, passing it to her along with a greeting from Didier: "He's down in Aveyron, but he'll be up in a couple of weeks." Alain didn't know everyone, but everyone seemed to recognize him. He was like a friend or an older brother, the unofficial mayor of the corner. And that's when it hit me. Didier and Alain, they were fixtures of the community. Le Mistral had been in the neighborhood for over half a century, a family institution. People hadn't stopped coming because the cousin was shy or because they couldn't smoke at the bar. They'd missed the brothers.

Calvin and I slid into a booth, an intimate corner table where we could linger over our meal. The waiter brought us a *pichet* of red wine, and we clinked glasses and grinned at each other. Calvin's crooked smile made my heart skip a beat. When the food arrived, I cut straight into the center of my steak, revealing a juicy, dark pink interior, the meat tasting of salt and brawn, of the grassy Aveyronnais plain. In an oval side dish sat an oversize pile of frites, glistening a little from the fryer. They weren't hand-cut, and they had almost certainly been frozen—Le Mistral has no pretensions of a four-star kitchen—but I relished the mix of crispy and salty, the crunch that gave way to a tender, mealy center. As Calvin and I ate and chatted, I could see my reflection in the mirror behind him: flushed cheeks, bright eyes, a smile that wouldn't leave my lips. I was intoxicated, and my drug was Paris.

Alain pulled up a wooden chair and joined us at our table as we finished our meal. Calvin poured him a glass of wine, and the two of them settled in to talk about the old days—the trip they took to Aveyron when it rained every day for two weeks, the unforgettable bottle of 1947 Châteauneuf-du-Pape that Alain's parents had poured at lunch one summer afternoon, the time Didier took a road trip to Holland and lost his parked car in a maze of city streets. They talked about Monsieur Alex, who had passed away a few years ago, new nieces recently born, old friends from the café.

After five years of marriage, I thought I'd met most of my husband's friends. But listening to Calvin and Alain chat, I was struck by the depth of this new cast of characters, all with poetic French names like Gilbert, Marie-Hélène, Michel, Agnès. For me France was new territory—albeit one that operated under an Old World code of politesse—and I still struggled to remember if a greeting should consist of two or three cheek kisses, or whether I needed to maintain eye contact while raising a toast. My husband, I realized now, already understood France with a fluency that went beyond language. At least I could rely on him for translation.

After dinner we stepped out of the café and paused at an intersection to peer around the corner of a building. "Look down there." Calvin pointed, and I gasped. From the top of Belleville, the city descended before us, the buildings receding in size. Far in the distance, I spied the Eiffel Tower, as small as a toy and twinkling madly. We flattened ourselves against the side of a building, away from the other pedestrians on rue de Belleville, and watched as the tower sparkled against the orange glow of the city lights.

"When good Americans die, they go to Paris," Oscar Wilde once said. I'd managed to get there a little earlier, and I still couldn't quite believe my luck. The future felt as glittery as the Eiffel Tower, brilliant with anticipation. Calvin's hand reached out to touch my arm. "Are you ready to go?" he asked, and I nodded.

Later I would realize the difference between us. Calvin had, in a way, come home. But I was on the brink of an exciting new adventure.

Bavette aux Échalotes

This is my interpretation of a set of loose instructions given to me by William Bernet. At his restaurant, Le Severo, most of the meat arrives at your table sauce-free. The bavette aux échalotes (skirt steak with shallots) is one of the few exceptions. Like many classic bistro dishes, this one relies on the quality of its ingredients. Bernet would encourage you to use aged meat.

Serves 2

For the steak

1 skirt steak, 9 to 10 ounces, patted dry
Salt and pepper to taste
1 tablespoon mild-tasting oil such as sunflower *or* grape seed

For the sauce

2 tablespoons unsalted butter
4 large shallots, peeled and thinly sliced
1½ tablespoons red wine vinegar
1 sprig fresh thyme
½ cup chicken *or* beef stock *or* water

Preparing the steak

Trim the steak of excess fat and season with salt and pepper. Place the oil in a skillet over medium-high heat. Test the heat of the pan by touching a wooden spoon to the oil—if the oil is hot, it will lightly sizzle. Place the steak in the pan. Cook for 2 minutes, until the underside is well seared and browned. Turn the steak and cook the second side for 40 to 50 seconds, or until medium rare. (Skirt steak is a thin cut, and the meat cooks very quickly.) Transfer to a plate, cover loosely with a tent of foil, and keep warm while you make the sauce.

Making the sauce

In the same skillet, heat 1 tablespoon of the butter with the meat drippings. Add the shallots and sauté over medium heat until golden brown, about 7 minutes. Add the red wine vinegar, thyme, and stock (or water), and bring the liquid to a boil. Cover and cook until the shallots have softened and the liquid has almost disappeared. Swirl in the remaining tablespoon of butter and add any juices released from the meat. Taste the sauce and adjust the seasoning, adding a few drops of vinegar if needed.

Slice the steaks against the grain into thin strips. Serve with the shallots spooned on top, accompanied by mashed potatoes or steamed green beans.

Chapter 2

Troyes / Andouillette

I had everything under control until I saw the ceramic Buddha. It appeared in the window on a gray and humid August morning, two burly movers sagging under its weight. *"On va le mettre où, madame?"* asked one, pointing with his chin at the rooms already stacked high with cartons.

My parents had thrust the statue upon me the last time they'd cleaned out their attic. It was about the size and weight of a Great Dane. I'd shoved it into storage hoping it might disappear, and it did—from my memory at least. Now—surprise!—it was in Paris, delivered along with the rest of our boxes and furniture, hoisted by crane up two stories and hauled through our dining room's French windows.

It had been five years since I'd seen most of our personal effects, which had been packed hastily during the panicked month that separated our wedding and our move to China. While we lived in a furnished apartment in Beijing and then a cramped one-bedroom rental in Washington, the cartons had done hard time in a storage unit in northern Virginia. But our apartment in Paris was unfurnished, and so now we were reunited with everything—for better or worse.

Sorting through the array of dusty boxes was like viewing my past life, the one I'd led before I met Calvin, back when I was just another New York editorial assistant slaving over a hot photocopier. As I tried to find room in the bookshelves for my waist-high stacks of paperbacks, I thought about my last day of work in publishing, when my colleagues toasted me with coffee and doughnuts and I surprised everyone, including myself, by bursting into tears. I didn't feel too different from that girl in her mid-twenties, the one who'd dreamed of running her own publishing imprint and who'd survived on grilled cheese sandwiches toasted on the waffle iron. Still, it felt as if a lot of time had passed since I'd gotten married and left New York.

I like to tell people that my husband and I met at a party, but the truth is we were set up. A mutual friend, John, introduced us, inviting me to accompany him to Calvin's holiday party so he could play matchmaker. The first thing I noticed when I walked into Calvin's apartment was the view—the dazzling drape of the East River, the red lights of the Pepsi-Cola sign reflecting in the water. The second thing I noticed was that no one was speaking English, not even my host. While I chatted with young diplomats from the United Nations and ate chunks of aged Gruyère cheese, I snuck occasional glances at Calvin's boyish face as he mingled with his guests in Russian, English, and . . . French?

"He speaks *French*?" I whispered to John. My Francophilia was on high alert.

"Didn't I tell you? He taught kindergarten in Paris for a couple of years, before he joined the foreign service."

A French-speaking diplomat who had lived in Paris and liked Gruyère and kids? What can I say? It was love at first sight.

Six months later we were engaged—so quickly that we felt a little shy about telling people—and a year after that we got married. And then, a month after that, we moved to Beijing. I quit my job in book publishing, the only work I'd ever known, a career I'd adored for six years, and leaped—into nothing.

Beijing sprawled in front of me, an enormous, vibrant, uncompromising metropolis. After an initial flush of sightseeing, reality set in. How could I fill the days? Shopping for knockoffs and cheap pearls held little appeal. I started taking Mandarin classes again, but they raised complicated memories of childhood coercion, when my mother had dragged me to Chinese school every Saturday. I considered working at the embassy, but the only jobs available for spouses were secretarial, and I had no patience for administrative work. My limited Chinese prevented me from finding a job locally. In any case our host government strongly discouraged diplomatic spouses from working or even volunteering.

I missed my friends and family, of course, but more than anything I missed my job. For more than half my life, I'd dreamed of working in publishing, ever since I discovered at the age of ten that creating books was a profession and that people called editors actually got paid to read. I'd spent the years since college on the humble path to editor, answering phones and sending packages, acquiring a few projects of my own, dreaming of one day shepherding a string of authors onto the *New York Times* bestseller list. Now, I was unemployed in Beijing, and my former ambition seemed like the pollution that smudged the sky, a great green cloud composed of a billion different particles of fear and uncertainty. Without a career I hardly knew who I *was* anymore.

I was terrified my friends and family would think I'd made a mistake in marrying so hastily, that I'd been immature and foolish for allowing my heart to carry me more than six thousand miles away. My weekends and evenings had never been happier, filled with late-night strolls through twisting Beijing alleys, Sunday afternoons spent basking in the rare calm of a Confucian temple, and feasts of pork-and-chive dumplings with new Dutch diplomat friends. But I dreaded Monday mornings when Calvin left for the office. The workweek spooled to infinity, my days an exercise in killing time. I dawdled over the weight machines at the gym, spent hours comparison-shopping at the grocery store. I cooked elaborate meals for dinner and wondered how the hell I—a self-proclaimed feminist—had become a housewife.

I tried to stay positive, writing to friends back home about China's vitality, picnics on the Great Wall, excursions to eat fried scorpions at the night market. In reality I struggled daily with identity issues—not only job-related but also cultural: I thought of myself as an American, but everyone else viewed me as Chinese. My Asian features were like a mask. Sometimes I felt grateful for the way I could slip into a crowded Beijing subway car, unnoticed as long as I remained silent. But most of the time, I elicited hostile disappointment, expressed in the double take when a taxi driver saw my face and heard my accent, the questions, always the same: "Where are you from?" The refusal to accept my response: "America? You don't look American. Americans have yellow hair and big noses." In a culture as ancient and proud, as trampled and reborn as China's, a little ethnic chauvinism was natural. But what shocked me were the privileges granted automatically to my Caucasian friends and husband, the respect offered because of their foreign features alone, the praise of their Chinese judged by a single *"Ni hao."* In contrast, there was hardly anyone lower on the totem pole than a woman who looked young and Chinese. And even though I wasn't that young, or that Chinese, when Calvin and I went out together, people took one look at us and thought I was his translator. Sometimes they assumed worse.

At least I had lunch to punctuate my days. For an hour or two each afternoon, I plunged into street markets to slurp up noodles and dumplings. I watched with fascination as a jianbing vendor swirled crêpe batter on a hot griddle and delicately cracked an egg on top. I scalded my tongue on soup dumplings and stuffed my cheeks with snow-white hunks of puffy mantou (steamed bread). At Calvin's suggestion I started a food journal, a dog-eared notebook where I recorded recent meals and other culinary adventures.

Salvation came one day in the form of a magazine rack in our apartment building's mail room. I can still picture it, a shoulder-high structure in dark wood, right next to the window where I dropped off the dry cleaning. I can still feel the filmy cling of the plastic-bagged laundry draped over my arm as I stopped to glance at the garish covers. They were expat magazines that existed primarily to sell advertising, the articles in hastily copyedited English. For months I'd ignored them, but that day I picked up a copy of each, took them upstairs, and examined them. By the end of the afternoon, I had chosen one—*That's Beijing*—as the best of the bunch.

And so I thought up some story ideas and e-mailed them to the address listed for the editor in chief. I hoped to write about food, but he wanted stories for the House and Home section, so I wrote an article about orchid care. I reviewed books that I'd purchased on vacation and pestered so many cabdrivers for their opinions that I feared they might issue an all-points bulletin banning me from the city's taxis. After I'd freelanced for several months at one RMB per word (the equivalent of eight cents), the dining editor left. When they offered me the job, I jumped into the seat. Yes, *That's Beijing* was a far cry from Manhattan book publishing—the magazine's ty-pos, which seemed to multiply as fast as we could correct them, made that abundantly clear. But I loved reviewing Beijing's restau-rants and writing about Chinese regional cuisine, experiences that would eventually inspire me to write a novel. Every day for lunch, my colleagues and I would try a new restaurant, often delicious and always dirt cheap, and slowly, over shared plates of stir-fried bitter melon and cumin lamb, these co-workers evolved into friends. They had chosen to build a new life in Beijing, and their enthusiasm for the city's relentless energy and hustle, its sense of possibility and quirky charm, was infectious. I started writing pieces for American magazines, just short, front-of-the-book articles—barely longer than three sentences but each one a step forward, tiny but sure. Food had become a bridge to a foreign culture and, maybe, a new career.

The thing about diplomatic life is that just as you've gotten settled, made a few friends, and grown confident at navigating a new country, your assignment is over and it's time to move on. After almost a year and a half at *That's Beijing*, cleaning out my desk proved harder than I'd thought. I sifted through the detritus—receipts and business cards, broken pencils and coffee-stained notebooks—separating it into piles to keep and piles to throw away. In the end I swept everything into a huge garbage bin. I would have to start afresh in our next assignment in Washington, D.C. New contacts, new article ideas—I would need to build everything from scratch. Now, a year later, in Paris, I found myself starting over once again.

The day before the shipment of our belongings arrived at our apartment in Paris, I walked through the empty rooms, mentally unfurling a carpet here, hanging a favorite photograph there, selecting a cupboard for wineglasses near the refrigerator and one for pots and pans next to the stove. Three overseas transfers in five years had made me savvy. The next morning I asked the movers to empty all the boxes and take away the bulky packing materials. Calvin and I gently unwrapped our wedding china and made a trip to IKEA to buy a new bookcase. As for the Buddha, I shoved it into the *cave*, the basement storage room that was supposed to hold our precious wine collection. There it remained, wrapped in a blanket, waiting for our next move.

With the apartment unpacked and the Buddha stored, we settled into a routine of *métro-boulot-dodo,* as the French call the daily grind: subway, work, sleep. Calvin immersed himself in his new job at the American embassy, and I worked on revisions to my first novel, which I'd sold a few months before our move.

I'd written a first draft of the manuscript in Beijing, weaving together descriptions of the city's vibrant cuisine with the story of a young American woman in China who happens to be Chinese. My agent called over the summer to tell me she had found a publisher for the book, reaching me in the midst of my French-immersion program. There I was, tucked into a jewel-box New England college campus, sworn to speak only French, sneaking off to an empty field so I could talk to her in English on my cell phone and shriek at the top of my lungs. Even now, several months later, the double happiness of publishing a book *and* moving to Paris made me shaky with joy and a little fearful that I didn't deserve my good fortune.

As I soon discovered, however, the only thing better than working on a novel in Paris was *not* working on a novel in Paris. The streets beckoned, their morning markets bursting with late-summer produce—fruits I'd never seen before, like tiny golden plums called mirabelles and vine peaches with dusty skin and scarlet flesh. There were *fromageries* to visit, bakeries to discover, baguettes to sample. I wanted to shop like *une vraie femme au foyer,* a market basket over my arm, buying only enough groceries for one day or sometimes, it seemed, a single meal.

"Ah, non, monsieur! C'est trop! C'est trop!" cried the little old ladies at the market. They liked to nudge in front of me with an adroit

maneuver of the wheeled shopping cart and bat their eyelashes at the vegetable vendor. *"Juste un TOUT petit peu!"* Just a LITTLE bit! *"Une POIGNÉE!"* A handful! *"Pas TROP!"* Not TOO much! *"S'il vous plaît!"*

I couldn't help but wonder, what were they cooking at home? What did real French people eat? I tried to peer into their market baskets, but the contents offered few clues. Out to dinner with Didier at a local café, I sat up in my straight-backed chair when he ordered off the *ardoise* chalkboard menu an unfamiliar plate, something called andouillette. Five spiky letters followed the word: AAAAA.

"What is it?" I asked.

"C'est un plat typiquement français," Didier told me as a television in the corner flashed soccer. *"Une charcuterie faite d'intestins de porc."*

A traditional French sausage made from pork guts? My curiosity faded.

"Les français adorent ça!" he said with a grin. The French adore it? I was pretty sure he was teasing me.

When the food arrived, Didier's meal looked innocent enough, a pale sausage in a creamy, mustard-grain-flecked sauce. But when he cut off a slice, I smelled it, a deep whiff that was reminiscent of the barnyard. Or a cow pasture. Or a baby's unchanged diaper. Or one of Paris's narrow, dog-friendly sidewalks. You catch my drift, right?

"Tu veux goûter?" Didier asked me, his fork and knife poised to offer me a chunk.

"Ça a l'air délicieux . . . Mais non, merci," I said. He shot me a look, as if I'd shown him my inner core and it was soft like a coward's.

Thus I was spared the hard lesson of the difference between andouillette, andouille, and the latter's smoky, spicy Cajun cousin of the same name. I didn't know what the letters AAAAA meant, but when I saw them on menus, I knew to steer clear. I wasn't proud of my timid palate. I didn't advertise it. But I wouldn't have tucked into a big, steaming plate of offal even if threatened by a gang of knife-wielding butchers.

I could have gone on avoiding tripe sausage forever. But one day I found myself preparing dinner for a group of friends—nine omni-vores and one vegan. As I devised a series of special animal-free courses, I couldn't help but feel a little aggravated, I admit it.

"Have you ever noticed that picky eaters never think *they're* es-pecially picky?" I asked Calvin. "Cate doesn't eat meat, fish, dairy, or soy. And yet the first words out of her mouth are always, 'I'm not that fussy, am I?'" I thrust a tray of red peppers under the broiler. "I'm tired of people who don't eat everything."

"You don't eat everything."

"Yes I do!"

"Offal? Sweetbreads? Brains?" He raised an eyebrow. "Andouill-ette?"

I swallowed hard. He had me there. I started thinking. And feel-ing a little hypocritical. How could I describe myself as an open-minded food enthusiast—not to mention a food writer—if I refused to sample andouillette, one of France's oldest, most traditional forms of charcuterie? After all, would Julia Child have turned her nose up at pork intestines?

"Why don't you find out more about andouillette?" Calvin sug-gested. "You could take a trip."

"By myself?" I dropped a clove of garlic, and it skittered under the stove. "I don't think so."

"Just a day trip? Why not?" He reached into a grocery bag and handed me a fresh head of garlic. "Who knows? You might even like the stuff."

That is how I found myself in Troyes, a city about a hundred miles southeast of Paris, in the southern part of the Champagne region. The capital of andouillette.

Do you know what tripe is? I didn't before I went to Troyes. It turns out it's stomach lining, a pale, wrinkly membrane used in digestion (hence the smell). Most of the world eats tripe. It's boiled up in spicy Chinese hot pots, chopped and stuffed into tacos, stewed with tomatoes and Pecorino Romano cheese—to name just a few of its global incarnations. If not cooked gently, it becomes tough and rubbery.

Though beef tripe is most commonly eaten—with four stomachs, cows have a lot of it to offer—tripe sausages in France are made of pork. There is andouille de Vire, smoky and chunky, which hails from Normandy. There is andouille de Guémené, from Brittany, made of rolled sheets of tripe that form a swirling pattern when cut across the bias. But the most famous of all tripe sausage, andouillette, comes from Troyes—a twist of tripe and stomach, mixed with onions, spices, and lots of salt and stuffed into *la robe*, another part of the pig's intestine.

The first thing I noticed when I entered the spotless *laboratoire* workroom of the *charcutier*, Patrick Maury, was the smell. It was muffled but persistent, an unclean whiff that pervaded the winter cold of the unheated space. The culprit sat near the large windows, a plastic bucket filled with pale pink intestines soaking in water. Other corners of the room hid gruesome surprises like sagging sacks of blood—used in the boudin noir, a type of black sausage—and bags filled to bursting with unidentifiable animal bits.

The second thing I noticed was the half a pig lying splayed on the counter like an anatomy model or a butcher's diagram. There was the hind leg, ready to be carved off and cured into ham. There were the ribs, racked as if on the barbecue. There was the belly, soft and striped with fat just like the bacon it would become. A scooped cavity in the center indicated the spot where the intestines used to coil. "I wanted to show you where the tripe comes from in the pig," Maury told me.

But the pig hadn't taken up residence for my personal edification alone. It was destined to become the array of prizewinning charcuterie that Maury sells in his store: jambon, boudin blanc, boudin noir, pâté de campagne, and terrine. Like his father before him, he makes 90 percent of his own merchandise, purchasing and preparing a whole pig every Wednesday. (During my visit he changed to Tuesday to accommodate my schedule.)

A visit to Maury's workroom was not for the faint of heart, yet being there felt also quite magical, like paying homage to an ancient and respected métier, one that is rapidly disappearing in France. I admired the accoutrements of the trade squeezed into a small space—a smoker in the corner, the commercial oven next to it, a large vat to boil andouillette, the basement's walk-in refrigerator where sausages were hung to age. The room was a paean to frugality, with every last edible morsel found, seasoned, and sold.

To make the andouillette, first Maury plunged the tripe and stomach into scalding water to clean them. He cut each organ by hand into zigzagging strips, interconnected so that they formed one long, narrow chain. Deftly twisting the intestines together, he sprinkled them with diced onions, salt, pepper, nutmeg, and a dash of his secret blend of spices. He finished with a drizzle of Champagne, which is produced in the region, and white vinegar—both unique to his recipe. "Usually we'd leave it now to marinate for two to three hours," he told me. But with an eye on the clock, he proceeded directly to the *enrobement*, grasping a piece of intestine casing and expertly sliding the twist of tripe and stomach inside. In the final step, he would simmer the sausages gently—they're very delicate—for at least five hours in a vegetable bouillon. "They lose about a third of their mass," he told me. "The best part is, they're cooked for so long that all the fat just disappears."

"What's your favorite way to eat andouillette?" I asked.

"Grilled on the barbecue. Or with a creamy mustard sauce, topped with a slice of Chaource"—a soft cheese, similar to Brie. "Stick it under the broiler for a few minutes to melt the cheese . . . eat it with a few steamed potatoes, maybe a little choucroute . . . *Et voilà. C'est très fin dans la bouche.*" He looked as if he might like to polish off a plate at that very moment. *"Voulez-vous en goûter un morceau maintenant?"* he asked me suddenly. "I could pop an andouillette in the oven. It would be done in a second."

I looked at my watch. It was nine-thirty in the morning. I hadn't yet drunk a sip of tea or eaten a crumb of baguette. *"C'est très gentil de votre part."* My voice squeaked a little. "But maybe next time. It's a bit early for me."

"C'est vrai," said Maury. Still, I thought he looked a little disappointed.

Andouillette has a pedigreed history. Louis II, known as "the Stammerer," served it at his 878 coronation banquet, held in Troyes. Centuries later Louis XIV also declared himself an admirer, stopping at Troyes after a battle in neighboring Burgundy to stock up for the victory feast. The sausage even had the power to seduce, as discovered by the French royal army in 1560. Attempting to conquer Troyes, royal soldiers breached the city walls and spread through the narrow cobblestone streets of the Saint-Denis neighborhood, where they suddenly halted en masse, drawn to the allegedly tantalizing aroma rising from the quartier's tripe shops. They lingered, stuffing themselves with andouillette, which gave the town's troops time to assemble and swoop to victory in a surprise attack.

As I strolled the same narrow cobblestone streets, I couldn't help but wonder, why Troyes? How did this charming town give birth to such a divisive delicacy? With its magnificent, flamboyant Gothic cathedral, its rows of medieval timber-frame houses decked in Easter-egg pastels, Troyes gives off an air of wealthy respectability. During the Middle Ages, the town was an important post of the Champagne fairs (named after the region, not the wine), graced by the rushing river Seine, which flows through its center. As Troyes's market attracted people from all over Europe—with, for example, the Flemish exchanging linens for Mediterranean silks and spices—the town dished up its specialty, andouillette, to thousands of hungry travelers.

The Lemelle andouillette factory is located on the city limits, a family business started in 1973, housed in a gleaming white building in the *zone industrielle*. Through a window onto the factory floor, I saw enormous blue vats of *boyau*, pork tripe, enough raw ingredients to produce eighty thousand andouillettes a day. Workers clad in caps, rubber boots, and gloves hefted enormous trays of sausages to the boiler room, where they would simmer the links in stock for hours. The factory has 160 employees working around the clock in shifts, stopping only from Saturday afternoon to Sunday night.

In his sunny office, I asked Dominique Lemelle, who together with his brother, Benoît, owns the factory, if he could explain the letters A A A A A, which I'd often seen used to describe andouillette. An American friend had told me never to eat any with fewer than five A's. "What do they stand for?"

"C'est l'Association Amicale des Amateurs d'Andouillette Authentique," he said. Loosely translated, it means "the Friendly Association of Authentic Andouillette Connoisseurs," nicknamed "5A" (pronounced *cinq ah*). The group, a sort of fan club, was started in the 1970s by five andouillette lovers and food critics—among them the celebrated French food writer Robert Courtine, who wrote under the pseudonym "La Reynière"—with the goal of protecting the standards of tripe sausage. Since then the club has doubled in size, meeting two or three times a year to sample andouillette from around France and award certificates of exceptional quality. "I once went to one of the tastings," said Dominique. "It started at noon and didn't finish until eight o'clock at night. We ate at least seven whole andouillettes, with a poached chicken in between each one to clean our palate."

Dominique showed me his framed AAAAA certificates, illustrated with five cavorting cartoon pigs, each representing one of the association's five founding members. "Every two to three years, the panel reviews our product," he said. A certificate is good for two years, as long as the *charcutier* doesn't change the recipe or method of production. (If necessary, a special written authorization can extend the award's validity until the next tasting.) "The 5A defends the valor of andouillette," said Dominique.

Though generally prized by *charcutiers*, the AAAAA award is not an official government mark of quality, and there are some who choose not to participate in the association's tastings. The independent *charcutier* Patrick Maury is among them.

"I don't want to be a part of that," he told me.

"Why?" I asked, surprised. He didn't seem shy of competition. I glanced at the shelves of his boutique, lined with dozens of trophies and medals—over seventy prizes—that Maury has won since taking over from his father in 1995. For four years in a row, the Compagnons de la Gastronomie Porcine, another gourmet appreciation society, has named his andouillette the Champion of France and Europe.

"Ninety percent of AAAAA andouillette is industrial," he explained. "If you participate, people think your products are made in a factory. I want to stay artisanal, personal, familial. I'm protecting the authenticity of the *veritable* andouillette of Troyes."

For a minute I wondered if his objections had the tinge of sour grapes. But I didn't detect any bitterness in his voice. In fact, his argument seemed to illustrate the current state of French cuisine, which teeters between factories producing food in gross quantity and tiny, family-owned boutiques and restaurants passed from generation to generation. Being in Maury's shop was like stepping back thirty years, to a time when supermarkets hadn't yet spread to every French village and housewives made the daily rounds at the butcher, baker, and greengrocer. During my morning visit, Maury was doing a brisk business—on average he sells between thirteen hundred to fifteen hundred pounds of andouillette a week. Given his long hours, however, not to mention the intense amount of physical labor, and the economic reality created by cost-cutting superstores, I couldn't help but speculate how his boutique and, indeed, the art of artisanal charcuterie, could endure another generation.

Every andouillette enthusiast I met in Troyes—and I met many—wanted to be *the* person who convinced me that andouillette is delicious. "A lot of people don't want to try it because of the smell," Dominique said to me. "The secret is in the quality of the products. If they're fresh, there's no smell at all."

I definitely smelled something, though. We were in the factory's *laboratoire*, and Dominique and an employee, Pascal, had just shown me their method for cutting tripe and stomach. My time had come. When Dominique offered to slice up some rounds of chilled andouillette, I knew I couldn't avoid it any longer. "It's easier to taste it cold," he said. "When it's hot, the flavor is much stronger."

Cut horizontally, the andouillette had a marbled effect, rosy with swirls of white and dark pink. Dominique offered me the plate, and I tried to summon the enthusiasm of my andouillette-loving friends in Paris. "Eating it makes me feel connected to France," said Guillaume, a Frenchman I met at a dinner party who had spent most of his childhood in the United States. "Like I'm part of the history and the *terroir*."

"Chunky goodness—*comme il faut*," said another friend, Sylvain.

With the eyes of Dominique and Pascal upon me, I bit into a slice. It tasted salty, highly spiced with pepper and nutmeg, similar to bologna. I started chewing, and the sausage squished between my teeth, at once soft yet cartilaginous, like a stretched-out rubber band. Dominique looked at me expectantly.

"*C'est pas mal!*" I said. And, really, the flavor was quite inoffensive. The slippery, ropy, chewy texture, however, seemed to encapsulate the very essence of tripe. I thought of the vat of intestines soaking on the factory floor and forced myself to swallow. The second bite was harder.

Dominique proffered the plate again. "Another piece?"

"*Non, merci,*" I said, feeling a little sheepish.

That night I met a local blogger, Céline Camoun, for dinner at Au Jardin Gourmand, a small restaurant in the town's historic center. A friend of a friend had introduced us. "Oh, you're going to Troyes? My sister's best friend's friend lives there. I'm sure she would be delighted to show you around." And she was. *Fier d'être français, et puis fier de ma région*—this was a sentence I heard over and over again while traveling in France. Proud to be French, and then proud of my region.

As a Troyes local, Céline would be an andouillette enthusiast, I figured. Not so. *"Je déteste ça,"* she told me after we'd exchanged cheek kisses. "My mother and my cousins love it, but I can't stand the smell."

We installed ourselves at a table in the cozy, book-lined room. Céline had selected the restaurant because it specialized in andouillette, and indeed the menu read like an encyclopedia of the stuff, with eleven preparations, some simply grilled or panfried, others with complex cream and cheese sauces, one with a crown of foie gras.

"I think I'll have the steak," said Céline.

Jacques Lebois, the restaurant's owner, approached our table. "My friend is an American. She's researching andouillette," Céline told him.

"Oh, I *love* introducing foreigners to andouillette," said Lebois, clasping his hands and practically rubbing them together with glee. "Do you know the story of andouillette de Troyes?"

"Hmm, I don't think so, no." Anyway, I didn't know *his* version of the story.

"During the Middle Ages," he began, "the town was under siege and surrounded by soldiers camped outside the city walls. Eventually, when there was nothing left to eat except tripe, people started making andouillette. The soldiers were so enchanted by the smell that they declared, 'We'll let you out as long as we can have some of what you're eating!'"

The three of us laughed. Behind Lebois a waiter passed carrying an armful of plates, all of them laden with fat andouillettes in a creamy sauce. The whiff was unmistakable.

"Are you ready to order?" Lebois produced a pen.

Céline ordered a steak, and then Lebois turned to me with a gleam in his eye. "May I suggest the andouillette with fromage de Chaource perhaps?" he said. "Or poached in white wine? That's also excellent."

"I think I'll have . . ." They both looked at me expectantly. "The grilled salmon," I said eventually.

"*Pas d'andouillette?*" cried Lebois. He turned to Céline. "She doesn't want to order andouillette?"

"Well, she's been tasting it all day," Céline said kindly. "She probably doesn't want to overdo it."

I could tell he was thinking, Is that even possible? Nonetheless, he brought me the grilled salmon. I have to admit, I enjoyed every bite.

With andouillette conquered—or, at least tasted—what was next? Back in Paris I luxuriated in the three years that stretched before us, contemplating the feasts that still lay ahead. We would roast a poulet de Bresse, and stack Brie de Meaux against Brie de Melun, and eat a perfect omelette aux fines herbes after the cinema, and taste an array of Burgundies from young to complex, and, and, and . . .

My running list of places for us to try—restaurants, pâtisseries, chocolatiers, charcuteries, *fromageries, boulangeries, cavistes*—was so long that I was afraid it would crash my hard drive. And then Calvin got the call.

Chief of staff at the U.S. embassy in Baghdad. It was a big assignment at an important embassy, the type of job that could make a diplomatic career. Calvin tried to remain neutral when he told me about it, but I could feel the excitement bursting from him, even despite the drawbacks, of which there were many. Danger, for one.

Danger. He shrugged it off, but when I imagined my husband in a war zone, my heartbeat shot into arrhythmia. Though the embassy was in the Green Zone, encircled like a prison, it was still bombed regularly by mortar fire. *Separation.* Baghdad was an unaccompanied post—meaning no spouses, no children, no family. If he took the job, we would be apart from each other for a year.

Calvin, however, listed the advantages. During his year away, I would be able to stay in Paris, in our Belle Époque apartment with its white marble fireplaces and antique parquet floors and flutters of crown molding circling the ceilings. He would take three vacations from Iraq, each lasting three weeks. And after a year away, he would return to Paris. Our three-year assignment would become four.

"But didn't we move to Paris to be together?" I crossed my arms. "After all the traveling you did last year?" During our year in Washington, Calvin had traveled for work almost two weeks a month.

"I have to be ready for service anywhere in the world. Anywhere. Even places where my family can't go. It's kind of like the military." He'd repeated the words so many times I scarcely heard them anymore.

"And I'd be here alone?" Anxiety rose in my chest—for Calvin's safety, for my own potential isolation.

"I know, it's not ideal. But at least you'll be in Paris."

"It won't be the same without you." The words tasted bitter in my mouth.

During the day, while Calvin was at work, I wept. I understood his ambition because I had it, too, burning inside me, at times as gently warming as a nursery fire, at others as acrid as an ulcer. We both had our own career goals and dreams, but—in my mind at least—we also had an unspoken agreement that marriage and family life came first. A year apart seemed to break that agreement.

One afternoon I found myself alone in the kitchen, snipping the stems of a bunch of tulips. I reached above my head to pull a vase off a high shelf, edging it past a row of wineglasses. But the shelf was narrower than I thought, and one of the cheap glasses fell and broke with a sharp pop and tinkle of jagged shards. I pulled again at the vase, and another glass broke, shattered by my careless gesture.

According to the American Foreign Service Association (the closest thing the diplomatic corps has to a union) the foreign service's divorce rate mirrors that of the general American population. What they don't add is that it's 50 percent. I mention this not because Calvin and I ever considered divorce—we didn't—but to illustrate how naïve I was about the institution of marriage. We had been so happy, so conscientious about making big decisions together—we fought so rarely—that I thought our marriage was indestructible. Sweeping up the shards of glass, I realized that it was as delicate as anyone's, which is to say, very.

Six months after our arrival in Paris together, my husband began to prepare for his departure. Neither of us wanted to spend a year without the other, but Calvin's dedication to public service and—yes—his ambition helped him shoulder the hardship. As for me, I finally agreed because . . . well, because I love him. And part of that love is admiration of his civic responsibility and his ambition and his belief in diplomacy.

In the two months before he left, the light-starved days of winter grew longer and milder, artichokes and asparagus replaced leeks and chard in the market, and our moods grew darker and darker. We didn't talk much about Calvin's departure because talking made it too real; on the contrary, we tried hard to ignore the dwindling time, the days, then hours. But the imminence of it loomed in the shadows of every evening, in a glass of white wine poured at cocktail hour, in the golden glow of the streetlamps when we exited an afternoon movie to streets already dark and wet. Calvin bought me tulips on his way home from work; I cooked a last batch of his favorite dinner, spaghetti and meatballs, and we clung to these thoughtful gestures, to our familiar routine.

I wanted time to slow down, to stop. But suddenly it was April and we were celebrating my birthday at one of my favorite restaurants, a sleek fish bistro called Les Fables de la Fontaine, where I gazed at my plate of perfect, firm-fleshed, brown-buttery sole meunière and wondered how I'd force the food past the lump in my throat. The next morning Calvin left. And then I wept for the rest of the day.

I tried to stop—I wanted to stop—the tears were embarrassing, not to mention messy. But my eyes kept betraying me, releasing a slow leak that increased with every human interaction. Already minimally weepy as I ordered a grand crème at our local café, my tears overflowed when the kind owner, Amar, patted me on the shoulder and whispered, *"Bon courage!"* I cried at the doctor's office, where the Australian receptionist urged me to keep my chin up. I cried in the stairwell of my apartment building when I ran into my downstairs neighbor, the male half of a tiny elderly couple. He paused in the middle of complaining about the water stains on his ceiling and asked if I would share a glass of wine with him and his wife from time to time.

I was making a spectacle of myself. Worse, I was confirming French stereotypes of Americans: that we're overemotional and indecorous, indiscreet about our personal lives. I had never seen a Frenchwoman crying on the métro. Heck, I had never even seen a Frenchwoman *eating* on the métro. Yet there I was on the platform at École Militaire with tears cascading down my cheeks. I longed to blow my nose, but my only tissue was already sodden.

When I got home, I found our apartment empty and forlorn, echoing every sound in the building. The neighbor's TV upstairs sounded like a furious mob; the métro below was like the deep-throated rumble of an earthquake. Though our windows shone with clear spring light, I went to every room and switched on all the lamps. The light reflected off the walls, making the voluminous, high-ceilinged rooms feel a little cozier. But the hours until dinner and bedtime stretched before me dry and uncompromising and lonely. Now that Calvin was gone, I had switched from willing the time to slow down to hoping it would race by until his return.

Desperate for distraction, I ransacked the fridge, where I saw the carcass of Sunday's roasted bird. It went into a big pot for stock, and I found some vegetables to accompany it, taking a long time to peel and chop the carrots, onions, and celery into a careful dice. I put them in the pot with the chicken bones, added cold water, and brought everything to a boil.

Standing over the stove, I skimmed the broth and then lowered the heat so that bubbles flickered across the surface. The stock perfumed the apartment with cozy, chicken-y warmth, a scent I remembered from my childhood, when my father used to simmer a giant soup pot late into the night. It was the smell of comfort and safety, of hugs and love and classic children's books—of home. At least for a few hours, I had managed to replace the clean, soapy smell of my husband with something almost as comforting.

Calvin and I had moved so often that I'd grown used to thinking of home as the place in the world where we lived together. But even without him, this was still my home, still a place of retreat, and I had never considered leaving it. Besides, where would I have gone? Calvin and I didn't have a permanent address; we didn't own any property. And though I loved my parents, I couldn't imagine moving in with them for a year.

"Try to take advantage of being in Paris," Calvin told me before he left. He'd said it partly, I knew, to comfort me, because he felt rotten seeing me so sad. But as I thought of him on the airplane, buckled into an aisle seat, hurtling across the sky to a country where he'd never been, I realized that his words were also the advice of someone who loved Paris and had left it many times, someone who knew the city and understood what it meant to live without it.

I stood at the window, peering through the swirled design of the wrought-iron balcony, at the cars whisking by on the boulevard Raspail. I reached out and plucked a cluster of dried petals from the bright geraniums in my window box. Sunshine flooded suddenly into the apartment, bleaching the carpets and the couch, shining on the parquet floor. Paris was still there, in all its elegant, decadent, luxurious beauty. And I was still in Paris, the city I'd dreamed about for so long.

Andouillette à la Sauce Maury

Patrick Maury's favorite way to eat andouillette is, he admitted, *costaud*, or heavy, with its creamy mustard sauce and gratinéed cheese. He told me that this recipe pairs well with a white wine like Chablis or the region's Champagne, which cuts the sharp scent of the sausage. In the States andouillette is made by gourmet-food producers like Fabrique Délices and sold by mail order nationwide. Fromage de Chaource is a soft and creamy cheese local to the area surrounding Troyes. If you can't find it, Brie makes a good substitute. The hit of ratafia—a strong alcohol, sometimes fruit-flavored—is optional. Finally, if you are not an andouillette enthusiast, this recipe is also delicious with poached chicken breasts substituted for the sausage.

Serves 4

4 andouillettes de Troyes
1 tablespoon unsalted butter
1 shallot, peeled and minced
¾ cup dry white wine
1½ tablespoons whole-grain Dijon mustard
¾ cup crème fraîche *or* sour cream
Ratafia (optional)
Salt and pepper to taste
½ pound fromage de Chaource

In a dry pan, or under the broiler, brown the andouillettes, turning them until all the sides become golden. Meanwhile, heat a sauté pan over medium heat, melt the butter, and add the minced shallot, sautéing until soft. Add the white wine, bring to a boil, and reduce the liquid by a third. Stir in the mustard, crème fraîche, and dash of ratafia, if desired, then bring to a boil and simmer for a minute or two. Taste and season with salt and pepper.

Turn on the broiler. Transfer half the sauce to an ovenproof baking dish and add the browned andouillettes. Cover them with the remaining sauce and top each sausage with a quarter-inch-thick wedge of Chaource cheese. Broil until lightly browned and bubbling, about 10 minutes. Serve with steamed potatoes and a little choucroute or sauerkraut.

Chapter 3

Brittany / Crêpes

The morning after Calvin left, I pushed myself out of bed and into a routine: gym, tea, breakfast, desk. I stared blankly at the computer screen until the clock in the corner told me it was time to catch the crosstown bus. My friend Elena had invited me to have lunch at Breizh Café, a *crêperie* in the Marais that featured a distinctly Parisian Franco-Japanese aesthetic, with minimalist cube tables, tatami mats on the floor, dabs of wasabi in the vinaigrette, and scoops of green-tea ice cream adorning the desserts. She was there when I arrived, sitting by the window with the light shining on her dark curls. We greeted each other with double-cheek kisses, a custom I'd noticed that all expats living in France seemed to adopt, no matter where they came from.

"How are you?" she said.

I hesitated before answering. "Fine." I had met Elena only a few months before, at a cocktail party in Neuilly thrown by a friend of a friend. We instantly discovered a shared New York history and mutual interest in good food—*la bouffe,* as the French call it—and the pursuit of eating adventures, heedless of our waistlines. Since then we'd seen each other a few times, swapping tales of expat miscommunication—Elena was American, with a Swiss husband—and sympathizing about the grim state of freelancing, whether in graphic design (her) or journalism (me). But we were only just creeping toward friendship. I still felt shy about revealing my problems.

"Have you heard from Calvin yet?" she asked.

I nodded. "He e-mailed me last night when he got to Amman." I swallowed, a hard, dry gulp of air, and fell quiet.

Elena was sensitive enough to let my silence pass. She handed me a menu, and we communicated in the way we knew best: by admiring, considering, and then dissecting our food options. Would I get the galette complète, a thin buckwheat crêpe filled with ham, cheese, and egg? What about the one with cheese and mushrooms? Should we order two different galettes and trade bites? And how about splitting a leafy side salad with wasabi dressing? I knew we would be friends—not just lunching acquaintances but real, secret-swapping, worry-soothing, laughter-exchanging friends—when she agreed with beaming enthusiasm to share everything.

"How's work going?" Elena asked after we had ordered.

"Pretty slow," I admitted. I had finished revisions to my novel a few months earlier and was now in the laborious, contemplative process of trying to start a new book. "I'm having trouble concentrating."

"Oh, honey, he just left. It'll get easier."

"I'm worried about spending too much time alone. You know what it's like working from home." I was grateful for the time and space to be able to write, but as a moderately social person I'd craved daily human interaction even before Calvin had left.

She nodded. "When Stéphane works late, I sometimes go the whole day without talking to anyone but the cat."

"I might start stalking our building's *gardienne*, listening for the vacuum, just so I can pop out and talk to another person for five minutes."

She laughed. "Call me, okay? Before you start stalking the *gardienne*, just give me a call. We can meet up for coffee or lunch anytime." She nodded a little bit to emphasize her words, to encourage me, and I felt a rush of gratitude. Calvin and I had several friends in Paris, both old and new, but we had socialized mainly as a couple. I was still trying to build that web of friends, colleagues, and neighbors that constitutes a community.

The food arrived, and Elena and I both pulled out our cameras and started snapping photos, not for any real reason but because the food looked pretty in the natural light. I admired the contrast of melted Emmental cheese against the thin pancake's dark and lacy beauty before picking up my knife and fork. The galettes were crisp, almost tough, difficult to cut, and chewy with the buckwheat flour's deep nuttiness offset by soft, oozing cheese.

We chewed in silence for a moment, then looked up from our plates, our eyes bright. I felt my mouth sweep into a smile, a real one. "How're the mushrooms?" I gestured toward Elena's plate.

"Shiitake," she said, almost reverently. "Do you want to taste?" We exchanged pie-shaped wedges and resumed eating.

After we'd cleaned our plates of every delicately dressed mesclun leaf, every tender mushroom slice, every last butter-crisped buckwheat crumb, Elena turned to me and uttered a word I was hoping to hear: "Dessert?"

I don't usually eat dessert at lunch. But you know what? It's not every week that your husband leaves for Baghdad. We flagged down the waiter. *"Deux crêpes au caramel beurre salé, s'il vous plaît."* Two crêpes with salted butter caramel.

"Du café? Du thé?" he asked.

"Qu'est-ce que c'est du thé au sarrasin?" Elena pointed at the menu. "Buckwheat tea—have you ever heard of that?" she asked me. I shook my head.

"It's tea from Japan," the waiter replied. "Made from roasted buckwheat grains."

"*On va essayer,*" Elena said. "Sounds interesting."

The crêpes arrived first, folded into triangles, each a contrast of crisp edges and spongy centers, drizzled with golden butter caramel sauce. I cut mine in half, and the liquid pooled into a golden, sticky, salty-sweet, faintly bitter puddle. Between bites we sipped the tea, a pale yellow liquid steeped in a small, heavy Japanese metal pot. "It tastes a little like toast," Elena said.

I breathed in the tea's nutty fragrance. "You know, I *have* had this before. At a Japanese restaurant in New York."

"Don't they make soba noodles out of buckwheat?"

"I think so, yeah." I took another sip. The tea, I realized, connected the Paris restaurant with its Tokyo branch, forming a sort of bridge between two cultures that use the same grain in very different ways. "But buckwheat seems like an unusual link between France and Japan."

"It grows everywhere in Brittany. Have you ever been? The coast is so wild and beautiful."

I shook my head. "I've always wanted to go, but we didn't have a chance before Calvin left."

Elena picked up the teapot to refill our cups and then set it down with a thump. "You should go! You should take a trip up there. Oh, Ann, you'd love it—it's so gorgeous—all green fields and jagged coastline. And the food! The crêpes are even better than here."

"Go to Brittany? By myself?"

"Why not? It's an easy train ride. And you could rent a car right at the station. You won't get lost with a GPS."

"I've never really traveled by myself before. Not overnight." Even as I said the words, I realized how silly they sounded. This was France, not West Africa or rural China. Traveling here wasn't that complicated; it didn't involve facing danger or hardship.

"Look." Elena put down her cup. "Your husband's away, but you're still in France. You'll only be here for a few years. Why not take advantage of it? *Il faut profiter,* as they say."

"*Profiter,*" I repeated, remembering Calvin's words before he left.

Later, after we had paid the bill and kissed each other good-bye, after I had taken the bus back home to my echoey apartment, double-locked myself inside, and turned on all the lights, I sat down at my computer and began to research train tickets to Brittany.

The first thing to take into consideration when you're planning a crêpe-eating expedition in Brittany is the region's size. It's enormous—divided into north and south and then divided again into *départements*—too big to visit in its entirety over a weekend or even during the span of a two-week holiday. No, tackling this territory requires careful planning and selection. Should one go north, to the seaside resort towns of Saint-Malo, Dinard, and Cancale, once the favored retreats of vacationing Victorians? Or should one venture south and west—far, far west—to the farthest tip of France? All the Bretons I talked to in Paris encouraged me to visit their province. But only one, Sophie Le Floch, pulled out her address book and wrote me a list of people to meet and places to visit.

"If you want to learn about crêpes, you have to go to Finistère," she said. As a native Bretonne and the owner of one of my favorite Parisian *crêperies,* the popular West Country Girl, Sophie certainly knew what she was talking about. She tore a page scrawled with names and phone numbers out of her notebook and pressed it on me.

And so I booked myself a ticket to Quimper, a modest city 350 miles west of Paris, the capital of the *département* called Finistère. The high-speed train from Paris tore through the countryside until Rennes, when it switched to the normal track and slowed. As we passed towns with Breton names—Vannes, Lorient, Rosporden—the other passengers disembarked. By the time we arrived in Quimper, the train's last stop, I was the only person in my carriage. Finistère doesn't mean "Land's End" for nothing.

Quimper has a quaint charm, with narrow streets, timber-framed houses, and enchanting little footbridges that span the three rivers flowing through it. At the train station, I picked up my rental car and headed toward the center of town with one destination in mind: place au Beurre. Translation: Butter Square. Yes, this town—arguably the crêpe capital of the world—values dairy fat so highly that it actually has a square named after the stuff. Once the town's marketplace, where salted butter was traded with great ferocity, it's now a pretty, pocket-size, cobblestoned hub that is the home to half a dozen *crêperies*.

I chose one of them, Au Vieux Quimper, for lunch. Inside, I found a dimly lit room with lace-covered windows, tables and chairs in honey-colored wood, and customers sipping apple cider from little bowls instead of glasses. My savory galette burst with cheese, bacon, and mushrooms cooked in cream, a heavy load of dairy and pork enclosed in a buckwheat wrapper of incredible delicacy. I wanted to scrape out the rich garnish so that I could better savor the crêpe's crisp edges and spongy middle and taste the rough, nutty graininess of the buckwheat itself.

Next to me a pair of older women gossiped their way through a lunch of plain buckwheat crêpes smeared generously with salted butter. One of them had a small bowl of something thick and creamy, which she ate with a spoon. What was it? Cream? Yogurt? She caught me staring, and I shifted my gaze. The waitress arrived to clear their plates. *"Désirez-vous un dessert?"* she asked the pair. *"Une crêpe au caramel au beurre salé, peut-être?"*

I was only midway through my savory crêpe but my ears pricked up at the mention of salted butter caramel.

"Du caramel? Dans une crêpe?" The woman across from me raised her eyebrows so high they practically touched her blue-tinted hair.

"C'est une sauce au caramel, faite maison"—a homemade caramel sauce—explained the waitress.

I began to feel confused. Weren't these women locals? Why weren't they familiar with salted butter caramel? Wasn't it traditionally Breton? One of the great sweetmeats of seventeenth-century corsairs (or something like that)?

"On peut tenter," the friend said after a lengthy pause. But she sounded pretty doubtful, even as she agreed to try it.

Ah, I thought, *they're tourists! They don't know salted butter caramel.* I congratulated myself on being more culinarily savvy than a French person. It didn't happen often.

The waitress came to remove my plate, and I asked for my own crêpe au caramel au beurre salé. When it arrived, I slid a knife through its center so that the sauce flooded the plate, a sticky, sweet-salty pool deepened with a note of brown butter. The pancake was finer than those I'd eaten in Paris, the sauce more sugary. And yet—did the caramel overwhelm the tender crêpe with its sugary richness? I scraped out the sauce and took a bite of plain crêpe, savoring its lacey edges and soft center.

What was wrong with me?

I would never have understood Brittany's true crêpe culture if I hadn't met Louise.

Louise Gesten is a proud Bretonne with short gray hair, a sturdy figure, and arms made strong from administering hugs and beating crêpe batter. I met her on my second day in Quimper, introduced by Hervé Floch'lay, a local cooking professor who was a friend of Sophie's and one of the many contacts on her list.

Louise was born in 1934, which doesn't seem that long ago, and yet she can easily recall a time when crêpes were made on a wood-burning stove. Her grandmother had an enormous *billig*—that's the Breton word for the round, flat griddle used for cooking crêpes—heated with bits of white-hot coal collected from the fireplace. Many Breton homes had a special stove for making crêpes, which was usually found outside the house in a small shed.

When Louise was a little girl living on her grandparents' farm, Fridays were known as *le jour de crêpe*, she told me. "Every family had a special day to eat crêpes. It was usually Friday, because that was a *jour maigre*"—a thin day, a fasting day—"and we didn't eat meat."

Preparing the crêpes took the better part of the day. Louise's grandmother used to start at nine in the morning, mixing the batter by hand—she actually stuck her hand into the bowl of ingredients and beat everything together—and she didn't finish frying the last crêpe until three o'clock. "There were so many of us she had to serve the meal in two batches," Louise said. "Eight children, plus the farmhands. . . ." They ate so many crêpes that after the heavy lunch everyone would pull out blankets, curl up on the floor, and take a nap.

"But *how* did you eat the crêpes?" I pressed Louise for details.

"Plain," she said.

"Plain, with cheese?"

"*Non, nature*. Plain, with a little salted butter. Or sometimes *graisse salée*"—a highly seasoned preserved pork fat local to the region. "It was less expensive than butter."

The idea of a crêpe stuffed to bursting with different fillings was so ingrained in my culinary sensibility that at first I had a little trouble accepting the idea of a plain one. "What about a crêpe complète?" I asked, citing the version popular in restaurants across France: egg, ham, and cheese.

"Oh, I make that for my grandchildren," Louise said. "But honestly, Bretons like to taste the crêpe—not the filling." I thought back to my lunch at the Quimper *créperie* the day before, when I'd scraped out the rich bacon and cheese filling and eaten just the thin pancake. Perhaps a Breton spirit had been guiding me.

"And to accompany the crêpes," Louise continued, "we drank bowls of *lait ribot* or *gros lait*."

I knew that *lait ribot* was buttermilk, the thin liquid left over in the butter churn. But what was *gros lait*, which translates literally to "fat milk"?

"C'est une spécialité bretonne, un vrai délice!" Louise assured me.

Later I discovered that *gros lait* was halfway between yogurt and fromage frais, tangy, thick, and creamy. In fact, it was probably what I'd seen my neighbor eating at the *créperie*, a traditional accompaniment to crêpes in Brittany yet almost unknown outside the region.

Louise still uses her grandmother's recipe to make crêpes, combining buckwheat and white flour for the savory version, because it makes the batter more delicate. "Crêpes from Finistère are crisp and light," she told me. "In the north they're called galettes because they're made only with buckwheat flour. They're heavier—*costaud*." She frowned a little.

Sweet crêpes in both the north and south are made solely with white flour, which Louise called *beau blé*—beautiful wheat. She serves them for dessert brushed with melted butter and perhaps a sprinkle of sugar.

"Not caramel au beurre salé?" I asked.

"What's that?" she said.

Before I left her house, Louise disappeared into the kitchen and returned with a stack of crêpes pulled from the freezer. "Take these home with you," she insisted. They were perfect, a mottled golden color, as thin as tissue paper.

"Oh, I can't," I protested. Even with today's modern conveniences, I was sure it took a lot of effort and energy to make crêpes. After all, Louise had just finished describing how she beat the batter with her hand for at least ten minutes, to "bring it to life."

But she insisted, finding a plastic bag to wrap them in and pressing them into my hands. "I have more!" she assured me. "I always have more. If I don't have any in my *frigo*, I crave them."

Her need for crêpes reminded me of my Chinese mother, who can't go more than a day without a bowl of rice, or my Italian friend Gianfranco, who requires regular infusions of pasta, or even Didier, who once told me that he missed cheese so much on a trip to South Africa that he ate an entire wheel of Camembert on the airplane home. Crêpes, I realized, were a Breton's comfort food.

"You can't make a good crêpe without butter," Sophie had said. "It provides the flavor." Her words spurred me on as I tried to hunt down a local dairy farm, driving in circles through endless stretches of green pastures, making U-turns again and again and again, obeying the GPS as it repeated itself tonelessly: *"Faites demi-tour. Faites demi-tour."* But with no real address to punch into it, I had no real directions to follow. When I called, all I could hear was the sound of mooing cows.

I was trying to find the Ferme de Kerheü, an organic, family-run farm near Quimper. Valérie Guillermou, the dairy farmer's wife and butter maven, had offered to explain the secrets of her special cultured butter. But like so many locations in rural France, the farm had no actual address, just a name and a nearby village, Briec. I flagged down a passing car and asked if there was a farm nearby. One farm? There were several. I spelled out the name, and the guy gave me directions, repeating them three times. When I finally found Valérie, she greeted me with warmth even though I was more than an hour late. Inside her stone farmhouse, we sat at the dining table while she explained *beurre de baratte:* Breton butter.

It begins, she told me, with cream, which is fermented so it's thick and slightly tangy. It is beaten in the butter churn, not an old-fashioned, hand-cranked wooden apparatus but a modern industrial machine with a deep metal basin and lethal blades that whip the fat out of the liquid "until it forms grains." She then drains the thin liquid and washes the butter, dousing it with water at least three times. "The trick to good butter is to rinse it really well," she said. "The residue of *babeurre*"—buttermilk—"is what makes it turn rancid."

After the rinsing comes the *malaxage*, or kneading, which works the butter grains by machine into a smooth mass, and then the salting—a generous sprinkling of coarse, gray sel de Guérande, which is collected on Brittany's coast.

"Breton butter is always salted," Valérie told me. "In the past, salt wasn't taxed, so they used a lot of it to preserve food."

It's the combination of this flaky, minerally salt and tangy, soured cream that makes Breton butter so desirable and delicious, with its soft texture and faint flavor of toasted hazelnuts.

The butter-making process takes about two hours from start to finish, from buckets of soured cream to molded sticks. Valérie, along with her husband, Stéphane, and their team of five employees produce about 140 pounds of the stuff a day, along with yogurt, raw milk, *gros lait*, and *lait ribot*—products that are sold at supermarkets in Finistère.

Before we said good-bye, I asked Valérie about her crêpe-eating memories. "I'm Canadian," she said. Her accent, which I had assumed was Breton, was actually Quebecois. "I immigrated to France ten years ago." But because she married into a Breton family, crêpes were woven into the fabric of her domestic life. "*Le jour des crêpes* is like an institution. Friday is for crêpes. Saturday you eat the week's leftovers. And Sunday you make a whole new meal for the family to eat until Friday."

"Do you have a favorite recipe?" I asked.

Silly question. Valérie and her family—like many of the people I met in Finistère—used to own a *crêperie*. She had perfected the professional crêpe maker's smooth, assured twist of the wrist while practicing over a *billig*, with a three-liter tub of batter by her side. "They say there are as many recipes for crêpes in Bretagne as there are people who make them," she said before rattling hers off by heart.

Indeed, everyone I met in Brittany had a crêpe recipe to share. Each formula was unique—some added milk, others an egg, a drizzle of honey, or a spoonful of sugar—but each used the same basic formula of buckwheat flour, liquid, and salt. And every person recited her recipe from memory, like a favorite poem or a prayer.

People who love food tend to speak a common language, easily exchanging ideas and culinary traditions. But what touched me most in Brittany was the generosity I encountered, the willingness to share personal memories and family recipes, down to the minutest detail. I spent one morning in Brittany at Hervé Floch'lay's house swapping cooking techniques, learning about kouign-amann, a buttery Breton cake, and telling him about my father's pork-and-cabbage dumplings.

Hervé is Breton *de souche*—from the stump—born in Finistère with Celtic roots that stretch back generations. He is a cooking professor at a local vocational school in Quimper, and in his spare time he gardens and raises chickens, makes his own cider with his own apples, and collects honey from his own beehive. His house, bright with oversize windows, is part of a small outcropping of buildings above the village of Briec, and he had invited me there to meet his family and eat homemade crêpes. On the day of my visit, he had a fire burning in the living room and a crêpe-making station set up in the kitchen, with a *billig*, deep bowls of savory and sweet batter, and a *rozelle*, the slender, T-shaped tool used to spread the mixture on the searing surface of the griddle.

I sat at the kitchen table while Hervé made crêpes, confidently swirling the pale batter over the black *billig*, allowing the batter to brown, and then turning it with a sharp flip. "What would you like in it?" he asked.

"Just butter."

Hervé stabbed a hunk of yellow butter with a fork, slid it around the hot surface of the crêpe, which he then maneuvered to a plate. It looked like dark, shining lace, a contrast of deep brown buckwheat against clean white porcelain. I cut into it and the edges shattered under the pressure of my knife, crisp bits softening to a toothsome chew, the melted butter offset by a wholesome buckwheat tang. It was a classic crêpe, a perfect marriage of crunch and tenderness. I devoured it in two minutes, and when I was done, Hervé was at the ready with his ladle and *rozelle* and wooden spatula to make me another. This time I asked for *graisse salée*. I had never knowingly enjoyed pure animal fat, but this was different: savory with onions and salt, studded with cracked black pepper, the lard melted into the crêpe, giving it a porky richness brightened by the relief of spicy bursts. By this time Hervé had made his own crêpe with *graisse salée*, and we ate them together, savoring each bite in appreciative silence.

We cleansed our palates with a few leaves of green salad, and Hervé told me crêpe tales of yore. As a little girl, his wife used to walk to the village *crêperie* bearing her own pats of butter on a plate—one for each of the pancakes she would eat. And Hervé still remembers the unique payment system at his boyhood *crêperie*: Before serving, the owner would pinch a corner from each of the crêpes consumed, then tally them up at the end of the meal to calculate the bill.

Hervé smeared only melted butter on his dessert crêpes, but they didn't need anything else. The contrast of sweet dough and salted butter, of brittle and spongy, was a study in textures and flavors, decadent simplicity. But what about the famous sauce au caramel au beurre salé? Whenever I'd mentioned Brittany and crêpes to friends in Paris, they'd breathed the words "salted butter caramel" before slumping into a swoon. Yet no one in Finistère seemed to know what I was talking about. As Hervé and I swiped the last vestiges of butter from our plates, I finally uncovered the story.

"When I was a kid, there was no sauce au caramel au beurre salé," he said. "We had caramels—individually wrapped sweets—but not a sauce for crêpes."

"So it was something created for . . ." I could scarcely bring myself to utter the word.

"Tourists? *Ouais*." Hervé nodded. "People have the impression they're eating something classically Breton. But the truth is, fifteen years ago it didn't even exist. That doesn't mean it's bad," he added, seeing the shocked expression on my face. "It's not traditional. But it tastes good, it's easy to prepare ahead of service. Personally, I really like sauce au caramel au beurre salé."

Still, I couldn't help but feel a little disappointed.

During my spring visit to Brittany, I kept looking for buckwheat fields. I asked Louise if she remembered them from her Breton childhood, and she described endless acres of white flowers with red stems and an exquisite perfume. However, as I drove around the Quimper countryside on my final afternoon in Brittany, I didn't see a single leaf of the plant. Why? I asked Youenn Le Gall—a local farmer and owner of the buckwheat-producing Ferme de Kerveguen—and he guffawed. *"C'est une plante d'été,"* he said.

"A summer plant? *C'est-à-dire . . .*"

"You sow it in mid-June and reap in September. It only takes a hundred days," he explained patiently. "It grows very, very fast. Faster than weeds."

Buckwheat is a plant native to East Asia. It came to Western Europe in the twelfth century (some sources say later), traveling in the food sacks and saddlebags of soldiers fighting in the Crusades. In fact, the French word for buckwheat—*sarrasin*—is the same one used during the Middle Ages to refer to Muslims; doubtless there was a racially tinged connection between *blé noir*—the darker flour made from *sarrasin*—and the darker-skinned immigrants who imported it.

With a resistant, fast-growing nature and its ability to thrive in anemic soil, buckwheat long ago earned a reputation as a food of the poor. "When the earth is poor, so are the people," Youenn said. But as commercial transport increased and white flour became more available, the dark and heavy *blé noir* eventually lost favor. In the

1960s, when the French government decided to make Brittany a dairy-producing region, the focus of local farmers switched to cows and buckwheat production decreased dramatically. By the 1990s local *crêperies* found themselves importing Brittany's traditional staple from Canada. That's when some Breton farmers formed a cooperative and started growing it again.

In recent years nutritionists have touted buckwheat as a miracle food, full of amino acids and other beneficial compounds. But Bretons have long known the nutritional benefits of this hardy plant. After all, over five hundred years ago it saved them from famine.

During the fifteenth century, Duchess Anne of Bretagne first planted crops of buckwheat in the region. A Breton noblewoman, Anne loved her native country with a fierce loyalty, so deeply that—despite marriage to two kings of France—she fought to maintain its independence as a duchy. Part of this independence was self-sustenance, and as a wise and prescient ruler she encouraged the cultivation of buckwheat, recognizing it as a nutritious plant that grew quickly and easily in the area's poor soil. Thus buckwheat spread throughout the region, and Anne established herself as a beloved ruler. After her death she became the patron saint of Brittany.

For three centuries buckwheat continued to flourish in Brittany. "Wheat was taxed," Youenn said. "But not *blé noir*." This explained, in part, its wide appeal.

"But why use it to make crêpes?" I asked. "Why not bread?"

He regarded me with a bemused air. "You can't make bread from *sarrasin*. There's no gluten in it. The dough is too heavy. It won't rise."

"Well, what about . . . ?" My mind raced over the cooking options. Aside from bread, it was difficult to think of another really satisfying, hearty, nutritious food that could be made from flour. "Can you make porridge?"

"In the north of Finistère, they make kig ha farz," he acknowledged. "It's a kind of stew. They stuff a piece of cloth with buckwheat dough and boil it with the meat so that it absorbs all the fat." I could tell from the way he described it—with a little moue of distaste—that he did not consider kig ha farz to be a dish worthy of exploration.

"So that leaves . . . crêpes."

"*Oui.*"

"Because people had nothing to eat but *sarrasin*. And the only way to eat *sarrasin* is as a crêpe."

"*Oui.*"

Later, driving back to my bed-and-breakfast in the gray drizzle of a spring afternoon, I considered the paradox: One of France's most beloved dishes—a food that had come to symbolize the country around the world—had begun as a product of penury and survival, of sustenance. It was the story of the world's staple foods, from corn to oats to rice—out of hardship had come innovation, and out of innovation had come enduring bounty.

It sounded, actually, like a pretty good philosophy for life.

Galettes de Blé Noir

Of all the crêpes I ate in Brittany—and there were many—Hervé
Floch'lay's remain my favorite. He offered me his recipe in exchange
for one of mine (for Chinese dumplings), and though I tried to faithfully replicate his, I found the pure buckwheat-flour batter frustrat-
ingly difficult to handle. Without any gluten, the crêpes were stodgy
and thick; they broke easily and stuck to the pan. Through trial and
error, I discovered that a fifty-fifty mix of buckwheat and white
flours creates a silky batter that produces delicate crêpes with crisp
edges. (Buckwheat flour, by the way, is available at health-food
stores, produced by special mills like Bob's Red Mill, which also offers mail order nationwide.) I like to eat galettes plain with a little
salted butter, but filled crêpes are a beloved, inexpensive meal in
France, especially the complète: cheese, ham, and an *oeuf miroir*, or
sunny-side-up egg.

Keep your pan lightly oiled (if it's too greasy, the batter won't
spread evenly) and continue adjusting the heat until it's at the correct temperature—not too hot or cold. This requires some patience,
but as they say in French, the first crêpe is always *ratée*, or failed, the
one you feed to the dog or cat. Actually, for me the first three or four
are flops, but I eat them anyway.

Serves 4

1 cup buckwheat flour
1 cup all-purpose flour
Pinch of salt
Salted butter

Crêpe fillings

Grated cheese (Emmental or Gruyère is traditional), thin
slices of ham, eggs, sautéed spinach, caramelized onions,
goat cheese—let your imagination run wild!

Mixing the batter

In a large bowl, stir together the buckwheat and all-purpose flours
and a pinch of salt. Add 3 cups of water. With your hand (yes, your
bare hand), stir the ingredients vigorously and continuously for 2
to 3 minutes until a smooth and homogeneous batter is formed.
Cover the bowl with plastic wrap and refrigerate for at least 2 hours
and preferably overnight. (This is an important step; it allows the
buckwheat to absorb the water and creates a batter that spreads
more easily.)

Cooking the crêpes

Stir the batter. If it seems too thick, add a small dash or two of water
until the batter's consistency resembles light cream.

Heat an 8-inch nonstick skillet over a medium flame for a minute
or two (you want the crêpe to cook quickly, but you don't want the
butter or batter to scorch). Stir the batter thoroughly. Melt a tiny
sliver of butter in the pan. Using a ladle, pour about ¼ cup of batter
into the pan, swirling and shaking in order to spread the batter
across the surface and create a very thin, even layer. This takes
some skill and also requires a hot—but not too hot—pan. (If the
batter is too thick, and doesn't spread fluidly, stir in more water, a
tablespoon at a time.) Cook for 60 to 90 seconds, until the edges

73

start to brown and curl away from the pan. Shake the pan sharply—if the crêpe detaches, it's ready to be flipped. If it sticks, allow it to cook for a few more seconds. Toss the pan to flip the crêpe or slide a spatula underneath and turn it over. Cook the other side until golden, about 30 seconds.

For a galette complète

Place a small handful of shredded cheese and a thin slice of ham in the center of the crêpe. If desired, crack an egg into a small dish and add it to the center, using a spatula to contain the white and prevent it from running everywhere until it has set. Cook over medium heat until the cheese has melted and the egg is done. Form a little package by folding two sides of the crêpe around the egg as best you can, like a loose burrito, taking care not to cover the yolk. Serve immediately.

Chapter 4

Lyon / Salade Lyonnaise

Some ideas appear in the shower, magically whole and crystal-clear perfect. Others creep up on you gradually, sucked up through the subconscious the way a carnation absorbs dyed water, slowly drinking through its stalk until all the petals are blue. My idea to find a job was of the latter variety.

I know. I was supposed to be writing—another novel, a flurry of magazine articles. I should have been pitching travel stories until my fingers fell off from typing. But establishing freelance credentials in another country takes time, and I was still new in town, still trying to separate the fresh ideas from the clichés. Protective of their territory, my fellow American-expat travel writers hadn't exactly welcomed me with open arms or shared lists of e-mail contacts (not that I expected them to). And my editors, used to articles from me about Asia or Washington, D.C., were confused by my shift in focus. I heard the word "no" a lot: No, thanks. Not for us. I'm not seeing this. Or—the most common form—silence.

As for my new novel . . . Well . . .

"Did you make any progress today?" Calvin's voice, transmitted from Baghdad over the Internet, sounded tinny and echoey through my computer's speakers.

"On Le Projet? Not really." Le Projet was my second novel, the one I was allegedly writing—all fifteen hundred words of it.

It was my favorite time of the day—cocktail hour—when I poured myself a glass of wine, shook some cashews into a little bowl, and met my husband. Virtually, that is. Every evening we chatted by Skype, our voices and images transported over two thousand miles in the blink of a modem. Baghdad is one hour ahead of Paris (two in the winter), and so we started and ended our days at about the same time, a confluence of schedules for which I was grateful. Somehow sharing almost the same time zone made him seem not quite so far away.

"It's so weird," I continued. "Every morning the same thing happens. I make myself a cup of tea, sit down at my computer, and . . . log in to Facebook." We laughed, but I was serious. Ever since Calvin's departure a month ago, my discipline had been washed away by a sea of cat videos. The life of a writer was not for the faint of heart, or the thin of skin, or the flighty of mind. But I am only human, and I wrestled with bouts of self-doubt and sensitivity and entire afternoons lost to Google searches for narwhals. And now, without Calvin, I struggled with something else: isolation. I had a few friends whom I saw as frequently as social boundaries allowed, perhaps once or twice a week. But I interacted with no one on a daily basis, not even—as I had hoped—the apartment building's *gardienne*, who left our mail on the doormat. I craved human contact, to be part of a community. And so, being American, I set out to find one the only way I knew how: work.

"Have you heard back from any bookstores?" Calvin reached to pour another glass of wine, and the image on my monitor distorted, his tender blue eyes and generous mouth dissolving into a blur.

"*Nyet.*" I had left my résumé with a handful of anglophone bookshops in the hopes that someone was looking for a clerk. So far none had responded.

"Well, *perviy blin komom.*" Calvin had several Russian phrases that he trotted out from time to time. They all sounded the same to me.

"Uh, never drink vodka on a Moscow balcony in January?"

"The first pancake is always a flop."

I hit my head with my hand. "How do I always forget that one?" If Calvin had been standing next to me in the kitchen, I might have leaned over and given him an affectionate squeeze. But as we were gazing at each other through our laptops, a pixelated smile had to suffice.

"How about you?" I asked. "How was your day?"

He launched into a tale of office politics, which I followed as if it were a soap opera. I found Calvin's colleagues fascinating, though I'd never met most of them. I often thought about them at the gym or while washing dishes, wondering if Anjali had eaten at any of the restaurants I'd recommended in New York or if Timothy had chosen Addis Ababa or Kuala Lumpur for his next assignment. Clearly this was another sign that I needed to get out more.

"And then," Calvin continued, "just as I was heading back to the dorm from the DFAC"—the military dining facility—"a duck-and-cover alarm went off, and I had to wait in a bomb shelter for the all clear. That's why I was a little late tonight."

"Were there any bombs?" I took a sip of wine and resisted the urge to down the whole glass.

"I did hear some this time," he admitted. We both fell quiet, and the silence stretched between us, broken by faint electronic creaks and scratches. "Don't worry," he said eventually. "I don't think there were any direct hits."

This, then, also haunted my solitude: fear and worry, twin demons that crept through my thoughts, darkening my imagination. I tried to smother them, tried to distract myself by looking for a job or worrying about the whiteflies attacking my window-box planters. But there were words I couldn't bring myself to say: Mortar fire.

Body armor. Car bombs. Attacked convoys. Rationally I knew that Calvin spent most of his time in a fortified embassy compound in the protected Green Zone, reportedly one of the safest places in Baghdad. When he traveled within Iraq (which was more often than I liked), he and his colleagues rode in armored vehicles, accompanied by armed bodyguards. But this was my *husband* we were talking about—my nearsighted, kindhearted, beloved husband. My favorite person in the world. My anxiety knew no rationality.

"Should we talk the same time tomorrow?" Calvin pushed down the top of the empty Styrofoam take-out box that held his dinner and moved it to the side of his desk.

"Oh, I can't! I almost forgot—I'm volunteering tomorrow night."

"Where?"

"At the American Library in Paris." The English-language library was near the Eiffel Tower. Edith Wharton used to be a member—and Gertrude Stein. "They host weekly author readings. I'll be helping with the drinks, pouring wine and passing around peanuts."

"Mmm, red wine and peanuts. That reminds me of . . ."

"Peanut butter and jelly?"

"*Doesn't* it? Do you think everyone thinks so?"

"Maybe I can conduct an impromptu survey tomorrow night."

"I can't wait to hear all about it."

I smiled at him, and his eyes crinkled in response, just for a second losing the shadow of perpetual fatigue caused by the pressure of his job, the seven-day workweeks, the worry that his wife was too isolated.

"I think this is a great idea." It was almost imperceptible, but in his voice I thought I heard a faint note of relief that I was finally getting out of the house.

* * *

Calvin was right. Volunteering at the American Library was a great idea. No, not just great. Utterly fantastic. A lucky break. Because if I hadn't volunteered that night, I would never have known about the job opening for programs manager, the person in charge of inviting writers to talk about their books. It was a part-time job so perfect I would have eaten a big plate of andouillette to get it. Happily, all it took was an interview, during which I managed to convince the library director, Charlie Trueheart, that my experience as a former editorial assistant and first-time novelist meant I was highly skilled at handling the special neuroses unique to authors. When he offered me the job, I felt giddy with happiness.

Now it was early summer, and after a couple of months of brainstorming meetings, gossip over the electric kettle, birthday cakes, and happy hours, I felt enormously grateful to be part of a team. Sure, there were small crises—like the time a famous, bestselling author forgot about his speaking appearance, leaving me scrambling to find a replacement at the last minute. Or the time I miscalculated metric centiliters and spent an entire month's wine budget on three cases of *half bottles*. But these mishaps were tiny compared with the comforting exoskeleton of routine the job gave me.

My colleagues were a mix of French people who had studied in the United States and Americans who had dual citizenship with Ireland, which gave them the right to work in Europe. (I have never met so many Americans carrying Irish passports as in Paris.) They were all friendly and collegial, chatting with me in English and using the informal *tu* right away when we spoke in French. And yet, despite the bilingual setting, the office felt comfortingly American, right down to the communal kitchen that smelled of stale coffee and the flock of fresh-faced summer interns imported straight from New

England. I had been too proud to admit it to anyone, but ever since Calvin's departure I'd struggled to feel at home again in Paris, where the telemarketers repeated themselves loudly and slowly to me as if I were a child, where the cashier at the grocery store refused to break a fifty-euro note, where a polite smile was often met with a blank stare. I sank into the American Library's friendly familiarity, so lulled by it that I had no idea I was making an enormous cultural gaffe every single day.

I began to get an inkling of the error of my ways one sunny afternoon, when I'd been on the job for a few weeks. I had picked up a salad for lunch—stepping out into beautiful mid-June sunshine and crisp breezes—and brought it back to eat in the office. At my desk I speared a piece of cucumber with one hand and checked my e-mail with the other.

"Ooh, that looks good." Elizabeth, the children's librarian, appeared, weaving her way around the desks that made up the open-plan back office. "Did you go to the Greek *traiteur*?"

"Mmm, yes. Thanks so much for the suggestion." I pointed to my plastic container of Greek salad and stuffed grape leaves. "I'm so happy to find a light lunch around here. I was having this recurring dream where I opened the office-supply cupboard and found a chopped-salad bar."

She laughed. "Have a good lunch!" she said before tossing her purse over her shoulder and heading out the door.

I resumed scrolling through my e-mail, pausing when François, the quietly intimidating collections librarian, hurried by my desk. "*À plus tard!*" I said to his swiftly retreating back.

"*Bon appétit!*" called the reference librarian, Lisa, as she breezed past, a plastic bag swinging from one hand. Was it my imagination, or did she shoot a disapproving glance at the food on my desk?

Silence descended in the office, which was normal—this was a library, right? But it felt odd without the companionable click of other keyboards. I got up and walked over to the adjoining room of the office and out into the reading room. Even the front desk had a skeleton crew of volunteers. Where was everybody? I checked the kitchen, where I found José, the elegant, gray-haired circulation manager, eating a sandwich and reading a magazine. "Enjoy your lunch," I whispered, backing out of the room.

How do you spend your lunch break? I'd always thought of the noonish hour as a chance to step outside, run errands, and pick up a salad or a sandwich, which I'd scarf down back at my desk.

As it turns out, in France the lunch hour is used for . . . well, eating.

According to recent studies, 60 percent of French people enjoy their daily midday meal in a restaurant. Compare this with almost 60 percent of Americans, who eat at their desks while continuing to work. I was one of them. Every day I lunched at my desk, trying hard not to drop crumbs on my computer keyboard, and every day I became increasingly aware of the silence around me.

Though a flurry of recent news articles has reported the demise of the traditional French lunch break, I witnessed the inverse among my colleagues. Even when they heated up leftovers or nibbled on a baguette sandwich, they preferred to dine in the small office kitchen, seated at a table, with a napkin and proper cutlery. After they finished eating, they read a book or took a walk and didn't return to their desks until the entire hour had elapsed. No one ever said anything to me, but their daily disappearance spoke volumes. So did the employee regulations, which encouraged a lunch break in muscular language. The idea of eating mindlessly and hurriedly in front of the computer was unwholesome to the point of being unhealthy.

Of all the meals eaten in France, I'd argue that lunch is the most important. It's an opportunity to draw a line between morning and afternoon, a chance not only to satisfy hunger but also to refresh the mind. French children are taught the art of lunch, dining every day in the school cafeteria on four courses, including cheese. For adults a government-mandated, employer-sponsored program helps fund the midday meal, distributing meal vouchers called *tickets-restaurants* (nicknamed *tickets restos* and accepted by restaurants and take-out shops) to workers whose offices lack a canteen. According to the Code du Travail, or French labor code, employers are required to offer a *pause déjeuner* for every six hours of work. In contrast, only twenty-two American states—fewer than half—require a meal break.

Are the United States and France two nations separated by the midday meal? Even our differences in lunch vocabulary seem to indicate our diverging attitudes. Take, for example, the salad, a typical lunch choice from Washington to Paris, Chicago to Lyon. In France there is the *salade composée*—a pile of lettuce topped with organized piles of cheese and cubes of ham, or flaked tuna and blanched green beans. The very name, that word—"composed"— is that a message? Eat me, the *salade composée* says, and you will be as serene and unruffled as my name implies. In contrast are American salads: tossed. Quick and convenient, thrown together at a bar, they're a combination of ingredients and dressings that each person chooses for herself.

The longer I worked at the American Library, the more I thought about lunch. And the more I thought about lunch, the more I contemplated salad. American salads, like chilled iceberg wedges draped in creamy blue-cheese dressing. French salads, like my favorite, lyonnaise, with its contrasts of bitter frisée and salty bacon, tart vinaigrette and quivering poached egg.

"Stop! Stop!" Calvin protested as I described the latter during our nightly Skype chat. "You're making me too hungry. Any talk about food is like torture." Calvin ate three meals a day at the embassy's dining facility, which offered a completely inoffensive menu of bland American classics.

"We'll eat some when you come home," I promised.

"I can't wait." He smiled at me, and for a moment it felt as if we were in the same room together, as if I could reach out and touch him.

"How many weeks until your vacation?" I glanced at the calendar on my desk. "Five? Oh, no, six."

We both fell silent. It felt like forever.

"Maybe you could take another trip before I get back," Calvin said eventually. He leaned forward a little in his chair. "You could go to Lyon and see if they really eat salad."

"You mean launch a pressing investigation into whether or not Lyon is the cradle of . . . *the work lunch?*" I laughed. "That sounds like just an excuse to travel around and eat."

"Well," Calvin raised an eyebrow. "Why not?"

Some serious eating occurs in Lyon, I noticed right away. In this town dining out requires a special vocabulary, even for French people. It's a place where nuggets of fried pork rind, *grattons,* replace cocktail-hour peanuts, and a scoop of silk worker's brains, cervelle de canut, refers to herb-flecked farmer's cheese. Here restaurants are called *bouchons,* a word with many meanings: cork, plug, or a bunch of packed straw once used to wipe down a sweating horse. In fact, Lyon's classic eateries take their name from these handfuls of hay, used during the days of carriages and stagecoaches, when the city was an important rest stop between the treacherous mountains of the Alps and the Massif Central. Tired travelers would stop at roadside inns to eat, sleep, and groom their weary horses. Over time these simple establishments became known simply as *bouchons*.

At least that's one version of the story. Other accounts were either more simplistic (*bouchon* refers to the cork of a wine bottle) or strangely complex (a long tale involving Bacchus, branches of pinecones evolving into bunches of hay, and wordplay). Whatever the legend, it's true that at some point before the twentieth century these convivial, warmly lit bistros became the signature eateries of Lyon, renowned for excellent food, a casual ambience—and a special midmorning meal called the *mâchon*.

On my first day in Lyon, I learned all about the *mâchon* from two members of the Confrérie des Francs-Mâchons, Emmanuel Peyre de Fabrègues and Christian Proton, respectively the organization's president and vice president. Rooted in the Lyonnais tradition of secret societies—the group's name is a pun on *francs-maçons*, or freemasons—this brotherhood of forty men strives to preserve the tradition of the hearty morning meal, meeting one morning a month to sample a *mâchon* at an untested *bouchon*. At the end of the year, they bestow awards to Lyon's best establishments: a small plaque emblazoned with Gnafron (a satirical figure, like Punch or Judy) and the words *authentique bouchon lyonnais*.

"*Un vrai bouchon* always serves the *mâchon*," said Emmanuel. "At nine in the morning, you can sit down to a selection of salads"—lentils, pickled herrings, *clapotons* (sheep's trotters), and salade lyonnaise, to name a few—"followed by a big hot dish"—like andouillette, poached *tête de veau*, or calf's head—"and then some cheese."

I gulped. Nine o'clock in the morning? "Does that mean the *mâchon* takes the place of lunch?" I asked.

"Oh, no!" Emmanuel said cheerfully. "They eat again at noon!"

I felt the waist of my pants pinch a little, just at the thought of all that food.

Emmanuel, with his rimmed glasses and dark jeans, his royal purple sweater and double-cuffed shirtsleeves, his job as an advertising director, is what the French would describe as *bobo*, short for the young, self-consciously chic, often reviled slice of society known as *bourgeois-bohème*. In contrast, Christian was an *ouvrier d'état*, a local mail carrier with a bald head and the sturdy frame of a rugby player.

The two had invited me for lunch at Chez Georges, a Confrérie-approved *bouchon* (I saw the plaque on the door), where it's possible to tuck into a plate of stewed tripe at nine in the morning. We squeezed into a corner table covered in paper, and I took in the dining room's classic *bouchon* ambience, a mix of lace curtains, vinyl tablecloths, and wooden chairs. The walls were covered in chalkboard menus, copper pans, straw hats, and other bric-a-brac.

"The *mâchon* was eaten by laborers, mainly *canuts*"—silk workers—"who began their workday very early, around four or five in the morning," said Christian. He explained that the meal dates to the nineteenth century, when Lyon was an industrial center and silk production dominated the local economy. After a morning of manual labor, these workers needed a hearty and caloric spread of food, which they washed down with a *pot* (or two or three) of the region's Beaujolais wine.

Over salade lyonnaise and a quenelle de brochet, Emmanuel waxed rhetorical. "Why is Lyon considered the capital of French gastronomy?" I listened as I sliced off a piece of the rather solid fish dumpling and dabbed it in the coral puddle of crayfish sauce Nantua. "Just look at a map of France," he answered himself.

Indeed, the city sits at an epicurean crossroads, surrounded by several famous food-producing regions, all of which stock its larder. The sun-warmed produce and olive oil of the south, the butter and cheeses of the north, the beef from the Massif Central, poultry from Bresse, wines from Beaujolais and the Rhône Valley, not to mention imports from neighboring Italy and Switzerland, are all easily obtainable. "When the products are good, people like to eat. When people like to eat, they like to cook," concluded Emmanuel.

In 43 B.C. the Romans founded a colony here, Lugdunum, centered on two rivers, the Saône and the Rhône. The town quickly grew into a commercial hub, eventually becoming the capital of the Roman Empire's region of Gaul, second in size only to Rome. By the fifteenth century, Italian merchants had arrived, constructing pastel-colored Renaissance mansions—many still grace the city— and introducing a series of silk markets, similar to the trading fairs of Troyes. Under their influence Lyon blossomed into the economic powerhouse of France.

The greatest evolution in Lyonnais cuisine occurred during the first half of the twentieth century, with the advent of the Mères Lyonnaises. "They were often quite fat, with very strong personalities," said Christian. "And they really, *really* knew how to cook."

The kitchen skills of the *mères* had their roots in the grand bourgeois homes scattered throughout Lyon. As servants and cooks for those wealthy families, these women used the region's fine ingredients to create meals that were simple yet perfect. After World War I, however, the French economy crashed, the bourgeoisie closed or sold their mansions, and many of the women found themselves unemployed. With their work experience limited to the kitchen, they turned to restaurants and *bouchons*, staffing establishments that served a few dishes cooked exquisitely. The advent of automobile travel brought customers from far and wide, and eventually word of Lyon's exceptional cuisine spread throughout France, helped in large part by the celebrated French food writer Curnonsky, who in 1934 declared Lyon "the world capital of gastronomy." Some women—like the famed Mère Brazier—even saw their restaurants earn Michelin stars.

Today, although there are few of the original *mères* left in the kitchen, their influence endures. I discovered evidence of this *cuisine de femmes* at one Lyonnais restaurant, La Voûte Chez Léa, even though a man, Philippe Rabatel, currently owns it.

Rabatel has the kind eyes of someone who loves to feed people and a heavy frame possibly made heavier from the cream-laced and butter-rich dishes he prepares. In 1980 he bought Chez Léa from Madame Léa, taking over the kitchen that she first established in 1942. "She was the last *mère* to open up a restaurant in Lyon," he told me. "I spent six months with her, learning all her recipes." Even after her retirement, Madame Léa lived in an apartment above the restaurant until her death several years later.

Many of Madame Léa's recipes still appear on the restaurant's menu, including her salade lyonnaise. I asked Rabatel if he knew its origins.

"Who knows?" He shrugged. "It could have been the washer-women who invented it." In the days before refrigeration or washing machines, he said, laundresses carried loads of soiled clothes to the river's edge, along with picnics of bacon, hard-boiled eggs, and bread. Perhaps, Rabatel suggested, they gathered wild dandelion leaves along the way and tossed everything together into a big salad at the lunch hour.

Though this theory seems dubious, a few details give it a shred of credibility. First, salade lyonnaise *is* traditionally made with dan-

delion leaves—Rabatel serves them in season. Second, in local par-
lance dandelion is called "lion's tooth," or *dent-de-lion*. Somehow,
over the ages, could this mouthful of words, *salade de dents-de-lion*,
have been shortened to salade lyonnaise?

Madame Léa's version, as interpreted by Rabatel, arrived in a
large glass bowl with sides cloudy from vinaigrette. Inside, a pile of
curly frisée leaves tumbled with slivers of lardons, garlic-rubbed
croutons, and a soft-boiled egg gently broken so that its yolk trick-
led into the receptive crags of lettuce and bread, the whole *just* over-
dressed *à la française*. I took a bite, and the tang of vinaigrette hit my
palate, followed by the flush of bacon and something else deep and
sumptuous. Smoked herring? As I ate, I thought of Madame Léa,
and tried to imagine her as a young kitchen maid. At age sixteen she
was sent into service at a bourgeois home, Rabatel told me, working
for the same family for eight years. Was her hand evident in the vinaigrette, with its audacious hint of smoked herring? Had she boiled
her eggs this way, with the yolk at that creamy point between soft
and hard?

Even as I ate, I considered something else Rabatel had said: "No
one ever invents a recipe. All the best chefs get their greatest recipes
from their grandmother's kitchen." So, then, was this Madame Léa's
grandmother's salad? Even with a recipe, a dish can never be re-
created exactly. It will always be filtered through the hands of the
cook, her memory of taste, the ingredients available, the weather,
and a hundred other factors. Eating Madame Léa's salad was a little
like reading the *Odyssey* and straining to hear the voice of an ancient
Greek poet—evident in some spots, in others maybe not at all.

Despite the multitude of organizations that exist to defend and protect them, *bouchons* have suffered in recent years. No one I spoke to

wanted to declare that they were vanishing, but everyone acknowledged that *"vrais bouchons"* were becoming scarce. When I asked the Lyonnais I met if they ever dined in *bouchons*, their answer was almost uniformly the same: Yes, but only when we have friends visiting from out of town.

Only Emmanuel and Christian, who enjoy a monthly *mâchon* with the Confrérie, professed to be steady *bouchon* diners. But even they made this assertion with a slight air of embarrassment. "Sure, we eat at *bouchons* all the time—can't you tell?" Christian joked, patting his solid midsection and chuckling. Yet somewhere in his self-conscious smile, there was an acknowledgment that a regular diet of *bouchon* cuisine was not sustainable, even though, as he'd declared, "in Lyon pork is a vegetable that's eaten with everything."

So who frequents the *bouchons*?

The answer: tourists.

The experience of eating in an authentic *bouchon* is, arguably, Lyon's top tourist attraction. And, as with any successful endeavor, imitators have followed. Yves Rivoiron warned me about these knockoffs. "There are many *bouchons* that aren't real *bouchons*," he said.

Rivoiron is the owner of the Café des Fédérations and a former member of the Association de Défense des Bouchons, a preservation society that is now defunct. His *bouchon*, nicknamed La Fédé, is considered a Lyonnais institution, established, as the sign painted on the windows indicates, *"depuis bien longtemps"*—a very long time ago.

"When I took over, the previous owner told me, 'Make an evolution, not a revolution,'" Rivoiron said. "I'm very careful to preserve the authenticity." It was midafternoon, the witching hour between the lunch and dinner services, and we were sitting in the empty dining room. He gestured at the tables covered in checked cloths and butcher paper, the bare fluorescent bulbs on the ceiling. "But how can we evolve?" he asked. Behind the restaurateur's mask of smiling good cheer, his eyes were shadowed with genuine concern.

For Rivoiron the answer has been to expand his dining room and increase the restaurant's hours. "I'm thinking of opening on Sundays and throughout the month of August," he said. This was not, I knew, a small decision for a French employer—especially a small-business owner—considering the financial restrictions imposed by the thirty-five-hour workweek. Employers pay high rates of social-security tax for every employee, and many can't afford to hire extra help. Nevertheless, Rivoiron explained, "being in a tourist zone means being in a service industry."

There are those who accuse La Fédé of being *too* touristy, an assertion that made Rivoiron bristle. "I don't like the negative connotation of the word," he said. "Tourists these days are intelligent and well read. We welcome them, but that doesn't mean we're not preserving our traditional spirit."

Later, walking the curved cobblestone streets near the Hôtel de Ville, I considered his theory. *Bouchons* seemed to be perched on every corner, glowing with old-fashioned bonhomie, yet only a scattered few featured the true sign of authenticity, the plaque of Gnafron. "But even if the majority of customers are tourists, these places are still authentic. Yes," Rivoiron had said.

When I thought back to my own vacations, however, to the hours spent plotting itineraries, right down to the last crumb of designer macaron, I couldn't help but question his conviction. The slightest hint of a tourist trap—touts at the door, menus in English, the bright blue and yellow of a Rick Steves guidebook—could turn a culinary discovery banal. Authenticity sometimes seemed as elusive as a unicorn. And foodie tourists are an exasperating and exacting pack, influenced by rumors and legends and online forums, determined to capture the mythical beast and document it with a digital camera.

Perhaps, I thought, Emmanuel and Christian and the Confrérie des Francs-Mâchons had it right all along. Maybe the survival of the *bouchon* is linked to that of the *mâchon*. If *bouchons* exist to serve the *mâchon*, then the *mâchon* must continue. Suddenly consuming three thousand calories at nine in the morning didn't seem like a gluttonous indulgence. It was a sacrifice.

My favorite meal in Lyon was at Chez Hugon, a mother-son *bouchon* (she's in the front, he's in the kitchen) where I ate lentils dressed with bacon and a quenelle de brochet that resembled a small football and had a texture reminiscent of a cloud's. The restaurant was almost empty that evening because it was a four-day holiday weekend, yet the customers chose to sit clustered together instead of spreading throughout the small dining room. In the fluorescent lighting, with a paper napkin spread across my lap, I slid a fork through the quenelle's airy sponge, served from a family-style platter, and relaxed against the chatter of my neighbors. The room reminded me of a conversation I'd had earlier in the day, with Gérard Trachet, president of the Société des Amis de Lyon et de Guignol, a Lyon preservation organization (yes, another one). I finally felt I was witnessing the true spirit of a *bouchon*, where strangers sit "elbow to elbow," as he had described.

To really understand *bouchons*, Trachet had explained, one must first understand the industrial fervor that swept Lyon between the fifteenth and nineteenth centuries, when the town lived and breathed for only one thing: silk. Italian merchants had introduced the precious cloth during the fifteenth century; by the eighteenth century, Lyon supplied the whole of Europe with bolts of heavy brocade and meters of gold-embossed ribbon.

Locals still call the Croix Rousse, the former neighborhood of the silk weavers, *la colline qui travaille*—the hill that works. (In contrast, adjacent Fourvière, with its watchful basilica, is known as *la colline qui prie*—the hill that prays.) The area still bears the marks of industry, with boxy, high-ceilinged lofts built to accommodate massive weaving machines and secret passageways, called *traboules*, which allowed workers to transport bolts of cloth without going outside. (Decades later the Resistance, too, used this hidden network of alleys during the Nazi occupation.) Silk weaving was a laborious process, one that required strength, skill, and hours of physical toil. The weavers, called *canuts*, existed under dismal conditions, working fourteen hours a day for a miserable wage.

In the pyramid that was the nineteenth-century Lyonnais silk industry, wealthy merchants, called *soyeux*, sat at the top, followed by a larger layer of master weavers, followed by thousands of workers, apprentices and women among them. The world of the *canuts* rarely overlapped with that of the *soyeux*, who financed the manufacturing. But there *was* one place where bourgeois and workers alike gathered to eat, drink, and socialize: the *bouchon*. Here the wine flowed freely, everyone tucked into humble dishes like tablier de sapeur, a sort of chicken-fried tripe, and men addressed each other as *tu*, not *vous*. Though merchants and workers didn't necessarily share their meals together, they did sit elbow to elbow, equals in the same establishment.

Over time *bouchons* evolved into social centers, where *canuts* met their colleagues to enjoy the morning *mâchon*, a bit of wine, and good gossip, discussing the price of silk and whether their work, which was paid by the piece, was being fairly compensated. With silk prices determined by the *soyeux*, the weavers were largely powerless. Still, things continued fairly peacefully until 1831, when an economic crisis hit Europe.

Demand for silk sharply declined, and silk prices tumbled. The *canuts* became anxious to protect their salaries, lobbying the *soyeux* to establish a fixed price for silk; the *soyeux* refused, saying it would hamper their trade. In November 1831 a group of frustrated *canuts* organized a violent revolt, halting silk production for weeks. In the end, however, their efforts proved unsuccessful. By December the national army had swept in and crushed the insurrection. The idea of the fixed price was swept away, and normal life resumed.

Until the next rebellion occurred, in 1834. And the next one in 1848. During the first half of the nineteenth century, the *canuts* organized three major revolts. Though the national army squashed each one, these events paved the way for the *canuts* to create trade unions that would protect their rights and salaries. "The entire population went on strike," Trachet told me. "And in the end they succeeded."

But what does this have to do with the *bouchon*?

Remember that for most nineteenth-century *canuts* life revolved around the *mâchon*, the morning meal that was often the bright spot of an otherwise dreary workday. It was in the *bouchon* that they chatted, networked for jobs, complained about their silk prices, debated local politics—and, in all likelihood, plotted demonstrations. Is it too big a leap to suggest that some of the world's first organized labor movements were fueled by salade lyonnaise?

Lest you think that I'm grasping at straws, I'd like to refer to an article, *"Sur un coin de table, le mâchon lyonnais,"* by Bruno Benoît, from the French journal *Le Dossier: Casse-croûte*, which posited this very theory that silk workers hatched the *canut* revolts over the *mâchon*.

The daytime meal, whether the *mâchon* or lunch, was more than just a chance to refuel between morning, noon, and night. It was more, as well, than a restful pause during the day—more even than a chance to laugh with colleagues and commiserate over the evil boss. It was—for the *canuts* at least—an opportunity to gather, debate, and organize, to try to change their world. I imagined their motto could have been "If you want to go fast, eat alone. If you want to go far, eat together."

It was so simple. Obvious, really. Salad, lunch, and work—they had been linked all along, a sturdy triumvirate of food, rest, and camaraderie. It took a trip to Lyon to remind me that food has the power to unite, that the act of eating can create a community.

And wasn't a community what I'd been looking for all along?

In Lyon I had faithfully learned the importance of lunch. But a few weeks after my trip, back in Paris, my lunches remained the same: a small carton of Greek salad, some hummus spread on a few crackers, eaten alone at my desk. I usually enjoyed the quiet time, reading the newspaper online or catching up on e-mail. But as the days and nights without Calvin wore on, as my evenings at home continued to mirror my lunches—a bit of food eaten in front of the computer— the loneliness started to engulf me once again. At the office I listened to my colleagues make quick phone calls about grocery lists—"*Oui, chérie,* I'll pick up some lemons, *pas de problème*"— before bustling home to walk the dog. In the métro I saw couples on their way to dinner parties, juggling large bouquets of flowers; in the street I passed groups of friends cheek-kissing each other hello.

I had hoped that through my job, I would find a community—and, to a certain extent, I had—but it hadn't lifted me out of my solitude.

"Why don't you invite one of your colleagues out for a drink after work?" Calvin said one evening over Skype. "Marie-Claude? She sounds nice."

"Oh, no. I don't think so."

We were having a difficult video chat. Already our connection had broken twice, which always made me extra anxious, and now my patience felt brittle.

"Why not?"

"It's not that kind of office culture. People don't socialize outside of work. They go home and spend time with their families." I didn't try to hide the note of resentment in my voice.

Calvin pushed his chair back. "It's almost August. I'll be home for vacation in two weeks," he said evenly.

"I know. I'm sorry, I know you want to help." I hated the anger that flashed through me sometimes, the self-pitying feelings of abandonment. I wanted to move away from those emotions, but too often they pinched me, little demons with sharp fingers. I didn't want to fight with him, not about a decision that had been made months ago. How could I argue with him while he was in a war zone working twelve-hour days and I was living a life most people—including, at one point, myself—only dreamed about?

"I know you're not having an easy time. I really, really do." His brow furrowed into familiar lines, and as I looked at his face, so beloved and dear, my shoulders dropped. I would have given anything for a hug from him at that moment. But at least we had Skype.

I felt awful the next morning, guilty and sad the way I always did after snapping at my husband. But as the day wore on, Calvin and I exchanged jokey e-mails about our downstairs neighbors—the tiny couple who complained constantly about . . . well, everything—and my mood started to brighten. By lunchtime I was ready for a little salad and a few quiet minutes to send Calvin another e-mail.

"I'm going out now. Do you need anything?" Marie-Claude appeared by my desk. *Une femme d'un certain âge,* she'd worked in the fashion industry before becoming an office manager and still wore high heels every day.

"No, thanks. I brought my lunch."

"*À tout à l'heure,*" she said, and turned toward the door, before hesitating. "I've been meaning to ask—where do you buy that salad? It looks so fresh."

"There's a Greek *traiteur* on rue Jean-Nicot. You don't know it? Elizabeth told me about it."

"It is where, rue Jean-Nicot?"

"It's a little side street off of rue Saint-Dominique. If you go out of the building and turn right . . ." I paused. "You know what? I'll come with you and show you where it is." I stood up and reached for my handbag.

"Really? Oh, *c'est gentil*! Thank you! I would appreciate that so much!" She held the door open for me. "I love Greek food. My brother lives in Athens," she said as we walked out into the bright summer day together.

It wasn't lunch. It wasn't even *le mâchon.* But it was a start.

Salade Lyonnaise

During my visit to Lyon, I ate salade lyonnaise at every meal except breakfast. The city's *bouchons* usually serve it as a rib-sticking first course—often followed by a hearty hot dish like stewed tripe—but it can also be a satisfying lunch or a quick supper, especially because except for the lettuce, all the ingredients are kitchen staples. For a truly classic version, use dandelion leaves instead of frisée.

Serves 4

2 heads frisée lettuce *or,* if in season, 2 bunches of dandelion
    leaves
¼ pound bacon (unsmoked is traditional, but I like a slight
    tang of smoke)
Vinaigrette (recipe follows)
4 slices pain de campagne *or* rustic sourdough bread
2 cloves garlic, peeled
4 eggs, at room temperature

Wash, sort, and dry the lettuce. If using dandelion leaves, remove the hard stems and tear the leaves into bite-size pieces. Cut the bacon into lardons, or ¼-inch-thick matchsticks. Prepare the vinaigrette. Lightly toast the bread and rub one side with a clove of garlic. Cut the bread into ½-inch cubes for croutons.

To prepare the coddled eggs, bring a large pot of water to a boil. Lower the eggs gently into the boiling water and cook for 5 minutes, adding 30 seconds if your eggs are jumbo. Drain them immediately and run cold water into the pan to stop the cooking and to cool the eggs so you can handle them. Gently crack and peel the eggs, taking care not to tear the white—the yolk should still be runny. Rinse the peeled eggs to wash away any bits of shell.

In a frying pan over medium-high heat, cook the lardons until they start to crisp and most of their fat has rendered. Remove them from the pan. With the flat side of a chef's knife, lightly crush the remaining clove of garlic. Add it to the remaining bacon fat in the pan with the bread, turning the cubes so that they are lightly toasted on all sides.

In a large bowl, toss the lettuce with the vinaigrette. Scatter the croutons and bacon over the salad. Arrange the eggs on top and serve family style.

Vinaigrette

2 tablespoons red wine vinegar
1 teaspoon Dijon mustard
4 tablespoons mild-tasting oil, such as olive *or* canola
Salt and pepper to taste

In a small, lidded jar, combine the vinegar, mustard, and oil; cover and shake to combine. Season to taste (but not too much, given the saltiness of the salad's other ingredients). Taste with a piece of lettuce and adjust the seasoning if necessary.

Chapter 5

Provence / Soupe au Pistou

I used to sleep through the night—seven, eight, nine hours of pure rest, curling beneath the downy duvet on our bed, lulled even further into my dreams by the deep, even breaths of my husband next to me. Our bedroom windows edged the courtyard, and the room was dark and quiet, a calm oasis of retreat, unlike the rest of the apartment, which faced the busy boulevard and was bright and noisy. I loved our bedroom, loved changing into my pajamas and crawling between sheets that smelled of laundry detergent, loved reading a few pages of my book until my head started to droop, whereupon I would turn out the lamp, kiss my husband, and drift away. But then Calvin left, and I stopped sleeping.

Insomnia. It was like a foreign movie I never wanted to see, filled with dark images that ran on an incessant loop through my exhausted brain. I worried about the dangers of Iraq—helicopter crashes, enemy fire, friendly fire—each fear exploding in my mind with a blinding charge. I worried about Calvin's health: the constant pressure, the cafeteria diet of fried food, the lack of exercise. And then there were the other worries: my aging parents, my stalled writing projects, my health—dear God, my health. My stomach growled. Did I have an ulcer? I felt dizzy. Was it the flu? Or was I having a stroke? I searched phantom symptoms on my cell phone, the glow of the screen lighting up my face, driving sleep further and further away.

I avoided bedtime, watching TV or surfing the Internet, staying up later and later until the clock edged past one o'clock, two o'clock, late enough for me to hope that I'd fall asleep as soon as my head hit the pillow. Eventually I'd crawl into bed, read a few pages of my book hoping my eyes would close—they never did—turn out the lights and stare at the ceiling for a couple of hours. I'd finally drop off around four o'clock in the morning and then force myself to wake up a few hours later.

But on the night before Calvin came home for vacation in August, something else kept me awake until the small hours—not just anxiety but also excitement. By the time I climbed into bed, his flight from Baghdad had landed in Amman and he had begun the final leg of his thirty-hour journey home. I stared at the ceiling as time dripped away in a slow leak, impatient to throw my arms around him. Even though we had chatted with each other every evening by Skype, even though we knew the minutiae of each other's life right down to what we'd eaten for lunch, even though Calvin seemed unchanged—brimming with encouragement, quick with a pun—I needed reassurance that our months apart hadn't distanced us. I needed the wobbly image on the computer screen to become real again.

Calvin arrived home in the soft violet light of early morning, before the city had started to shimmer in the noonday heat, waking me with a lively trill of the downstairs bell. It seemed to take him forever to walk up the stairs, but then there he was, his brown hair slightly ruffled, with scratchy cheeks and the faint eyebrows that were so incredibly dear to me. I saw only a glimpse of them before I flung myself into his arms for a hug that squeezed all the anxiety of the last few months out of me.

"Did I wake you up?" His voice was muffled against my hair.

"I was so excited last night I couldn't sleep. I finally drifted off at about four. Are you tired? Hungry?"

He mumbled something else. "Hungry," I thought he said. Or maybe he said "Happy." They both made sense. For the first time in months, I felt genuinely hungry and happy, too.

Parisians take croissants very seriously. So seriously that some will never, ever reveal the address of their favorite *boulangerie* for fear it will become too popular. I'm willing to bet that friendships have been lost over diverging viewpoints on the ratio of crunch to yeasty tenderness. But I promise you there is no croissant as crisp and flaky or as sweetly buttery as the one you eat, still warm from the oven, on your first morning in Paris after a long absence. Outside Poilâne bakery I watched Calvin eat his, shattering the shell to reveal supple layers of pastry. One, two, three bites and it was gone, leaving only a drift of golden flakes as evidence. He licked the crumbs from his fingers, and when he smiled, his whole face seemed to relax.

As we walked past the prim boutiques that line the rue du Cherche-Midi, I bit into my own early-morning treat, a pain au chocolat, and brushed the crumbs from my shirt down to the sidewalk. For once there were no Parisians to censor me for eating on the street, no sarcastic calls of *"Bon appétit!"* as I walked and chewed. Lost in its early-August haze, the city was empty.

We turned the corner onto rue de Vaugirard, passing a gaping construction site, a lone bustle of activity. Suddenly a booming crash destroyed the calm—a falling load of concrete debris perhaps, or a backhoe knocking the metal edge of a Dumpster. Beside me I felt Calvin jump, a sharp, quick movement as if I'd pinched him.

"What's the matter? Are you okay?"

"It was just kind of loud." He shrugged, but his eyes looked wide.

I squeezed his arm, but the truth was, his reaction had made me feel a little wide-eyed myself, all quivery limbs and nervous energy. Now I realized that the endless days and weeks, the duck-and-cover alarms and convoy attacks, the safety and suffocation of an insulated compound, the complete absence of children's voices and leafy trees and cooking smells, the sixty-five-year-old roommate jockeying to use the bathroom first every morning—it had all taken its toll. I would never truly understand Calvin's life in Baghdad. His experiences there, both the prosaic and profound, were shared by his colleagues, not by me, his wife.

While I kneaded my fretful thoughts, Calvin seemed awfully quiet, too. We paused at an intersection to wait for the light to change.

"I wanted to ask you something." He fixed his gaze on the oncoming traffic.

"Sure." My hands felt damp and I surreptitiously wiped them against the hem of my shirt.

"Could you make spaghetti and meatballs for dinner tonight?" Now he glanced over at me, his face brimming with hope, as if only I could help him.

I grabbed his arm, hugging it close. "Of course!"

The light changed, and we crossed the street, heading in unspoken agreement toward the grocery store, where we bought ground meat and canned tomatoes, parsley and Parmesan cheese. After all, life-changing work experiences come and go. But homemade meatballs and red sauce are forever.

That night we gorged ourselves on wine and meatballs and glorious forkfuls of tomato-drenched, cheese-dusted pasta. We stored the remaining meatballs, along with their precious sauce, in the freezer. Because the next morning we were off, following a heavily trodden path toward sunshine and dry heat, droning cicadas and the

purple haze of blooming lavender fields. Like so many Parisians before us—like all of them really, if the city's empty streets and métro
were any indication—we were heading toward vacation.

I know it's a little, well, cliché to be captivated by Provence, a region
that has made the fortune of not a few travel writers. But I am—I
can't help myself. These are some of the things I love: Proud pink
villages perched on hilltops. The relief of moving from sharp light
and heat into cool shadows. Unapologetic ice cubes tinkling in a
glass of rosé. Hell, unapologetic enjoyment of rosé. The gusty wind
known as the mistral, rough and cleansing. Unfiltered olive oil decanted into recycled juice bottles, bought at a roadside stand.
Lavender-scented breezes tumbling into car windows. Tangy Provençal accents. Vineyards and fields shadowed by the looming bulk
of the Luberon Mountains. And most of all, the thing I dream about
fifty weeks of the year: open-air markets that brim with bright summer produce—speckled beans, soft-skinned peaches, mint-scented
tomatoes—all bursting with delicious possibility.

We had first visited the village of Bonnieux four years earlier,
when we were living in Beijing. Back then I could barely pronounce
the word *merci*, yet the Luberon region, located between Avignon
and Aix-en-Provence, instantly felt familiar and beloved. Partly it
was the hot desert brightness, reminiscent of my Southern California childhood. Or maybe it was the food and wine and the sweet art
of doing nothing. Whatever the reason, I felt at home there. And yet
there was also something else, a European exoticism that captivated
me—a cheese course before dessert, shops shuttered in the afternoon heat, a game of *boules* played in the dust of the village square.

On that first visit, we inhaled soft air into our scarred lungs, rev-
eled in the stars and silence, devoured plates of fresh fish, salad, and

fruits, raw and unpeeled. When our vacation ended and we left Provence, I felt like weeping. "We'll come back," Calvin promised, partly as a way to comfort his overemotional wife but also because he'd loved it, too. And we had come back. For four years in a row, we'd rented the same stone house from a friend's mother, who had also become a friend. Now we were back once again, more in need of a vacation together than ever before.

At the Avignon TGV station, we stepped down from the train and into a blast of air so arid and hot it could have come from a hair dryer. We found our rental car at an agency located just steps away from the station and headed east toward Apt, whizzing along country highways, searching for familiar landmarks. There was the cornfield that bordered the road, the red-earth cliffs cresting against the sky, then the olive grove with a vintage truck parked outside. Each of them felt significant, concrete proof that our vacation had begun.

The engine of our tiny Smart car strained as we ascended the hill to Bonnieux. We passed the *pigeonnier* and, across from it, the farm stand run by the white-haired woman who'd given me a recipe for courgette-flower fritters. On our left the solid church, built during the late nineteenth century and considered ugly by locals; straight ahead a roundabout. And then, in rapid succession, the newsstand, the hotel (the nice one), the other hotel (the not-so-nice one), the baker, the butcher, the café, the pharmacy. I ticked off each shop as we drove by, relieved to find they'd all survived another off-season.

I parked, and we climbed out of the car, clambering down a steep road, picking our way between potholes and slimy patches of figs fallen from the tree above. We retrieved the key from its hiding place and entered the refreshing darkness of the house, breathing in the clean scent of lavender that filled the entryway. For a minute I hesitated. What should we do next? Unpack our bags? Walk to the village *épicerie*? Drive into Apt to stock up on wine? But then the cool silence of the house crept through me, and I allowed myself to stand there for a long time, rooted to the stone floor in the hall. After all, we were on vacation.

The French love of vacation is well documented, an institution as sacred as Sunday lunch *en famille*, one that's alternately mocked and sighed over by other, non-European nations. It's true the French take a lot of leave—at least five weeks a year, compared with the two enjoyed by most Americans—parceled out in the summer, at Christmas, in the February ski season, at Easter, and at Toussaint (an autumn holiday I'd never even heard of before moving to France). But the right to a vacation is in fact a rather recent French institution that dates from the 1936 Matignon Agreements, which made *congés payés*, paid holidays, a legal obligation. In contrast, the United States has no federal law requiring employers to grant annual leave.

Les Accords de Matignon were a pet project of the Popular Front, the 1930s leftist political party led by Prime Minister Léon Blum. The laws gave workers a broad range of rights, increasing wages, introducing the forty-hour workweek, raising the school-leaving age to fourteen, and recognizing trade unions. But the most popular, enduring symbol of the Popular Front's commitment to social reform was the guarantee of two obligatory weeks of paid vacation, which over the decades stretched to five.

In the summer of 1936, floods of working-class travelers took advantage of the new policy, streaming south to resort towns previously the exclusive domain of the bourgeois. The government encouraged the exodus, organizing price reductions for holiday train tickets and creating newsreels of happy travelers crying *"Vive la vie!"* Blum patted himself on the back, saying he had "injected a little beauty and sunshine into lives of hardship." And thus the French tourist industry began to blossom.

With the spread of automobiles, more people headed south to the Mediterranean Sea—Charles Trenet even wrote a song, "Route Nationale 7," which paid homage to the "highway of vacations" that led from Paris to Italy. These sun-bronzed vacationers ignited an interest in regional cuisine—particularly for Provençal cooking— that eventually became a French passion.

I, too, had heard its siren call years ago, long before I ever set foot in Bonnieux, when I was only twelve years old. I had begged my parents to let us take a family trip to Provence that summer. Why? What about the south of France could have appealed to a girl who hated hot weather and insects, one who preferred reading over bicycling to the playground with the other neighborhood kids? Actually, I suspect that's the answer—I'd probably read something in a magazine or a book, some clever sketch of words, now long forgotten, that captured the region's beauty.

Despite my zeal, my parents were dubious. They'd been wary of my travel enthusiasms ever since suffering at my hands the previous summer, when I'd begged them to make a three-hour detour to visit the Tillamook cheddar-cheese factory in Oregon. I had pictured hand-pressed wheels of cheddar, spotted cows, and three-legged milking stools. Instead we encountered fractious families crowding the windows overlooking the factory floor. The gift shop marketed its cheddar so aggressively that even my cheese-averse mother felt coerced into buying a wheel. (Over twenty years later, my parents *still* haven't let me live that one down.)

But my uneven track record wasn't the only thing stopping us from donning berets and hopping the next plane to Marseille. There was also the problem of France—or rather my mother's aversion to it. She still bore deep emotional scars from her childhood in Shang-hai's French concession, remnants of the psychological abuse meted out by her half-Chinese, half-French stepmother. Niang had worn her Frenchness like a fur coat, preening and posing with it, stroking it to a high luster. Never mind that Niang's father had come from Corsica, the rugged island that had struggled for independence from France, or that he'd probably moved to China to escape pov-erty and cultural prejudice. In 1920s Shanghai anything was possi-ble for a foreigner, even for a Corsican who wished to reinvent himself as a Frenchman. By the time Niang was twenty, slim and beautiful and stepmother to five children she detested, she had be-come French. She gave my mother a French name—Adeline—and sent her to a French kindergarten, before packing her off to board-ing school and never allowing her to come home during the holi-days.

For my mother, carrying this colossal load of unhappy child-hood memories, France became like an allergy, something she pre-ferred to avoid as if it made her eyes itch and her nose run. At age twelve I didn't really understand why, but her aversion was obvious, displayed in crackly little blasts. "You want to visit *France*? My *step-mother* was French," she'd say, in the same tone she used when I brought home a B on an algebra exam. Perhaps Freud would say that was part of my *attraction* to France—that tinge of the taboo, the temptation of forbidden fruit.

As the school year dwindled down and my mom signed me up for an intensive SAT prep course—"You can never start too early!" she'd said, even though I was only finishing seventh grade—I be-gan to brace myself for the lonely summer months ahead. My parents worked long days, my mother as a physician and my father as a microbiology professor, and now that I was old enough to stay at home alone, there seemed to be an awful lot of hours to fill outside of college-preparatory work. I had just resigned myself to a few months of algebra drills (relieved by a secret stash of Sweet Valley High novels) when my parents surprised me with a late birthday present—plane tickets! What made them change their minds? Had I actually convinced them of the educational value of a trip to France? I'm still not sure. Whatever the case, several weeks later the three of us found ourselves in Aix-en-Provence during an August heat wave.

France surprised me. It was hot; I remember that so clearly, a kind of airless, choked heat that I had felt on our trip to Paris seven years before. The heat settled in the antique crevices of our rented apartment, drawing close and unrelenting at night, especially with the flocks of French mosquitoes feasting on us. By day the sun was so strong it shimmered, causing a haze around Mont Ventoux. We sat under the plane trees on the Cours Mirabeau and drank tall glasses of lemonade, ordered up by my mom. That was the other surprise—my mother could speak French! I hadn't remembered that from our other trip. I couldn't believe she'd allow the devil's tongue to fall from her lips, and yet there she was, booking bus tours of Roman ruins and interrogating the waiter as to whether there was cream in the potage aux légumes.

"Mom, you speak . . . *French*?"

"Just a few words that I learned in kindergarten." She shrugged and shot me a look that said, *Don't get any ideas, buster.*

Most of our meals were, I'm sorry to say, totally unremarkable. This was long before the term "foodie" had been coined, before Internet chat forums, Zagat guides, or even Rick Steves. Unfamiliar with the city, we found ourselves dining in mediocre restaurants planted squarely *on* the beaten path. And yet food is so ingrained in French culture—especially in fertile Provence—that I still came away from that trip with three indelible gastronomic memories.

The first took place at the home of Simone and Jacques, the French cousins of one of my mom's medical-school classmates. They invited us to their home in Marseille, where we sat in the garden and watched the sun drop into a grove of umbrella pines. Simone and Jacques were Jewish, part of Marseille's vibrant Sephardic community, and for dinner they had prepared a chicken tagine with preserved lemon. I can still taste its bitter, tart brininess, so clean and exotic—so contrary to what I thought of as French food and yet, Simone assured us, very typical.

The second unforgettable meal was at another home, that of Bernard and Véronique. Bernard had been a student researcher in my father's microbiology laboratory at UCLA. After a few years in Los Angeles, he'd returned to his native Provence, to the brush-covered hills that formed the *arrière-pays,* or backcountry, above Marseille. We sat in the garden at a long table under a grape arbor, and Véronique, Bernard's wife, served us roasted birds, as tiny as golf balls. We ate them with our hands, pulling the miniature limbs apart, crunching the bones between our teeth. The birds were called ortolans, and Bernard had caught them himself, baiting small traps with winged ants just like his father and his grandfather and probably his grandfather's father before him. I didn't know it then, but a meal of ortolans was a local tradition, one memorialized in Marcel Pagnol's tender memoirs of his Provençal childhood, a celebration of the hunting, trapping, and boyhood high jinks set in the high hills above Marseille.

My third food memory from that vacation is of the morning

market in Aix-en-Provence, the beautiful *marché traditionnel* brimming with flowers, vegetables, fruit, honey, and cheese. My parents and I wandered through its shaded stalls breathing in the peculiar aroma of lavender soap and roasting chickens, stopping to admire displays of cherry tomatoes tucked into straw baskets, the flash of yellow courgette flowers against dark-skinned squash. Unlike the chilled produce section of our grocery store at home, this market was alive with smells and wasps and people haggling over the price of a kilo of eggplants. My father eyed the piles of sun-warmed vegetables with the itchy longing of someone who loves to cook. Alas, our vacation rental's primitive kitchenette prevented him from buying sacks of food and whipping up a feast for twenty. Instead he contented himself with just one purchase—a giant, fragrant bunch of basil. We displayed it in a vase on the dining table so its perfume could drift across the apartment.

After a couple of weeks, we returned home to Southern California, back to air-conditioning and ice machines and our double-doored refrigerator. School started again, and so did Chinese school on Saturdays. I stopped daydreaming about France. But somewhere in the back of my mind, I guarded those food memories, taking them out from time to time to give them a polish. They seemed to represent another existence, one of tradition, of history, of continuity, rooted in a small sliver of the world. In contrast, the tract homes and tidy sidewalks of our American suburb, the shrink-wrapped Asian vegetables at the Vietnamese grocery store, the strawberries available in January and the napa cabbage that appeared in July, all of it offered little connection to the land on which we lived. Instead of traditional recipes, the food we cooked and ate combined a hodgepodge of cultures and cuisines. Over time I came to realize the great freedom in this diversity, as well as the loss.

* * *

Thirty years ago you'd have been lucky to find a bunch of basil in Paris, even at the height of summer. Basil was a plant of the Midi, the colloquial name for southern France, and its fragrant leaves didn't really travel north. For thousands of vacationers—including even my family—the aromatic herb represented summer holidays in Provence. And one dish in particular showcased its refreshing perfume: soupe au pistou.

I heard about the chunky vegetable soup during my first vacation in Bonnieux with Calvin. I was at the market, moving slowly so I could inspect the produce in each stall. The village hosted the market each Friday, attracting a mix of vendors and shoppers wielding baskets. Some were regulars, like the older woman with a zippy Provençal accent who greeted the salesmen with a *"Bonjour"* and a hearty handshake. Others were clearly tourists, like the young couple in shorts and bedraggled hair who paused before a pastel stack of overscented soaps. The stalls overlapped without reason—cheap and cheerful tablecloths fluttered next to rows of goat cheese; piles of espadrilles stood next to jars of honey. A display of fresh pasta smelled of egg yolks and raw flour, and a hint of marijuana emerged from the back of the vendor's van. At the fish stand, the *poissonnier* could have leaped from the set of a Pagnol film, with his curled mustache, straw hat, and striped shirt. In front of him, a row of shiny fish stared blankly at the underside of the striped awning, the crushed ice below them dripping slowly into a dirty bucket.

At the vegetable stand, I spotted something unusual: pods shaped like green beans but longer and fatter, some a delicate, pale greenish yellow, others splashed in magenta and white.

"C'est quoi?" I tried to ask.

"Voulez-vous des cocos blancs ou des cocos rouges, Madame?" asked

111

the *vendeur*. He had a blurry look in his eyes, clearly hungover from rising too early after a why-not-one-more-glass-of-rosé kind of evening. Actually, so did everyone in the market. Come to think of it, so did I.

"Comment? Cuisine?" This was before I could speak French, and my cheeks burned at the sound of my cavewoman grunts.

The woman standing next to me in line took pity on me—or maybe she just wanted to hurry me along. "You can make zee soupe au pistou," she said. "Like a vegetable soup. You need some of zis." She handed me a couple zucchini. "And some beans and a beeg, beeg pot of *basilic*. Vairy, vairy deeleecious." She paused, searching for words. "Eet is zee essence of summair."

Before I knew it, she had dictated a recipe, selected my vegetables, picked out exact change from the handful of coins I produced out of my pocket, and sent me on my merry way.

When I got home, I split open the pods and discovered a strand of fresh shell beans inside, as round and plump as if they'd already been cooked, the white ones tinged pale green, the red ones—called borlotti, or cranberry beans—spattered in hot pink. This was how beans grew, I realized with a jolt—encased in these beautiful shells. As a city girl, bean horticulture was something I'd never before considered.

When it came time to prepare the soup, the woman's voice swirled faintly through the foggy recesses of my hungover brain. Did I cook the beans first? How should I cut the zucchini? And as for the beeg, beeg pot of basil . . . well, I had no idea what to do with *that*. I cobbled together a vegetable soup of carrots, leeks, beans, zucchini, and a few roughly chopped leaves of basil floating on top. It tasted earthy and wholesome, kind of like minestrone. But comparing it with the essence of summer seemed like a grandiose exaggeration.

"I must've gotten the recipe wrong," I said glumly, transferring the leftovers to a vat-size plastic container. "That soup was more like essence of Progresso."

"I really liked it," Calvin said. (Four meals of soup later, his enthusiasm had dimmed considerably.)

Even after a few more summer vacations in Provence, soupe au pistou continued to elude me. I longed to taste this "essence of summer," and yet every time I asked for it in a restaurant, I was told it was a *plat de famille,* cooked and eaten at home. Now, on our fourth visit to Bonnieux, I was determined finally to taste it. But . . . how? Unless I kidnapped a Provençal grandmother and held her hostage in the kitchen, it seemed unlikely. And then one morning, while buying milk at the village *épicerie,* I spotted a fluorescent yellow poster. *FÊTE DE SOUPE AU PISTOU À BONNIEUX,* it announced in uneven handwriting.

I pounced on Calvin as he examined bars of milk chocolate. "The village is having a soupe au pistou party!" I said breathlessly.

"Hmm? Oh, that's nice."

"We have to go! This is my chance to finally taste the essence of summer!" I held up my phone. "Let's call and reserve right now!"

Calvin took a step back, but after six years of marriage he knew better than to question me when I had the excited, slightly rabid gleam of culinary obsession in my eye. He took the phone, called, and left a message.

But then I started thinking. What if instead of simply *eating* soupe au pistou at the fête, I actually helped *prepare* it? What if I cooked soupe au pistou for the entire village?

That is how I found myself chopping and peeling vegetables with a group of formidable Provençal women. At five-thirty in the morning.

* * *

The head chef of Bonnieux's soupe au pistou fête is a diminutive, deeply tanned woman named Mauricette. She has soft brown eyes and a sweet smile, but she runs a very strict kitchen. Whenever she came over to inspect our chopped vegetables, an anxious undercurrent ran through the group of volunteers.

"Are these potatoes the right size, Mauricette?"

"Am I peeling enough skin from the courgettes, Mauricette?"

"We're supposed to remove the seeds from the tomatoes!" one woman said accusingly to her neighbor. "Isn't that right, Mauricette?"

About ten of us had gathered at the home of Xavière, a robust woman who played soup producer to Mauricette's director. The sky was still dark when I parked my rental car on the edge of a fig orchard and made my way to the cement patio next to the house. In the dim light, I saw a long table groaning with tubs of white and cranberry shell beans, as well as haricots verts, or snap beans, cut into segments. A few feet away, under a grape arbor, stood two industrial-size pots of water, each perched on a powerful portable gas burner. This cooking area was Mauricette's domain. In the six hours it took to prepare the soup, none of the other women approached it.

As the sky brightened, the volunteers arrived one by one, each armed with her own cutting board, knife, and vegetable peeler. They were all local Bonnieulaises, all members of the Association la Boule Dorée, a local *pétanque*, or *boules*, club that organized the village soup fête as an annual fund-raiser.

Mauricette introduced me to the group. "She's an American journalist who wants to learn how to make soupe au pistou." At the words "American" and "journalist," eyebrows rose and a chill descended. Only a Parisian would have received more scrutiny. I tried to look as friendly as possible, mostly by smiling a lot, though this had the danger of making me seem simple. *Don't slip up and call them* *"tu,"* I reminded myself. *Vous, vous, vous.* Switching from the formal to informal form of "you" was a delicate decision, even for French people. Unfortunately, I had the bad habit of confusing the two when I got nervous.

We began by preparing the zucchini—about 130 pounds of it—peeling the dark skin away into tiger stripes. I helped chop the squash into a large dice, adding the pieces to a communal bowl. I could feel the eyes of the other women watching my knife move across the cutting board, and I concentrated hard on not cutting myself.

"Votre couteau n'est pas trop grand, Ann?" said a white-haired woman with eyes like a hatchet.

She thought my knife was too big? I glanced down at it, a dainty chef's blade. *"Tu . . .* uh, *vous trouvez?"* I stammered. Really? She thought so? *"Non, ça va aller."* I gave her a mild smile. She puffed her cheeks up and went back to peeling squash. A teenage girl with goth-black eyeliner handed me another pile of vegetables to chop and pulled a little face, as if to say, *Ignore her.*

Obtaining an introduction to the party of soup-making volunteers had seemed more difficult than wrangling an invitation to a White House state dinner. I'd summoned all my American resourcefulness and puppy-dog charm, calling the local tourist office, befriending the village on Facebook, all to no avail. Finally the manager of our rental house, a dynamic woman named Solange, took pity on me. Three phone calls later, I had an interview with Mauricette to present my soup-making credentials. Solange came with me to smooth the path—and to provide French vocabulary before my own could fail me.

"Si je peux vous aider, je serais ravie," I said with my most earnest

expression. If I could help you, I'd be delighted. . . . *"Je suis entière-ment . . ."*

"Disponible," Solange inserted neatly.

"Disponible," I agreed. Available. For soup. Exactly.

I'm still not sure if it was the introduction from Solange, Mauricette's curiosity, or the bottle of pure, grade-A maple syrup that I brought her (I'm not above a bribe, not when it comes to secret recipes), but somehow I was deemed acceptable. Mauricette took me under her wing and vowed to teach me her soup. As I was discovering this morning, however, an alliance with the boss can alienate you from other members of the team. Especially old hatchet eyes. She needled me with questions couched as concern. "You're not cold?" she asked me, eyeing my thin sweater. Later she told me, "Watch out for your sleeves!" though they were nowhere near the food. I sent a sympathetic thought to her daughter-in-law, whoever and wherever she was in the world.

We finished chopping the courgettes and potatoes and moved on to plucking basil leaves—"No stem!" instructed Mauricette—the heavy fresh-licorice perfume competing with the raunchy odor of peeled garlic. As the sky lightened into a pale grayish blue, so had the atmosphere around the table. After tiny cups of weak coffee, everyone looked more cheerful.

I finally felt brave enough to pose a question to the group. "Do you ever add any other vegetables to the soup? Carrots or leeks?"

"Mais NON!" The table erupted. *"Jamais de carottes, ni de poireaux!"*

"This is a summer soup, made with only summer vegetables," the woman across from me explained. "Courgettes, tomatoes, haricots verts, beans—fresh, never dried—potatoes, and pistou. *C'est tout*. Winter vegetables like carrots or leeks don't belong in soupe au pistou. And we *never* add meat."

"I once had soupe au pistou with meat," Mauricette said in a musing tone. "My cousin's wife made it. It was all pasta and cubes of ham!"

The other women stared, their mouths open in horror. *"Oh, la-la-la-la,"* someone said faintly.

"It was good, but . . ." Mauricette shook her head. "It had *nothing* to do with soupe au pistou." Everyone clucked in agreement. "I still don't know why she didn't just ask for *my* recipe." I eventually discovered that a ham bone, or a smoked pork knuckle, *is* sometimes added to soupe au pistou, namely in the rocky, mountainous region of the Alpes-de-Haute-Provence—a climate too cold to raise olive trees—where the meat probably replaces the calories and flavor traditionally added by a lazy drizzle of olive oil.

"What happens to the basil?" I asked.

"The leaves are blended with garlic and olive oil to make a sauce—pistou. That's what we mix into the soup," said Xavière.

"Ah, it's pesto!" I exclaimed.

"Pistou," Xavière corrected. She pronounced the word with care: *"Pee-stoo."*

"Yes, like pesto. From Italy?"

Silence fell around the table. "The Italians can call it what they want," someone sniffed.

Pistou, I later read, is the Provençal version of pesto; indeed, the word comes from the Italian *pestare,* which means "to pound." It's a sauce of crushed basil and garlic mixed with olive oil—a combination as ancient as the Roman ruins that dot the dry Provençal landscape. The poet Virgil wrote of pistou in the *Eclogues,* describing it as a mixture of herbs and garlic ground in a mortar. Today it's more commonly made in a food processor—even in rural Provence, even by traditionalists.

There exists perhaps no greater culinary rivalry than the one between Italy and France. But no matter who invented the fork or first perfected the béchamel or balsamella sauce, it is true that the two cultures have influenced each other enormously, especially in Provence. Greek Phocaeans founded Marseille in 600 B.C., bringing with them olive trees and grapevines. Julius Caesar claimed the port less than five hundred years later, leading troops of Romans through the region. They built aqueducts and arenas, created cities like Arles and Avignon and Aix-en-Provence, and cultivated lavender, the flower that still defines the landscape.

Centuries after the decline of the Roman Empire, parts of France and Italy remained loosely entwined—neighbors who sometimes slept together—as in the case of Nice, which remained protected by the counts of Savoy (and, by extension, tied to the Italian Piedmont and Sardinia) until the late nineteenth century. By this time Nice was a bustling port, fiercely competitive with its northern neighbor Genoa. Is it any surprise that Liguria's prized culinary invention—pesto—traveled about a hundred miles southwest to Provence?

The basic ingredients of pistou and pesto sounded similar to me, but I didn't dare mention this opinion to the Bonnieux soup volunteers. I had an idea what they might say: *"Je veux pas être chauvine, mais . . ."* Already this morning I'd heard the phrase many times, always followed by an inexorable opinion. "I don't want to be prejudiced, but . . . soupe au pistou is better than minestrone." Or, ". . . Parmesan cheese and pine nuts have no place in pistou." Or, ". . . you can't call it soupe au pistou unless all the vegetables come from Provence." I admired their loyalty even as I recognized the faint insularity. Because if you came from a region as stunningly beautiful and naturally abundant as Provence—a region that has been both saved and spoiled by the summer tourist season—wouldn't you be fiercely proud and protective of it, too?

At this point we had started crushing the tomatoes into puree—an exciting process that involved grinding them through a hand-cranked contraption that removed the skin and the seeds—and some of the ladies were gathering up their cutting boards and knives to go home. I lingered and watched Mauricette stir pistou into the giant pots of soup with a wooden spoon attached to a long stick. The liquid turned from softly rust-colored—leached from the bright skin of the cranberry beans—into a vegetal green, velvety with melted courgettes.

"The end is always the hardest part," Mauricette said, huffing a little bit. "Once the cheese is added, you can't stop stirring."

The soup's final ingredient, Emmental or Gruyère, is a controversial addition. Some add it directly to the soup, while others pass a small bowl of it at the table, while still others don't use any at all, feeling it detracts from the refreshing herbal punch of the pistou. Mauricette scattered a handful of shredded cheese across the surface of the soup and gestured to Fabrice, a visiting relative with strong arms, to come stir the vats of thick, bubbling liquid. "Don't let it burn on the bottom," she told him, and he respectfully obeyed her.

As she sprinkled and Fabrice stirred, Mauricette reminisced about her husband, who had passed away a few years before. "Wasn't he handsome?" She'd shown me his photograph at five-thirty that morning when I'd come to her house to follow her car to Xavière's.

I nodded. *"Il était très beau."* And he had been, with a youthful bronzed face and a relaxed smile.

"Oh, how he loved soupe au pistou!" exclaimed Mauricette. "I used to make a big pot in the morning, and he'd look forward to it all day long." She tipped the last shards of cheese into the steaming pot. "This soup, it's a celebration of summer, you know." Her eyes met mine, dark and serious.

Less than an hour later, I joined the crowd that had gathered for the fête in the village square. Rows of picnic tables covered in white butcher paper and dotted with plastic pitchers of rosé wine filled the sunny space. I could tell who the locals were because they stood in small clumps, gossiping in lowered voices while the vacationers picked their way around them, trying to find a spot to sit. Calvin and I joined Solange and her friends at a shaded table and unpacked the soup bowls and silverware we'd brought from home. Dotted throughout the crowd, I spotted the ladies from the soup-making committee, now attired in pretty summer garb. We waved at one another like old friends.

Mauricette arrived, clad in a fresh, bright T-shirt. (I was the only one who hadn't taken the time to change out of my pistou-flecked clothes, I noted with some embarrassment.) And close on her heels came an enormous soup pot, swaddled in a blanket and tucked into the back of a van. We crowded in front of the pot like Dickensian orphans, bowls in hand, and received ladles of fragrant soup. I dipped my spoon in and scooped up a mouthful of tender vegetables in a broth laced with the heady scent of garlic and basil. The fresh beans were like none I had eaten before—thin-skinned and exquisitely creamy, with a faint flavor of chestnuts—while the more toothsome green beans contrasted with the smooth texture of melted courgette. It sang of summer, the soup, a product of the nourishing sun, the Provençal soil, a shared moment in a village square, high in the Luberon hills. When we finished our first bowl, there were seconds, and even thirds, and with each bite I discovered a bitter undernote of unfiltered olive oil, a robust burst of cheese. I ate because the soup was delicious but also, perhaps, to prolong the moment a little longer.

As a dry breeze blew across our table and the *pichets* of rosé emptied, Calvin chatted with a retired Swiss diplomat and Solange and her sister argued the merits of their mother's soupe au pistou recipe. The crowd acknowledged Mauricette with enthusiastic applause, which she accepted without any pretense of modesty. People began to wander off, some to take naps, others to join the fiercely competitive *boules* tournament starting in a dusty square next to the church. Sleepy from lunch, I gazed a little blankly at the remaining crowd of village families and tourists. I kept thinking of something Mauricette had said earlier, when I'd asked her why she gave her time and energy to organize the village fête each year. *"Pour faire plaisir,"* she'd replied without hesitation. To give pleasure.

The village soupe au pistou fête marked the midway point of our vacation. We still had about a week, but now our slow breakfasts at the kitchen table, our languid afternoons by the pool felt a little less luxurious. One morning we got up early to follow the market to Gordes, parking at the edge of town and joining the line of people climbing to the village center, buying a basket of tomatoes for dinner, a few lavender sachets for gifts. Another day we explored the ruins of an ancient Roman fort, scrambling down a secret staircase carved into a side of rock. We lunched at my favorite local restaurant, a simple café with a view of a hayfield where the omelets were plump and tender and laced with finely chopped herbs. We read Tintin comics and swapped them with each other; we sipped rosé wine in Solange's thick-walled Provençal house; we listened to the Beatles while cooking dinner; we ate in the garden at a table aglow in candlelight. And suddenly the days had dwindled and we had only three left, then two.

That evening, as I sat in the garden, an ice cube bobbing gently in my predinner glass of rosé, I had a sinking feeling, as if everything was slipping away too fast. Soon we'd return to Paris, and I'd return to working at the library and preparing for the launch of my novel, and a day later Calvin would board a plane to Amman and then continue traveling east in his return to Iraq.

I sipped my wine, ate an olive, black and oily, and tried to focus on the silky air, my hair still damp from a late-afternoon swim, the bats swooping in the fading light. But an urgent flutter descended forcibly into my stomach. Vacation would be over soon, and with its end came the frisson of excitement and anxiety brought on by the thought of work. Calvin felt it, too, I could tell, a growing itch to get back to the office and continue the ambitious march.

During the past two weeks, we had indulged in love in Provence—love of place, of pastimes, and of each other. But without work to anchor me, I was beginning to feel a little unbalanced. And yet going back to work and the daily routine also meant being thousands of miles away from my husband. Without love, my work felt a bit meaningless; just as when I cooked for myself—the food never tasted as good.

The next morning I lingered in the market as if selecting the perfect pincushion goat cheese could erase the nine months that remained of Calvin's tour in Iraq. At the vegetable stand, I looked for all the ingredients for soupe au pistou—fresh beans, tomatoes, courgettes, basil—checking them off a mental list even though I had no intention of making the soup. But when the *vendeur* hovered over a pile of *cocos rouges*, I suddenly heard myself asking for five hundred grams of them. And five hundred grams of the white beans.

A kilo of courgettes, a kilo of haricots verts, a big pot of basil. I lugged everything home, carried a bowl into the garden, and started shelling beans. Calvin came and joined me, and we worked together, pausing now and again to take photos of the pink-speckled beans against the green glaze of their pottery bowl. We trimmed green beans, crunching a few squeaky segments between our teeth, peeled and chopped zucchini, and plucked basil leaves until our thumbnails turned black.

I told myself I wouldn't think about anything but the soup—the beauty of its ingredients, the scent and sizzle and simmer of them as the heat softened their color and texture. But of course that was impossible. Living mindfully and in the moment is a learned skill, one I hadn't yet developed. Also, soupe au pistou takes a really long time to make.

I could feel my anxiety rise as we accomplished each step and moved on to the next one, shelled the last bean, peeled the last squash, plucked the last basil leaf. Calvin started to feel it, too; his shoulders appeared tense.

"I'm starting to get a little sad," I admitted in a small voice as we picked sprigs of wild thyme from a corner of the garden.

"Me, too," he said. "Don't think about it," he added.

Instead we ranked all the meals on our vacation, from the porcini mushroom lasagna we'd eaten on our first night to the lunch of omelette aux fines herbes, the hamburgers grilled on a bed of rosemary, the soupe au pistou at the village fête.

"That was my favorite meal of the trip," I said.

"Yeah, mine, too. Definitely."

His voice sounded as wistful as my own. And with the courgettes disintegrating in the simmering soup and the pistou oxidizing slightly in the blender, I knew that we needed to reassure each other.

We couldn't hide our sadness about the coming months apart, nor could we indulge it. All we could do was keep moving forward, because the only thing that would end our separation was time.

A few hours later, we emerged from the kitchen a little disoriented, blinking at the dirty knives and spoons and cutting boards piled on the counters, the plastic bags of empty bean pods, the slimy strands of zucchini peel clinging to the sink. A pair of wasps circled the air with intent, zeroing in on the bowl of grated Gruyère.

And then there was the soup. It stood in an orange enameled cast-iron pot, cooling gently on the stove, waiting for the evening when we would eat it for dinner. It filled the kitchen with a perfume at once delicate and hearty, a basil-scented work of love, a profusion of summer vegetables made tender with time and patience, a small moment of pleasure to look forward to for the rest of the day.

Soupe au Pistou

There are as many recipes for soupe au pistou as there are soup cooks in Provence, but they all share a common ingredient: fresh white and cranberry beans, available only in summer. For most Provençal cooks, it would be unthinkable to use anything else. After conducting an informal social-media straw poll, however, I discovered that fresh beans are not widely available outside France. I've included a variation of the recipe that uses dried beans (just don't tell Mauricette).

Serves 6

For the soup

- 1 pound fresh, unshelled white beans (also called cannellini) *or* ½ cup dried white beans, sorted and soaked overnight
- 1 pound fresh, unshelled cranberry beans (also called borlotti) *or* ½ cup dried cranberry beans, sorted and soaked overnight
- 2 pounds zucchini
- 2 to 3 medium waxy potatoes
- 2 pounds green beans, trimmed and cut into 1-inch segments
- 1 cup elbow macaroni
- Salt and pepper to taste

For the pistou

- 1½ pounds ripe tomatoes
- 1 large bunch basil, washed and dried

2 to 3 cloves plump garlic
¼ cup olive oil plus more to taste
Pinch of salt

1 cup grated Gruyère *or* Parmesan, *or* a combination

Preparing the soup

If using fresh beans: Shell and rinse the white and cranberry beans. In a large Dutch oven or soup pot, add the beans and cover them with 2 inches of cold, salted water (about 2 quarts). Bring to a boil over medium heat, skimming the foam from the surface. Lower the heat and simmer for 15 to 20 minutes, until the beans start to soften.

If using dried beans: In a large Dutch oven or soup pot, add the white and cranberry beans and cover them with 2 inches of cold, unsalted water (about 2 quarts). Bring to a boil over medium heat, skimming the foam from the surface. Lower the heat and simmer for about 1½ hours, or until the beans are tender. The cooking time for dried beans varies greatly, so make sure to test the beans for tenderness before proceeding with the recipe.

While the beans are cooking, peel the zucchini, leaving half the skin on in stripes, and cut into 1½-inch dice. Peel and cube the potatoes into the same size. Add the zucchini, the potato cubes, and the segmented green beans to the pot of cooked beans. Bring to a boil, lower the heat, and simmer gently until the zucchini disintegrates (about an hour), using a fork to mash a few pieces of potato and zucchini against the side of the pot, to thicken the soup. Raise the heat slightly and add the macaroni, cooking until very soft. Taste and season the soup.

Making the pistou

While the soup is cooking, make the pistou. Peel and seed the tomatoes and blend them into a sauce or pass the tomatoes through a food
mill. Pluck the basil leaves from their stems. Peel the garlic and chop
it roughly. In a blender or food processor, add the basil leaves, garlic, olive oil, and a pinch of salt. Blend, pausing intermittently to
scrape down the sides of the work bowl. Add the crushed tomatoes
and puree into a smooth sauce, adding more olive oil if necessary.

Remove the soup from the heat. Stir in the pistou and combine thoroughly. Taste and adjust the seasonings. Serve, passing the grated
cheese at the table. Soupe au pistou can be made in advance and reheated; it's also delicious chilled.

Chapter 6

Toulouse, Castelnaudary, Carcassonne / Cassoulet

After weeks of summer indolence, Paris awoke with a start. One day it was sunny and still, people were licking ice-cream cones while their feet dangled over the banks of the Seine, and Calvin and I dragged our heavy bags back from the Gare de Lyon, closing our apartment's *volet* blinds against the blazing afternoon light. The next day the calendar page flipped to September, the métro was crowded, the cafés were packed at lunch, and my husband kissed me good-bye and began his long journey back to Iraq. The apartment felt empty, as ghostly as the August streets of Paris, and yet now that it was September, those very streets had come to life again. I took comfort in their bustle, even as I squared my shoulders to begin again without Calvin.

La rentrée was like an alarm clock without a snooze button. Children returned to school and adults to work, people made resolutions for the New Year, pharmacies stocked their windows with diet pills. Dry cleaners unlocked their doors again, liberating clothes that had been held hostage for the entire month of August. Friends met at *rentrée* cocktail parties, falling into one another's arms as if they'd been reunited after a natural disaster, not just a few weeks of summer holidays. *La rentrée* is a season of lunch dates and gallery openings, of new clothes and good intentions.

In the spirit of the moment, I made my own vow: I would start cooking more. And yet only a few days after Calvin left, I had already fallen into my old habits without him. Insomnia. Meals in front of the computer. An empty fridge. A diet that consisted solely of . . . well, I'm a little embarrassed to say.

Three times a week—on Tuesdays, Fridays, and Sundays—an open market unfurled right below my living-room windows, stretching along the center island of boulevard Raspail. It was a beautiful market, a double column of stalls spilling with clear-eyed fish, pyramids of bright produce, cheeses oozing at room temperature, bins of olives that filled the air with briny pungency. If you wanted fresh pumpkin, the vendor would hack off a slice from a Cinderella-size gourd. If you wanted fresh oysters, the fishmonger would teach you how to open them, taking your hand in his to show you how much pressure to apply and where. If you wanted local strawberries, the produce guy might tell you, "Wait until next week. They'll be sweeter." I adored the market. It was one of my favorite things about living in Paris, a cook's nirvana. And I had stopped going.

I could have blamed my schedule, which was busier now that the fall season of author lectures had begun again at the American Library. Marketing in France takes eons. You must wait in long lines, vigilant for impatient customers who edge in front of you. When it's finally your turn, you must announce your desires to the vendor, describing the required ripeness of your avocados or the exact thickness of a salmon steak. Everything must be prepared for you— the tomatoes must be bagged for you, the globe artichoke plucked from a pile for you, the chicken breasts sliced into escalopes and lightly pounded for you. By the time you've visited three vendors, a whole morning has elapsed. (In fact, there are no quick transactions of any kind in France. A trip to the dry cleaner's involves watching the woman ahead of you explain each stain on each item of clothing. Buying an ice-cream cone on a warm day means waiting for the server to beat air into each well of *glace* before scooping. When he was a student, Calvin used to dread borrowing the vacuum cleaner from his neighbors because it always entailed an invitation for coffee and an hour of small talk.)

So yes, shopping at the market is a slow endeavor. But even though I was busy juggling work and writing, I could have made time for it, because shouldn't we make time for our favorite things in life? Instead, every Tuesday, Friday, and Sunday, I listened to the action unfold through my apartment windows—the bustle and slam of early-morning setup, the swooping call of the vendors hawking their wares—and I avoided it. Why? I thought I loved to cook, but with Calvin away I had an embarrassing epiphany: What I really loved was cooking for an audience. And now that I was cooking for one, I wasn't doing much cooking at all.

Please note that I didn't say eating. I was still doing plenty of that, at lunch with my colleagues, at restaurants with friends, or on my own at home. But in the kitchen I had regressed to the simple foods of my single days—scrambled eggs, pasta with butter and Parmesan, baked beans on toast. Peanut butter on toast. Avocado on toast. Buttered toast. Any kind of toast, really. Sure, I was making a few different versions: Toast spread with ricotta cheese and drizzled with honey. Toast with almond butter. Toast with a poached egg. There were even some international variations: Bruschetta, Italian toast rubbed with garlic and dribbled with high-quality olive oil. Or its Spanish cousin, pan con tomate, which swiped the bread with the cut side of a tomato and was particularly delicious on a hot night with a glass of white wine. Nevertheless, no matter how you sliced it, no matter the fancy vocabulary you spread on it, the truth was this: I had the once-in-a-lifetime opportunity to live for a limited period in cooking paradise, and the only thing I was cooking was . . . toast.

I started viewing Paris through toast-colored glasses, if you will. Strolling around my neighborhood, I began to rank the stores by the type of bread they sold, or rather by how well that bread performed in the toaster. The old-fashioned gilt-and-black *boulangerie* that sat squarely on a busy corner of rue de Rennes had wonderful baguettes—I liked the *tradition,* nicknamed *"tradi,"* crusty and chewier than its *ordinaire* counterpart—but they were a toaster failure, getting trapped in the slots and burning. The gourmet-food mecca known as La Grande Épicerie—where I regularly saw groups of female Japanese tourists squeal over bricks of salted butter—sold adequate loaves of pain de campagne, good in a pinch, though I found them a bit too salty and the crumb too soft. No, my favorite toast-supply store was Poilâne, perhaps the city's most famous traditional bakery, squeezed into a tiny, jewel-box boutique on the rue du Cherche-Midi. *"Une demi-miche, coupée en tranches,"* I'd order, and receive half a round loaf, cut by machine into thin, wide planks, which, though delicious raw (that is, untoasted), became, when grilled, a paragon of crunch and chew.

One morning I took a tour of Poilâne's kitchen, climbing down a narrow staircase into a brick-walled basement room so small I would have mistaken it for a storeroom but for the cavernous wood-burning oven dominating the back. A skinny young man clad in a white T-shirt and long white shorts toiled away in the blazing heat. His name was Jean-Michel, and he was one of five master bakers who worked here in six-hour shifts around the clock, a continuous cycle of dough-to-bread punctuated by the regular stoking and feeding of the wood oven, which burned twenty-four hours a day. The oven dated to the seventeenth century, when the Couvent des Prémontrés occupied the site (or perhaps even earlier). Like many religious buildings, the convent was destroyed during the French

Revolution, but the oven endured, serving one *boulangerie* after another until Pierre Poilâne discovered it. He opened his bakery here in 1932, bucking the trend of white-flour baguettes to produce oversize round loaves made of wheat flour, water, sea salt, and sourdough starter, the same recipe used today. In the 1970s his son, Lionel, joined the bakery, expanding it to three shops in Paris, one in London, and a factory in Bièvres. When Lionel and his wife died in a helicopter accident in 2002, their daughter, Apollonia, succeeded them, the third generation to run the business.

In Poilâne's basement kitchen, the heat caused little rivulets of sweat to run down the nape of my neck, soaking my hair and making me want to pant. But it didn't seem to affect Jean-Michel. He worked in a blur of constant motion, whirling around with practiced efficiency and always, always returning to the oven, the nexus of his activity. I edged as close as I dared, peering through the ferocious orange light to glimpse the loaves of bread baking within the domed space. The oven had been rebuilt several times over the centuries, but in shape and principle it remained the same as the original— similar even to ovens from ancient Egypt or Mesopotamia—a large beehive chamber, heated from below. Jean-Michel tended his loaves with a long-handled paddle, turning and manipulating them so that they browned evenly within the radiating heat. People had been baking bread this way for centuries, a task so central to French culture that many villages still preserved a communal oven. Jean-Michel thrust his paddle into the oven, gave a quick jerk, and then another, and whisked out of the heat two loaves, each dark, golden, and crackling a little. It was all so beautiful—the fresh loaves of bread, Jean-Michel's balletic strength, the history flowing through the space—that I almost applauded. Later we went upstairs and ate sugar cookies and slices of raisin bread. Sometimes, I thought, living in Paris was like living in a museum—beautiful and poignant and untouched by time.

That evening I was in the kitchen making dinner—that is, waiting for the toaster to pop—and I couldn't stop thinking about the oven that had helped produce my meal. Though I had loved witnessing Poilâne's traditional bread-making process, it felt archaic, disconnected from the modern world, just as I still felt a little disconnected from Paris, an observer of the city rather than a participant. I spread some goat cheese on my toast and added a few slices of cucumber and I wondered, how can I make Paris feel more like home? Cooking was the obvious answer—but cooking what? I searched my mind for the most comforting dish in my repertoire. Lasagna? Matzo-ball soup? My dad's mapo tofu? No, though I loved them all, none of them was quite right; each required special ingredients that would be difficult to get, making them too awkwardly foreign rather than organic and local. The dish, I decided, should be French, a recipe that had evolved over centuries from the *terroir*, something to cook slowly and fuss over. The description could have fit any number of French specialties, but when I closed my eyes and tried to picture the epitome of French comfort food, one thing came to mind: cassoulet.

The first time I had cassoulet was in Paris, at a restaurant on the boulevard Saint-Germain called Aux Fins Gourmets. At the time Calvin and I were living in Beijing, but we'd come to France for a week's vacation, to drink wine, revel in a city built on a human scale, and breathe in the golden, blue-skied spring weather. Our friend Adam had grown up around the corner from the restaurant, and his mother had recommended it to us—it had been a family favorite during Adam's childhood. I loved it as much because I could imagine him there as a kid—scribbling on the paper-topped table between bites of roast lamb—as for its own outlandish, outmoded charm.

Aux Fins Gourmets had yellow walls stained from the smoke of ten thousand cigarettes, floors of worn tile, and, in one corner, an accordion-doored phone booth whose rotary telephone still accepted only French francs. Large mirrors reflected the bulbous bistro lighting as well as the clientele, an aging, elegantly dressed crowd—Madame in lipstick and coiffed hair, Monsieur in a corduroy jacket and a floppy cravat—who received the hearty handshake reserved for regulars when they entered. The menu came in a little folder, like something you'd use to present a school report, and had been typed—with a typewriter, if that were possible—onto sheets of ancient, yellowed stationery. The food was classic and sober, with entrées like leeks in vinaigrette or museau de boeuf (head cheese, I found out the hard way) or pickled herrings served *à volonté* from an immense terrine. Main courses were equally plain—omelets, roast chicken, steak frites—and some of them reflected the owner's southwest-French heritage, like the confit de canard, served with an avalanche of sautéed garlic potatoes, or the cassoulet, which came with the promise of extra beans if you wanted them.

We sipped a little wine and discreetly watched the other customers in the restaurant's mirrors. Was that handsome man with flamboyant hair Bernard-Henri Lévy? Calvin thought the life-size, well-preserved Barbie doll by the gentleman's side might be the actress Arielle Dombasle. We were discussing what a French philosopher and his impossibly thin wife might find to eat on the menu when our food arrived, an enormous crock of cassoulet, bubbling gently around the sides of its golden, bread-crumbed crust. Calvin broke in with a spoon, scooping up a wealth of tender white beans in a rich sauce, digging deeper to unearth chunks of sausage and confit de canard. The beans were hot enough to scorch, but they had a plush texture, and their flavor—once they had cooled enough to taste them—unfolded in a luxuriant richness, redolent of pork, duck fat, and a subtle hint of cloves and nutmeg. The hunks of garlicky sausage and confit de canard, which was really just duck preserved in salt and cooked in its own fat, added a toothsome heartiness, but it was the beans that I loved most, creamy and lush.

At first we ate with restraint, conscious of our long-suffering arteries. But as the level of cassoulet dipped lower and lower, we began to rationalize. "How many times in our lives will we have the opportunity to eat cassoulet in Paris?" Calvin asked. (As it turns out, a lot. We just didn't know that then.)

"What about the red wine we're drinking? Doesn't that counteract the fat?" I took another sip to illustrate my point. After this argument, of course, we felt obliged to order another *pichet*, and before we knew it, between the extra sips of wine and just-one-more spoonfuls of beans, we had finished the entire vat of cassoulet—a small vat, but a vat nonetheless.

"Voulez-vous encore des haricots?" Our waiter hovered above our table.

More beans? I opened my mouth, and—perhaps I was drunk on wine, or legumes, or duck fat, or all three—I felt my lips begin to form the word *"Ou—"*

"Non, merci." Calvin interjected. *"On a très bien mangé."*

I heaved a small sigh of relief and a little disappointment. But it was true—we had eaten very well indeed.

I thought cassoulet came from Toulouse, but once I decided to travel there, to discover the dish's true story and secrets, I learned that an entire region of southwestern France claims it, specifically a cradle-shaped territory that forms the province formerly known as Languedoc. "Cassoulet is the God of the Occitan cuisine," wrote the chef, culinary lexicographer, and author of the first *Larousse Gastronomique*, Prosper Montagné, in his 1929 book, *Le Festin Occitan.* "A god in three forms: God the father is the cassoulet of Castelnaudary; God the son is that of Carcassonne; and the Holy Spirit is that of Toulouse." These three cities—Toulouse, Castelnaudary, and Carcassonne—lie in a line that curves gently eastward, connected not only by cassoulet but also by the seventeenth-century man-made waterway the Canal du Midi.

The territory of Languedoc takes its name from its language, the Latin-based *langue d'oc,* spoken there since the twelfth century. The word *oc,* which means "yes," distinguished the language from the *langue d'oïl,* spoken farther north, where the word *oïl* eventually became *oui.* Speakers of the language of Oc were called *oc-citan*—Occitan—and they once covered most of southern France. Today the *langue d'oc* is still spoken by about a third of the region's population, taught in the region's schools, and broadcast on television and radio.

Until the French Revolution, the kingdom of France was organized into provinces—like the Languedoc, or Burgundy, or Champagne—their boundaries delineated more by common customs and traditions than political decree. In 1790 this system was abandoned in favor of the administrative *départements* still used today. Languedoc was divided, and Toulouse, the province's ancient capital, became part of the Midi-Pyrénées, while the rest of the territory formed the Languedoc-Roussillon. This explained why my favorite French guidebooks, the Guide du Routard series, split Toulouse from Castelnaudary and Carcassonne.

Over the centuries Toulouse has enjoyed many waves of prosperity: as a central city of Roman Gaul, as a Visigothic and Carolingian capital, as one of medieval Europe's great artistic and literary capitals governed by the counts of Toulouse, as a center of the Renaissance dye trade, and today as the headquarters of Airbus, one of the world's largest aircraft manufacturers. Wandering the city in the famous southern sunshine, I noticed that everything and everyone seemed tinged with a rosy glow, the flush heightened by the reflection of sun on Renaissance architecture. They call Toulouse *la ville rose*—the pink city—and indeed the streets are a girlish paradise, ranging from sixteenth-century *hôtels particuliers* in shades of palest petal to the hot coral brick façades of the place du Capitole.

I kept searching for a hint of the town's status as the "father" of cassoulet, which the culinary historian Prosper Montagné had mentioned. The city, however, with its crowds of well-heeled shoppers and university students sauntering arm in arm, seemed to have other interests. Though many restaurants offered cassoulet—usually announced in a chalkboard scrawl reading CASSOULET MAISON TRADITIONNEL! which made me very dubious indeed—they all also specified that they served *"le véritable cassoulet de Castelnaudary,"* the authentic cassoulet of Castelnaudary. What about the cassoulet Toulousain?

"Traditionally cassoulet from Toulouse has a base of pork, with a bit of mutton and tomatoes," said Alain Lacoste, the chef and owner of Le Colombier, a local restaurant. "Of course," he added, "it was a dish that changed with the seasons, depending on whatever you had on hand."

At Le Colombier, Lacoste uses the recipe of the owner before him, the same recipe that's been prepared on the premises for a hundred years. He makes his own sausage and confits his own goose

("It's very hard to find these days," he told me) and simmers them together with the beans for hours.

Lacoste served his cassoulet in a *cassole*—the traditional terracotta bowl that I would soon learn more about—with a thin crust on top, composed not of bread crumbs but simply of the natural juice and starch and fat of the dish, sealed from the heat of the stove. It was good—better than good—with silken beans and generous chunks of meat, though I found the intense flavor of nutmeg overpowering.

"Well?" Lacoste stopped by my table with raised eyebrows.

"It was a fine example of cassoulet from Toulouse," I assured him.

"Toulouse? *Mais non!* This is a recipe from Castelnaudary!"

The message was clear: If I wanted to truly understand cassoulet, I needed to hop in a rental car and drive about an hour through the region's flat, dry farmland, eastward to the town of Castelnaudary.

In ancient Rome every home had a lararium, a small shrine that stood near the hearth or in a corner of the atrium. Though the shrines were simple, usually just a cupboard or a shallow painted niche, they were crucial to the family, for inside them dwelled the statues of the household deities, guardian spirits who watched over the happiness and security of the home. There were two different types of gods: the Lar Familiaris, the protector of the building and all who lived within it, from master to slave, and the Penates, who watched over only the master and his blood family.

The Romans honored their household gods with daily prayer as well as offerings from every meal, usually bits of food thrown onto the fire. And when they moved houses—and this was the part that fascinated me the most—they took their Penates with them, as if they were an extension of themselves. But the Lar Familiaris was tied to a house, specific to a place, and there it would remain.

The household gods had intrigued me ever since I'd learned about them on our honeymoon in Pompeii, though initially my interest was abstract. But as Calvin and I made one international move (and then another and another), I began to absorb the implications his career as a foreign-service officer would have on our marriage, as well as our lives as individuals. In recent months I'd started contemplating the household gods with increasing frequency, linked as they were to the concepts of cooking and family and home.

My brooding interludes usually began with a single question asked at a cocktail party: Where are you from? Simple enough, but I never knew how to respond. Should I say Southern California, where I was born and raised, where my parents and brother lived, where I still voted and spent every Christmas? Yet I hadn't lived there since I'd graduated from college almost fifteen years earlier. Should I say New York, where I forged a path as a young professional, where my closest friends still lived, where I'd fallen in love with book publishing, ethnic cuisine, and my husband? But because the city changed so fast, I sometimes felt like a tourist when I visited, the blocks stripped bare of familiar landmarks. Should I say Washington, D.C., the city in America where we'd lived most recently? But we'd spent less than a year there, not even enough time to retrieve all our belongings from storage.

In my twenties and early thirties, the idea of an itinerant lifestyle seemed adventurous and romantic. But now, as my birthdays mounted and the numbers crept up—thirty-four, thirty-five—I began to worry that my Penates were too lonely without a constant

Lar Familiaris. I wondered if it thought of all the lares we'd left behind and missed them as much as I did.

One gray autumn day—as autumn days in Paris often are—I stopped at a Chinese restaurant for lunch, a little treat since I was between appointments in a neighborhood inconvenient to our apartment. I had just settled in with my book, a plate of dumplings, a bowl of rice, and porc lacqué—a Frenchified version of char siu pork—when my cell phone rang. The number was blocked, but I answered it anyway because the restaurant was empty and in the shabby gloom I felt a little lonely.

"Ann?"

I knew her voice at once, high and bright. It was Nicola—calling from New York—the friend I used to lunch with almost every single day when we worked together in publishing.

"Can you smell the pork dumplings from there?" I asked.

"Where are you?"

I told her about the restaurant, and my lunch, and the book I had just spattered with black vinegar. And then I told her about the stocky man outside the métro who had tried to attract my attention by shouting *"Ni hao!"* at me. "Is that supposed to be attractive? Screaming hello in Mandarin Chinese?" We laughed, and my lunch was growing cold, but I didn't really care, because it was so wonderful to hear her voice again after so many months.

"How are you?" I asked, glancing at my watch. "It's so early over there!" With the time difference, it was only six in the morning in New York. And as I spoke the words, I suddenly knew exactly why she was calling.

"I have some news," she said. "I'm pregnant." Pause. "With identical twins."

"Congratulations! It's so exciting! I'm so thrilled for you guys!"

I exclaimed as loudly as I dared in the restaurant, which turned out to be pretty loudly, because the waitress poked her head out of the kitchen to see if anything was wrong. I repeated the words over and over, simultaneously trying to shake my head at the waitress. The news surprised me—especially the part about the twins—but didn't shock me. Nicola and I had discussed children many times, circling around and around the questions of identity and balance and ticking clocks and the imperfect choices that most women seem to face. She knew she wanted kids, I thought I might, but we both struggled with the question of when. How, I fretted, would a baby affect the house of cards that already seemed so precarious—the work that I loved balanced on the marriage that I cherished teetering on the overseas moves that occurred every three years? Yet while I had hesitated, Nicola had made a decision and moved forward, and I admired her for it.

She was about three months along, she told me, and feeling pretty good, just a little tired and maybe a bit overwhelmed by all the different tests and information and concerns that came with carrying multiples. Multiples! Already she sounded like an expert. We discussed the aesthetic delights of chubby babies in tights and the probability of the twins' developing a secret language in the womb, and then she had to go get ready for work. Just as suddenly as she had appeared, she was gone.

I wandered around for the rest of the day in a haze. Every time I passed a children's clothing boutique—which was often, because in Paris there are at least two on every block—I stopped to gaze in the window and ponder pairs of matching outfits. I kept marveling at the news—Nicola! pregnant! with twins!—burnishing it brighter and brighter. I was so happy for her, so excited to meet her beautiful, identical babies, to buy them striped French onesies and, maybe one day, to help introduce them to the pleasures of runny cheese. My joy was so buoyant I almost didn't notice the little hollow underneath it, but as the day continued and Nicola's news moved from surprise into reality, I started to feel it more keenly, a thimbleful of emptiness that stretched across the distance. One of my best friends was about to become a mother, and I wouldn't be there. Oh, we still had e-mails, phone calls, visits, but I would miss the small events—like visiting her in the hospital or leaving a tray of lasagna in her fridge—the mundane participation that is the true meaning of friendship. She was over there and I was here, and the circles of our daily lives overlapped less and less, until they barely touched at all.

I knew it wasn't her fault, or mine, just the natural consequence of distance. And yet recently the distance had started to loom unforgiving and unmanageable, shadowing almost all my relationships. I felt it when I saw photos of friends' new boyfriends-turned-husbands, with my baby nieces who were suddenly young girls weaving me pot holders, with my parents who grew a little grayer every time I visited. The people I loved most in the world were living the most important moments of their lives without me, and I was living mine without them. It took me a while to recognize the emotion, unfamiliar as it was, but when I did, it scratched at me with thorny immediacy: I was homesick.

For centuries, cooking historians have posited the theory that Catherine de Médicis established modern French cuisine in 1533, when the young Florentine bride to Henri II imported the world's finest cooks from her native Italy to France. (Also included among her retinue: pâtissiers, perfumers, specialists in fireworks, table items like the fork, and recipes for noodles as well as, possibly, ice cream.) Though in recent years modern scholars have debated the reach of

Catherine's influence—perhaps none more thoroughly than Barbara Ketcham Wheaton in her book *Savoring the Past*—it is true that during her reign as regent queen Catherine traveled widely throughout France, organizing festival banquets and teaching local cooks court recipes.

In 1553, Catherine became the Countess of Lauragais, claiming a section of the Languedoc province that reached from Toulouse to Carcassonne (in other words, cassoulet country). When she visited the region for a few months, she brought an entourage with her, cooks and servants, as well as provisions, introducing new foods and plants, among them the bean.

Haricot beans are a New World plant, native to South America. Christopher Columbus imported them to Europe sometime around 1510, and their cultivation quickly spread throughout Spain and Italy. Some considered the bean a symbol of fertility—something to do with wind and a puffed stomach—and perhaps this is why Catherine carried them in her retinue. (She did bear ten children.) After her visit to the Languedoc, the white bean took root, eventually spreading through the whole of southwest France.

Before Catherine de Médicis—before the bean—cassoulet was made with mature dried fava beans, or broad beans, which remained tough and fibrous even after long and slow cooking. Given this description, it's easy to understand why local cooks so eagerly embraced Catherine's *haricot lingot*, a type of white navy bean. Even today Languedoc natives claim that locally grown beans have a thinner, more delicate skin, making them easier to digest.

I headed east from Toulouse in my rental car, and as I approached the outskirts of Castelnaudary, I began to see large signs proclaiming the town "the world capital of cassoulet." According to legend, cassoulet was invented here during the Hundred Years'

War, an extended series of conflicts between England and France that occurred from 1337 to 1453. Under siege from the English, the town's starving inhabitants pooled their food stocks—pork, fava beans, sausage, fat—simmering everything together in a giant cauldron. After feasting on the ragout—I imagined them all sitting down together in the town square—the Castelnaudary soldiers became so invigorated by the hearty meal that they rallied to defeat the English, chasing them all the way to the Channel.

As I drove along busy streets, past gleaming strip malls, the town seemed more of a commercial center, a place of transit, rather than the cradle of the Languedoc's signature dish. Nevertheless, almost every storefront, no matter how large or small, advertised cassoulet *fait maison*, ready to be enjoyed immediately or packed sous-vide and transported home. A ring of factories dominated the outskirts—collectively, they produce 170,000 cans of the stuff a day—further confirmation of Castelnaudary's world cassoulet domination. In fact, I soon realized that the town's residents were deadly serious about the title of cassoulet capital—so serious that in 1972 they formed a society, La Grande Confrérie du Cassoulet de Castelnaudary, to defend and protect the dish.

The Confrérie has about forty-five chevaliers, or active members, who meet several times a year to taste cassoulets from various restaurants and judge them worthy of inclusion on their list. They wear medals, long robes in red and yellow, and tapered fezlike hats adorned with a yellow ribbon, meant to resemble a *cassole* being licked by flames. Every August the Confrérie organizes a Fête du Cassoulet, a weeklong event featuring concerts, demonstrations, and more than forty thousand servings of the celebrated dish.

But what distinguishes Castelnaudary's version of cassoulet? According to Jean-Louis Male, a former *grand maître* of the Confrérie, it is the *cassole*—in Occitan, *cassolo*—the earthenware bowl that gave the recipe its name.

"Castelnaudary has a tradition of pottery," he told me. "There is an exceptional native red clay found here, and its composition has a special capacity to retain heat. These dishes can last up to a hundred years."

The *cassole* is a deep bowl with sloping sides that make it narrow at the bottom and wide at the mouth—an inverted pyramid—a smooth-glazed interior, and a rough exterior. It traditionally sat on the hearth simmering continuously for hours, or even days, the peasant wife adding scraps of food at different intervals. This, then, was arguably the true origin of cassoulet, a humble pot of food that never stopped cooking. The layer that formed and re-formed on the surface probably contributed to the old wives' tale that the cassoulet's crust must be pierced seven times during cooking, Male told me.

"There's no bread-crumb crust?" I asked.

"*Jamais,*" he replied.

Until World War II, Castelnaudary was known as a center of pottery, but today only one establishment continues to make *cassoles* in the traditional manner—the Poterie Not Frères. Run by two brothers and a nephew, it is the oldest pottery establishment in southern France, a family business started in 1830. Their atelier, on the banks of the Canal du Midi, resembles a medieval shack, with the three craftsmen toiling away by the light of narrow windows. When I visited, I found the three men perched on high stools, poised above foot-operated pottery wheels, painstakingly shaping each *cassole* by hand, forming a small spout in its lip. Outside, I spotted a backhoe—used for harvesting the region's clay from a seam located steps away from the atelier—and a wood-burning kiln the size of a modest New York apartment, which one of the pottery's owners,

Jean-Pierre Not, told me burned for thirty-six hours at a time and took fifteen days to cool.

Here, amid the dust, and the man-powered pottery wheels, and the handcrafted bowls, I started to feel a little emotional, washed over by a wave of timelessness. I couldn't leave without a *cassole*. I picked one up from a low shelf and weighed it in my hands, admiring the solidity of its clay and its tradition, wondering how on earth I could transport it home to Paris in my carry-on luggage. I put it down. Picked it up again. Down. Up. Down. Up. I *had* to bring it home with me. And so I did. Perhaps this was one of my Penates, a kitchen god to move with me around the world.

Here are five things that I discovered about cassoulet in Castelnaudary:

1. *It's not so much cooked as assembled.*

     Obvious, right? And yet I didn't realize it until Philippe Dunod, the owner of the Hôtel de France, a cassoulet producer in Castelnaudary, gave me a demonstration. Cassoulet is kind of like lasagna. All the ingredients are precooked—the beans, the pork meat, the pork skin, the goose confit, the sausage—layered together in the *cassole*, and baked in the oven at 350°F.

2. *It's simmered again, and again, and again.*

     Piercing the crust seven times is a myth. But the experts I spoke to all agreed that after it's assembled, the cassoulet should be cooked, then cooled, preferably overnight, then cooked and cooled again—at least three times. "Nothing," said the Grande Confrérie's Jean-Louis Malet, "is more catastrophic than a cassoulet made at the last minute."

3. *But it can be overcooked*.

The beans should be tender and flavorful, but not mushy. "If the beans fall apart, the dish is ruined," said Male.

4. *You can never eat too much cassoulet*.

Male once ate *eleven* in one week, though he admitted, "I lost some years of my life during my term as *grand maître*."

5. *There is no difference between cassoulets from Castelnaudary and Carcassonne*.

Traditionally Carcassonne's cassoulet contained partridge, which bred wild in the town's surrounding grapevines. "Today there are no more vines in Carcassonne and no more partridge," said Male. Instead chefs use duck or goose confit just like in Castelnaudary.

Was this last point hubris or heresy? There was only one way to find out. I got in the car and headed east for Carcassonne.

The landscape between Castelnaudary and Carcassonne stretches dusty and flat, farmland baked dry by the generous sun that spills over the region. From the highway I saw the occasional hill town rising in the distance, left over from the Middle Ages when villages were built on high ground to help prevent attack. Between the eleventh and thirteenth centuries, the Cathars flourished in this region. A sect of Christianity descended from the Byzantine Empire, they embraced a rigid doctrine—forbidding meat and requiring celibacy. Cathars found tolerance in the Languedoc, constructing châteaus and citadels, amassing adherents—called "les Bons Hommes"—and weapons. They became such a concern to the Catholic Church that in 1207 Pope Innocent III dispatched a mission of papal legates to the region to slow their activities. When one of the envoys was assassinated, it was all the proof that Innocent needed to launch a religious crusade. The town of Carcassonne saw its share of blood during these wars, with a siege in 1209 that expelled the Cathars from its city walls. Decades of war and massacre followed, ending in a fiery inquisition that burned the remaining heretics alive. In 1321 the last Cathar was executed.

Today the old town still looks remarkably as it must have in the Middle Ages, perched on a hill, with turrets and moats and gap-toothed fortifications protecting a warren of steep cobblestone streets and thick stone buildings. Only a handful of residents live in the *ville haute*—as the upper section of Carcassonne is called. Rather it's given over to museums, shops selling cheap tourist knickknacks, and restaurants advertising cassoulet. Even so, I thought I caught a glimpse of the wretchedness and wonder of medieval life as I moved from the chilled shadows of a side alley to the harsh light of the town square.

In a small hamlet a couple of miles from Carcassonne, I met Jean-Claude Rodriguez, the chef and owner of the restaurant Château Saint-Martin and the founder of the Académie Universelle du Cassoulet, an association devoted to the promotion and protection of cassoulet. Yes, there's another one. And, as I soon discovered, while the Académie and the Grande Confrérie share a similar mission, they are bitter rivals.

Rodriguez founded the Académie in 2001, with the goal of "protecting the cassoulet made by restaurants with high-quality products from the region." Its hundred members also wear robes—in red and white—medals, and hats that look like saggy chef's toques, and they meet several times a year to taste cassoulet and judge them worthy of inclusion on their list. Sound familiar? Unlike the Grande Confrérie, however, the Académie has admitted chefs from other countries, such as Australia, the United States, and Japan.

These days very few chefs—even avid devotees like Rodriguez—prepare the traditional cassoulet of Carcassonne. "This used to be a country of vineyards, and in the vines we found partridges, wild hares, and other small game," he said. "But the landscape has changed. The cassoulet with partridge . . . it's a lost recipe. Once or twice a year, I make a version with wild game. The rest of the time, I use confit de canard." His voice drooped so dolorously as he admitted this that I didn't have the heart to ask him about its similarity to the Castelnaudary recipe.

I thought back to Prosper Montagné, the culinary lexicographer and cassoulet devotee, who had declared that Carcassonne was "God the son" of cassoulet. He meant that it embodied the dish's legacy, but now his words seemed to turn the recipe ghostly, lost to a changed landscape, a different way of life. *Nothing lasts forever*, I thought. *Not even cassoulet.*

At the airport in Toulouse, the woman at security pulled my hand luggage, and I knew why. "Can you open it for me?" she asked.

"C'est une cassole," I told her, unzipping the bag to show her the heavy dish.

She pushed it aside and started digging deeper into the corners of the bag. *"Qu'est-ce que c'est . . . ?"* I heard her mutter. *"Des haricots?"* She pulled out a box of white beans that must have looked dangerous in the X-ray machine, *haricots lingots du Lauragais* bought in a shop in Castelnaudary. "There are two boxes of beans?"

"To make cassoulet at home."

She nodded as if that were the most natural thing in the world.

After so many months of toast, it felt a little unnatural to spend two hours in the kitchen. But I had downloaded some podcasts, and they kept me company as I cleaned and chopped and stirred. I'd forgotten how meditative cooking could be, how free my mind felt to wander while my hands busied themselves with a knife and a pile of vegetables. I thought about Calvin and the care package I planned to send him, to cheer him along until his next visit home. I thought of Nicola, growing bigger every day, and the pretty pink invitation for her baby shower that had arrived in the mail a few days earlier. I would miss the party, but I had already made a trip to Bonpoint, where I spent a happy half hour among the tiny frilly underpants, flowered rompers, and plum-colored cashmere cardigans, buying two of the sweetest baby outfits I had ever seen. I hoped my friend would dress her daughters in them and think of me.

I thought of the homesickness that had gripped me like a migraine a few weeks before, leaving me shaky and pale. The feeling, so sharp and unfamiliar, had shocked me with its strength. But there was no cure for it, no pill I could swallow, no number of long-distance phone calls that could ease the ache. A couple of weeks later, the sting had lessened a bit, quieted by the distractions of daily life: an emergency visit from the plumber to fix a leaky radiator, a shared square of afternoon chocolate with my colleagues at the library, a laugh with my husband over Skype. But it still lurked, the homesickness, and I knew it would return, perhaps sooner rather than later, an unstoppable wave. I had made choices in my life, as we all must make choices, and I didn't regret them. But still, there were consequences, sometimes painful, and they would linger for the rest of my life.

I thought of Aux Fins Gourmets, which I'd walked by a few days earlier on my way home from work. I had glanced in the windows, wondering if I'd see Bernard-Henri Lévy. Instead I saw a darkened space lit by pools of candlelight, white cloths on the tables, an empty dining room. When I looked at the posted menu, cassoulet was no longer listed. The restaurant had been sold—one more remnant of Paris abandoned to the figment of my memory. It made me wonder how much of homesickness was merely nostalgia, a yearning for a perfect ideal that never really existed.

I skimmed foam off the simmering beans and added a bay leaf. At the last minute, I had decided to forgo cassoulet for a bean soup, a lighter, healthier dish that appeased my hypochondria, one I could freeze in small portions and eat over the days and weeks to come. The cassoulet recipe would wait for another, more festive occasion— I had saved the other box of beans to simmer with sausage and duck confit, to share at a dinner with family and friends. But tonight I cooked just for myself, an offering to our Penates and Lar Familiaris that came from me and no one else.

Cassoulet de Castelnaudary

Cassoulet is not a difficult dish to make, but it requires at least three days to cook. I adapted the recipe below from one given to me by the Grande Confrérie du Cassoulet de Castelnaudary. I find that dividing the process makes it easier to tackle. You can consolidate, but remember that the true secret of a good cassoulet is time. Confit de canard and saucisse de Toulouse are sold online by mail order from gourmet food shops like frenchselections.com or dartagnan.com.

Serves 4 or 5

1 pound northern beans

2 quarts chicken broth (if not homemade, use "no sodium" or "unsalted"), plus more for cooking the cassoulet

2 duck confit thighs, cut in half

½ pound garlic sausage (saucisse de Toulouse *or* saucisse à l'ail), cut into large chunks

¼ pound pork shoulder, belly, or knuckle, cut into large chunks

¼ pound fresh pork skin (optional)

2 to 3 cloves garlic

A 2-inch piece of salt pork

1 teaspoon nutmeg

Salt and pepper to taste

DAY ONE

Sort and wash the beans. Place them in a large bowl and cover with cold water by 2 to 3 inches. Soak for at least 8 hours, or preferably overnight.

DAY TWO

Drain the beans of their soaking water. Place them in a large pot and add enough cold water to cover them by 2 inches. Bring to a rapid boil and boil for 5 minutes. Remove from the heat and drain.

In a large pot, heat 2 quarts of the chicken broth. Add the beans, bring to a boil, and skim off any scum. Simmer gently, uncovered, for 45 minutes to 1 hour, until the beans are just tender but still whole and unbroken. Allow the beans to cool in their cooking liquid.

While the beans are cooking, prepare the meats

In a large sauté pan, gently brown the duck thighs over medium-low heat until golden, then remove. In the same sauté pan, brown the sausage in the remaining fat and remove. Brown the chunks of pork and remove. If using pork skin, cut it into 2-inch squares.

Peel the garlic cloves and mash them into a paste together with the salt pork. Add this paste to the beans and their cooking liquid, along with the nutmeg.

Assemble the cassoulet

Use a *cassole* if you have one. Otherwise you can use a 3½-quart Dutch oven.

Line the bottom of the vessel with the cut pork skin (if using). Drain the beans, reserving their cooking liquid, and season them lightly with salt. Layer a third of the beans on top of the pork skin. Arrange the duck confit and chunks of pork on top. Spread the remaining beans in a layer over the top. Add the sausages, poking them into the beans until just their tops are visible. Warm the bean-cooking liquid and pour enough of it into the cassoulet to barely cover the beans. Sprinkle a dusting of freshly ground black pepper across the surface. The cassoulet can rest here, covered, overnight.

Cooking the cassoulet

Preheat the oven to 325°F. Place the cassoulet in the oven and allow it to cook for 3 hours. While it is cooking, it will develop a brown crust on top. Pierce the crust and moisten the surface, taking care not to disturb the layers below. Allow the crust to re-form 2 or 3 times. If the beans start to look dry, moisten them with several spoonfuls of extra bean-cooking liquid or chicken broth. Remove the cassoulet from the oven, cool, and refrigerate overnight.

DAY THREE

Preheat the oven to 325°F. Cook the cassoulet for 1½ hours, breaking the crust with a spoon and moistening the surface at least twice. If the beans look dry, add spoonfuls of extra bean-cooking liquid or chicken broth. You can serve the cassoulet now or remove it from the oven and allow to cool. Refrigerate overnight.

DAY FOUR

Preheat the oven to 325°F. Heat the cassoulet for 1½ hours, moistening with extra bean-cooking liquid or chicken broth as necessary. Serve immediately in its vessel, gently simmering and unstirred.

Chapter 7

Alsace / Choucroute

I know very little about my paternal grandparents, who both died before I was born, but here are some of the things I've gleaned: They came to the United States in the 1920s, emigrating from Toisan, a coastal city in Guangdong province that lies at the heart of the Chinese diaspora. They owned a Chinese restaurant in Fresno, California. They had more than ten children, some biological, some adopted. They were Catholic, but their ancestors may have been Muslim (the name Ma, which they changed to Mah to appear more American, means "horse" and is common among Islamic Chinese; it sounds like Mohammed). They spoke a regional dialect, also called Toisan, a derivative of Cantonese. They passed this language to their children along with a love of plants, a taste for bitter melon in black sauce, narrow feet, and a predilection for heart disease.

Here are some things I don't know about my grandparents: If I look like them. If they missed China. If they were legal immigrants.

I'd been thinking about my grandparents ever since September, when I'd received a letter from the Office Français de l'Immigration et de l'Intégration, the French version of immigration services. As a diplomat's spouse, I was eligible for French working papers, but—though Calvin's job at the American embassy had smoothed my path considerably—I still had to navigate the application process.

The letter I'd received was a thin, photocopied sheet "inviting" me to a *visite médicale*, a medical examination, the first step toward exchanging my temporary working permit for official documents. And so several weeks later, on a crisp and bright October morning, I joined a line of people waiting outside a dreary office building in the eleventh arrondissement. The limp air of disinterested bureaucracy hanging over the block told me I was in the right place before I even read the sign.

Americans who move to France share two horror stories: acquiring a French driver's license and obtaining a *carte de séjour*. The former necessitates buckets of cash, the latter reams of paperwork; both require infinite reserves of patience. But even forearmed with this knowledge, I was surprised by my experience.

Inside the office the process was a series of petite mortifications, from the obligatory educational video on *laïcité*, France's policy of secularism, to the interview that assessed my language proficiency to stripping down and posing bare-chested for an X-ray meant to ensure that I wasn't carrying tuberculosis. Thankfully, I understood the separation of church and state, spoke French, and was free of TB.

As the authorities poked and prodded, squeezed and scolded, I thought of my grandparents almost ninety years ago. Because of them I had grown up in California, the child of an American born in America, with all the confidence and hubris that implies. But today I, too, was an immigrant, stripped of familiarity and fluency, and the experience left me humbled.

My language interview was held in a plain, windowless room not unlike the warden's office in a low-security prison. The *fonctionnaire* quizzing me had dark eyes and hair and a surprisingly warm smile. We chatted for a few minutes about my French studies, my work, and my husband's post at the embassy. Then she spent several minutes printing out a series of colorful *attestations*—they looked like the participation certificates handed out to a children's soccer team—and informed me that I needed to sign up to take the *formation civique*, a daylong class on French government, history, and culture.

"It provides knowledge of the principles of the French state," she said.

"La formation civique?" A civic formation? "I'm already formed," I joked.

She smiled faintly. *"Désolée."*

But her apology had revealed a chink in her armor, and I tried to push through it. "Do I still need to take the class even though I'm only here temporarily? My husband is an American diplomat," I reminded her. "His post ends in three years."

I could feel her wavering, but then she shook her head. *"Désolée. Tout le monde est obligé."*

Something in her voice told me that *tout le monde* was *not* obligated—that some people managed to slither out of it. Then again, this was a perfect example of French logic—all people are equal, therefore all people must take the *formation civique* (except those who don't have to). It followed the same logic as the policy of *laïcité* discussed in the video I'd just watched: Religion and government must be kept separate (except in certain circumstances such as the calendar of public holidays, which is still guided by Catholic feast days). Who was I to argue?

I joined a group of people in a dingy waiting room, all of us struggling to wrangle the unwieldy film of our chest X-rays. While we waited to see the doctor who would proclaim us fit or unfit, the people around me chatted in quiet voices, a soft carpet of languages I didn't recognize. The institutional atmosphere felt universal to waiting rooms around the world; I recognized the smell of stale coffee, the fluorescent-tube lighting, and scuffed linoleum from the DMV in California, the jury-duty room in lower Manhattan, a bank in Beijing. But then a number would be called—*cent quatre-vingt-douze!*—and I would be jolted back to Paris. Not the Paris of lacy wrought-iron towers and toy boats sailing in marble fountains but a grittier, gutsier city, one of new beginnings and pinched pennies and endless stacks of paperwork.

I was the last person to be called that morning. I waited, fidgeting as the room emptied, reading the pamphlets on HIV that the X-ray technicians had thrust upon me. My stomach began a quiet rumble, which grew louder as the minutes ticked toward noon. To distract myself I started speculating about the people who had been in the waiting room with me. Where did they come from? Why had they moved to France? And, perhaps most interestingly, what were they going to have for lunch? I imagined noodle soup perfumed with basil and cilantro or fine-grained couscous spiked with harissa.

Like all cuisines, France's did not develop in a vacuum. It absorbed flavors and techniques through its porous borders, via age-old rivalries with Italy, Spain, Germany, and Belgium (to name but a few), and by way of its former colonies in North Africa and Southeast Asia. A walk through Paris was like a stroll among the regions of France and her interests, the Savoyard restaurants near the rue Mouffetard that served fondue and raclette, the thirteenth arrondissement's fragrant bowls of phô—a Vietnamese word possibly derived from the French *pot-au-feu*—the Corsican *épicerie* that emitted a whiff of powerful cheese and dried sausages, the bakeries in the nineteenth selling tiny honey-soaked pastries, the bright Alsatian brasseries with their oversize goblets of beer and metal platters brimming with cured pork.

It was the last one that gave me pause now, as my stomach began its slow growl toward lunch. I thought of the region of Alsace in eastern France, a producer of fruity wine decanted into long-necked bottles, and the home of choucroute garnie: finely sliced, fermented cabbage (which looked an awful lot like sauerkraut) topped with sausages and ham. The dish stood between two cultures—was it French? was it German?—a culinary witness to a region that had changed hands several times in the span of only a generation. With each change in power, Alsatians were forced to swtich allegiances and languages, becoming strangers in a *familiar* land.

How does a cross-cultural seesaw affect a person's identity? Perhaps if I learned more about Alsace and its cuisine, I could better understand what might happen to me, an American of Chinese ethnicity who changed countries every three or four years. By the time my number was called, I had decided to travel east, to the Rhine River, to the border between France and Germany—to Alsace.

Alsace is nestled between the Vosges Mountains and the Black Forest, a protective topographic sandwich that shelters the region from harsh weather. It also means that when the fog settles in, it lingers, blanketing the plain in a chilly, swirling mist that seeps through the bones like an unhappy ghost. During my four-day visit in October— carefully timed to coincide with the end of cabbage season—the fog never lifted. It hung in the air, dulling the fall colors into a muddy blur, spurring my imagination to run wild with thoughts of battle-fields haunted by phantom soldiers—relics of a land that has suffered more than its fair share of carnage.

Instead of abandoned battlefields, however, I found actual fields, the agricultural kind. And instead of ghosts, they were filled with cabbage—acres and acres of it, planted in orderly ranks that stretched far into the distance. Piles of even more cabbage broke the horizon, heaping mounds that loomed over the farm equipment.

The amount of cabbage shouldn't have surprised me. After all, I had come to the village of Krautergersheim, located in the center of the Alsace region, because it is called the *capitale de la choucroute*. Twenty percent of all the choucroute produced in France is grown here—about twenty thousand metric tons a year. Even the village's very name refers to its livelihood. "*Kraut* is the German word for cabbage, *heim* means 'home,'" René Hoelt, the village mayor, told me.

With their rich and moist soil, the fields surrounding the capital of choucroute have produced beautiful cabbages for centuries. A crossbreed of the local variety, Quintal d'Alsace, the heads are heavy and robust, with wide, tender, spongy leaves that absorb flavor and shred into long, fine strands.

The word "choucroute" is a combination of French and German that translates literally as "cabbage cabbage"; in the Alsatian dialect, it's called *Sürkrüt*. Cabbage has been documented in the local diet as early as 1673, a reliable source of vitamin C during long, cold months lacking fruits and vegetables.

Every fall a craftsman called the *Sürkrüthowler*, or *Sürkrüt schneider*, traveled between farms, slicing each family's cabbage harvest with a lethal mandoline. The family gathered the cored and chopped cabbage into a wooden barrel or a stone vat, then liberally salted, pressed, and covered it and left it in the basement to ferment. Throughout the course of the winter, they dipped into their stash, which grew more acidic as the months progressed.

Industrial choucroute production came to Krautergersheim in 1874, when Martin Dell, a Swiss entrepreneur, saw profit in the fertile cabbage fields and opened the first factory. In the industry's 1960s heyday, there were fifteen producers; today only five remain.

They still make choucroute in the traditional way, the cabbage cored, grated, salted, weighted, and fermented for two to twelve weeks, depending on the weather—the warmer the temperature, the shorter the period of time.

"It's the ancestral method," said Jean-Luc Meyer, the director of the choucroute producer Meyer Wagner. "The same one my great-grandfather used when he started the business in 1900."

I got lost on my way to the Meyer Wagner factory, despite Krautergersheim's small size and the small number of *choucroutiers* in town. I couldn't keep my Weber straight from my Adès Weber, from my Meyer Wagner. I finally found the factory, a vast boxy building on the village outskirts, surrounded by fields. Outside, a conveyor belt delivered cabbages straight to the mouth of an open door. Inside, the immense space hummed with machinery and smelled of cut cabbage, a raw, lingering scent that wasn't entirely unpleasant.

Meyer led me on a tour, showing me the machines that sliced and salted, the cement fermentation vats sunk deep into the floor, before pausing at another, discernibly warmer section of the factory that fogged my camera lens with steam. Here choucroute simmered in giant vessels, the uncooked, fermented stuff becoming soft and pliable in its warm bath of wine, water, goose fat, and spices. Once the pride and provenance of Alsatian housewives—each with her own secret recipe and tricks for producing the tenderest, most aromatic cabbage—the choucroute-cooking process has today been taken over by the factory.

"Most people don't have the time or inclination anymore," Meyer said. Though the company still sells a small quantity of raw choucroute, the majority of their business is done in flat, sealed, plastic packages of the cooked stuff, ready to reheat and serve. Sometimes the traditional meat accompaniment—ham or cured pork belly—is even included inside.

It seemed a little sad to me, this disappearance of the cast-iron Staub pot of choucroute bubbling away gently in Granny's kitchen, but Meyer seemed perfectly cheerful about it. "In the mid-1970s or early '80s," he said, "the local producers had to decide whether or not to buy the equipment to cook choucroute." Today Krautergersheim's five remaining *choucroutiers* all sell it cooked. It turns out that cooked cabbage saved the industry.

During our conversation Meyer offered me a bit of linguistic instruction. I had been calling the dish "choucroute," but, as he pointed out, that refers only to the preserved cabbage. The official name is "choucroute garnie," or garnished choucroute. The "garnish" means—inversely—the sausages, salt pork, smoked bacon, and *knack*, or hot dogs, that make up the caloric bulk of the meal.

At Charcuterie Muller, a small shop located on the main street in Rosheim, the pretty, half-timbered village where I was staying, I inspected a long glass case stuffed with cuts of pork in varying shades of pink: smoked, freshly salted, fully cured, squeaky lean, or striped with fat. There were sausages fat and thin; white; black; some made of liver, heart, or blood. There was a mound of crimson ground liver, used to make poached quenelles, or dumplings. The shop clerk—a dark-haired woman who politely refrained from asking me any questions despite my appearance, accent, and avid curiosity—patiently explained all the different cuts and cures, the pieces that should be cooked with the choucroute and those that needed to be cooked separately. We spoke French together, but when an older couple entered the shop, they addressed her in Alsatian, and she snapped into the other language without dropping an umlaut.

I eavesdropped on their conversation, straining to catch the meaning. Sometimes, if I listened carefully enough—and if the interaction was about food—I could pick out a few words of a local dialect or even other Romance languages. But this was impenetrable, a thick wall of sounds that, to my tin ear, sounded indistinguishable from German. I could recognize only two phrases, *"Ça va"* and *"Ja, ja, ja."* They repeated them often.

The Alsatian dialect, I later discovered, is linguistically close to Swiss German, a hearty tongue that's still spoken widely in the region, especially among Alsatians *d'un certain âge*. It has noble roots—in the Middle Ages it was the literary language of troubadours—and in the nineteenth century Napoleon grandly tolerated it, saying, "Who cares if they speak German, as long as their swords speak French?" Its vowels and low cadences color the names of towns and villages, making them difficult for non-Alsatian speakers to pronounce (which causes much glee among the locals).

This Germanic influence has also left its stamp on the region's gastronomy, with its encyclopedia of sausages and dishes like Baeckeoffe, a casserole of layered meat and potatoes, traditionally cooked in the baker's oven by housewives occupied with the weekly laundry. It's evident in the soft, fat pretzels, called *bretzels*, stacked on hooks at the *boulangerie;* in the elegant, long-necked bottles of local Riesling and Gewürztraminer; in the robust sweets like Kougelhopf, a tender, yeasty cake studded with dried fruits and nuts.

As I wandered the old-fashioned center of Strasbourg—the region's capital and a seat of the European Parliament—I felt drawn into another era, one of gas-powered streetlamps and half-timbered taverns, of pretty canals lined with Renaissance gingerbread houses in La Petite France, the city's heart-stoppingly charming historic neighborhood. Another era? Perhaps rather another place, another country distant from France. The street signs in Alsatian; the young families bicycling politely along marked paths; the pastry-shop windows filled with Black Forest cake and tarts of *quetsches;* the *Plätze,* or *places,* named after German icons like Gutenberg; the cozy pubs, called *Winstubs,* that beckoned with promises of *vin chaud*—all of it combined to make me feel as if I'd entered into a foreign land.

Later I described Strasbourg to a French friend as feeling like "nowhere," but that came out sounding much harsher than what I wanted to express. No, rather it felt to me like a different dimension—not a mix of France and Germany but another creation altogether—a city of Mitteleuropa where I could communicate perfectly and yet understand almost nothing.

On a chilly, late-autumn evening in Paris, I went to a farewell party for some departing American friends and drank one too many farewell glasses of Champagne. It was a perfectly innocent mistake—innocent, that is, until the next morning when I overslept my alarm, woke up late with a tongue that felt pickled, and had to dash through a dense fog to the northeast corner of Paris. My *formation civique*—the obligatory class that would teach me about French history, culture, and values—was scheduled to begin at half past eight.

I raced through the métro, up the stairs, and along a wide boulevard in the twentieth arrondissement, dodging mothers pushing strollers, veiled women carrying heavy sacks of groceries, and groups of men smoking and chatting outside cafés. At the address marked on my letter of invitation, I found a modern cement building, the windows covered in blinds, the door locked.

The door was locked.

I glanced at my watch and double-checked it against my cell phone. According to both, I was three minutes late and thus fully deserving of having the door locked against me. Still, I struggled to contain my rising concern. What was I going to do? How could I reschedule my class? Was I even *allowed* to reschedule?

I stood on the street, buffeted by a sharp wind, berating my own stupidity. I was learning the first lesson of being an immigrant: Never be late for any meeting relating to your situation. I rattled the door with increasing desperation, barely registering the man who had dashed to my side.

"Formation civique?" he asked. At first I thought he was a security guard, come to shoo me away. But then I noticed his rolling accent; the color of his skin, toffee, as if he'd come from warmer climes; the note of panic in his voice that matched my own; and I recognized him as a fellow émigré. I had observed at my medical examination that almost none of us were white, myself included. Evidently he identified me by the same criterion.

"C'est fermé à clé." I gestured at the door.

He shook the handle, and when the door didn't budge, he did what my blushing, ladylike, middle-class American sensibility prevented me from doing: He started to pound on it, hard enough to make the windows shake.

Boom. Boom. Boom.

He paused, and we turned our heads to listen. Nothing.

BOOM. BOOM. BOOM. Still nothing.

He raised his fist again, but before he could continue, we heard the sound of a bolt turning in the lock. A woman sporting a dark suit and a disciplinary air stood before us.

"Formation civique?" the man said again.

She puffed up her cheeks and blew them out again, the epitome of French exasperation. I took a deep breath, prepared to argue until she let us enter, but she merely asked for our documents, looked them over, and then allowed us through the door, pointing wordlessly toward a classroom. Inside, fluorescent bulbs lit the eyes of about thirty strangers, who watched as I hunted for a seat.

Our instructor was another woman, wearing a similar dark suit and air of authority. She was *d'origine tunisienne* and born in France, she announced, and today she would teach us about this decentralized republic of twenty-six regions. We went around the room and introduced ourselves. Of the thirty people in the room, I was one of two Americans—the other was a female rock musician who spoke exquisite French and sported tattoos and dark eyeliner—and among a minority of women. The rest were men, many from Africa, places like Tunisia, Algeria, or Mali. Mauritius. Eritrea. Later, when I got home, I looked up these last few places on the map.

The lecture began, our instructor careening wildly among topics that I expected—presidential term limits, the French judicial process—to those that in a million years I would have never dreamed she'd raise: female genital mutilation, polygamy (both illegal in France, in case you were wondering). During the breaks half the class rushed outside to smoke while the other half stood about in the drafty hallway. The men gathered in clusters, chatting and laughing, already united by common acquaintance perhaps, or a mother tongue, or simply gender. The women sat silent on the edges, blown aside by the testosterone in the room.

Around noon lunch arrived on cafeteria trays, but I slipped out to a local café and escaped into my book. Fifty minutes and a croque-monsieur later, I made my way back to the classroom—the door was unlocked this time—where I found my fellow classmates looking as sleepy as I felt. We settled in for an afternoon of lectures, maybe some discreet dozing. But then our instructor appeared, vibrating with renewed energy, as though she'd spent the past hour lifting weights and popping cans of spinach. She announced we'd be taking a true-or-false test and started to read the questions aloud.

"*Vrai ou faux*. Homosexuals have the right to marry in France."

From my seat in the front row, I heard a collective intake of breath behind me.

"*Faux*," said a man in the back.

"*Oui, faux*," said the instructor. "But two men can join in PACS, a pact of civil union recognized by the state."

"Only a man and woman should have the right to marry," said another man.

"*Tout à fait!*" called out another voice. Exactly.

The room erupted in lively debate, with those in agreement facing off against the instructor, who shouted paragraphs from her manual. It continued so loudly for so long that we had to take another break for everyone to calm down.

After ten minutes of more weak coffee, more idle cell-phone scrolling, more hurried smoking, we reconvened in the classroom for another question.

"*Vrai ou faux*—" The instructor paused. "Women must obey men."

"*Vrai*," said someone, and a few of the men in the room laughed.

"*Vrai?* Why do you say that? In France men and women have the same responsibilities and rights. Haven't you been listening to what I've been saying all day?"

"*Oui, mais chez moi, c'est chez moi.*"

"Would you let your wife go to a café alone?" the instructor asked.

"*Ma femme? Jamais.*"

"Women can go to the café here in France. If they want to go alone, and order a coffee, sit and read the newspaper, that's their right. They also have the right to go to school, work, vote, and inherit property—the same as men. *C'est. La. Loi. Vous comprenez?*"

"*Chez moi, c'est chez moi,*" he repeated.

The instructor's eye caught mine, and she rolled hers slightly, as if to say, *Men!* I was too startled to respond. Two things surprised me: First, it had never occurred to me that going to a café by myself could be considered improper. Second, my life had been so sheltered I had never before encountered such overt chauvinism. Until now I'd only seen sexism lurking like a shadow, the transparent glass ceiling, the unspoken bias. Now here it was, a hulking mass standing defiant in the center of the room. Not even four years in China had prepared me for its ugly muscularity.

I twisted around in my chair to get a glimpse of the man, expecting to see a stature that matched his opinions. Instead I found someone nondescript, neither big nor small, with a beard covering most of his face.

"*D'où venez-vous, monsieur?*" asked the instructor.

"Eritrea."

"Things are different here in France. *Vous verrez.*" You'll see. It sounded like a promise—or a warning.

Later, after the class had ended, after the instructor handed out signed certificates of participation, after I had returned to my pretty, privileged corner of Paris, I continued to think about the *formation civique* and my fellow classmates. I could guess at the reasons that had brought them to France—Eritrea alone is desperately poor, with one of the world's worst human-rights records—but I would never completely understand them. Now they had entered into a brave new world, one that upended their stature, along with their traditional values. How would they accept France? And, just as important, how would France accept them, if at all?

After a year in Paris, I still flinched when I heard people described by their race: *le cafetier maghrébin*, *le plombier roumain*, *la petite chinoise*. This last referred to me, no matter that I was born, raised, and educated in the United States, as American as my second-generation (but white) husband. Roots traveled deep here, a tangible marker considered acceptable in polite conversation, unlike religion or work. In the United States, race and nationality are separate; in France you are either French—with all that implies—or a *citoyen français*, with all that does not.

In the refined sixth arrondissement where I lived, I sometimes pretended to be a local, at the bakery joking with the cashier about the weather or at the market when my favorite vegetable vendor slipped a few extra lemons into my basket. But I was obviously an *étrangère*, a fact made evident by my accent, the shape of my eyes, the darkness of my hair, the briskness of my walk. For me it didn't matter; I was just a guest, after all. But what of the real immigrants? The ones who wouldn't—or couldn't—return home? The complicated truth was this: They would spend the rest of their lives in France, yet they would never become French.

I had come to Alsace with the intention of eating choucroute at every meal. But whenever I sat down in a *Winstub*, the same thing happened: I looked at the menu, resolved to order the choucroute garnie, summoned the waitress, and asked for . . . something else. I was cheating on choucroute with tarte flambée.

Despite its fiery name, tarte flambée is not a pie filled with burning embers. It's a sort of pizza with crisp edges, topped with crème fraîche, onions, and bacon, cooked in a wood-burning oven. In Al-

satian it's called flammeküeche, or "flame cake," and was traditionally a *plat du pauvre*, prepared every two weeks on bread-baking
day, when the village's communal wood oven was lit.

"They made it before they baked the bread, while waiting for the
temperature of the oven to cool," Lydia Roth told me.

At L'Aigle, Roth's sprawling tavern in Pfulgriesheim, a village
outside Strasbourg, she still prepares flammeküeche using the recipe
of her grandmother, Mamama Anne, who opened the restaurant in
1963. A lump of dough is rolled thin, spread with luscious crème
fraîche, strewn with slivers of raw onion and bacon, and singed
golden in the kitchen's ancient wood oven. "It only takes one minute
to cook," Roth said. The restaurant also serves a nontraditional version, sprinkled with grated Emmental cheese.

I ate both the plain and gratinéed varieties under Roth's watchful eye, savoring the contrast of tangy cream against the luxuriant
salty-sweetness of smoked bacon and onions. Roth brought them
out one half at a time, waiting until I'd finished the first to produce
the second. "It's best eaten *hot!*" she admonished me when she
caught me photographing my food instead of eating it. And when I
had finished both, she wanted to know which I preferred.

"The first one, without the cheese." The flavors had been
cleaner, the crust a little crisper.

She nodded. *"Moi aussi. La gratinée, c'est plus bourratif et moins
traditionnel."* More filling, less traditional. It sounded like the slogan
for a beer commercial. And then Lydia Roth whirled off into the
crowded dining room, to deliver a stream of perfectly charred
flammeküeches to her eager customers.

The village of Truchtersheim is close enough to Strasbourg to be
considered a suburb, a small hamlet of half-timbered houses boast-

ing steep-pitched tiled roofs. I parked my rental car and crept along narrow streets, feeling a little like Goldilocks among the bears, peering at the chinks of light escaping from behind closed window shutters. A heavy door opened, emitting a gush of warm air and a rush of voices—the Truchtersheim cooking club was waiting for me.

There were six of them, six women with short, graying hair, broad smiles, and old-fashioned names—Anne-Marie, Suzanne, Georgette, Andrée, Maria, Yvette—names that could have been German or French. They had gathered in Anne-Marie's home, along with her son René, perching on the velour sofas of her *Winstub,* not a tavern this time but the farmhouse's living room, a wood-paneled refuge stuffed with framed sepia photographs and bits of antique china. These women had known one another since childhood, their lives forever entwined by their village, first as schoolgirls, then as brides, mothers, wives, and now widows. For more than forty years, they had met once or twice a month, to eat good food and drink good wine, to prepare and enjoy a feast together. Today they welcomed me, too, to share a choucroute garnie, *une vraie*—or, according to René, loyal to his mother's cooking, *"la meilleure,"* the best. The Choucroute among choucroutes.

At the table, Anne-Marie delivered The Choucroute, a casserole dish heaped with cabbage and meat, followed by two smaller platters of sausages and boiled potatoes carried by Suzanne and Yvette. Little murmurs rippled across the room, sounds of enthusiastic appreciation, as if these women hadn't seen the dish for decades, instead of dining on it at least once a month ever since they could chew. Anne-Marie served each of us, dishing up all the classic elements: slow-simmered sauerkraut, plump sausages, fat-striped hunks of pork belly—both salted and smoked—rosy slices of smoked pork loin, and boiled potatoes. It was farm fare, honest and robust, eaten with a dab of mustard. I alternated bites of pine-scented, tangy sauerkraut with cured pork belly and the high-spiced savor of sausage, enjoying the contrast of tart cabbage against smoked meat.

"When I was growing up, every family had its own stone barrel of choucroute in the basement," said Yvette, who was sitting next to me. "It was the only vegetable we ate for the whole winter."

The others agreed with a chorus of *"Ja."*

"But on the farm we didn't have so many kinds of meat." Georgette gestured at her plate. "Only pork belly."

"I remember on Sundays," said Andrée, "my mother would simmer the choucroute for hours. None of this precooked stuff."

The table erupted in exclamations of horror, which René attempted to translate into French, because when these women talked among themselves, they did so in their mother tongue, Alsatian.

"I always add a glass of Riesling to the cabbage," Suzanne said eventually.

"Only a glass? I add half a bottle!" said Georgette.

"My grandkids don't like the taste of wine, so I use water," said Maria. "You can't tell the difference."

Everyone else looked a little skeptical.

We continued eating The Choucroute. At one point Anne-Marie threw up her hands and exclaimed, "Oh, the *knack*!" and then rushed to the kitchen. She came back bearing a plate of skinny hot dogs, which she passed around the table. I declined—already I feared that I might have to discreetly undo the top button of my trousers, and we hadn't even gotten to dessert—but she looked so disappointed that I took a half.

The conversation undulated between French and Alsatian, the

two languages washing across the table. The women tried to re-member to speak in French, but I could feel them struggling not to lapse into Alsatian. Sometimes they would stop midsentence, sifting their minds for a forgotten French word. "How do you say . . . ?" they'd murmur urgently. And then the word would appear: "Cloves!" they'd exclaim in a triumphant voice. "That's the spice my mother always added to her choucroute."

These women were old enough to remember the stories of their grandparents, tales from the late nineteenth century, when Alsace was ceded to Germany, part of the spoils of France's humiliating defeat during the Franco-Prussian War in 1870. Under the new re-gime, any reference to France was banished, the language erased, school textbooks rewritten, street signs reprinted. Thousands of Al-satians sought exile in France or in her North African colonies in order to remain French. Those who stayed were required to become German in loyalty, manner, and speech. No matter that the region had been French for centuries or that it had, in 1792, inspired the French anthem, "La Marseillaise," or that an Alsatian, Baron Hauss-mann, had redesigned the French capital.

Less than fifty years later, the entire process happened again— in reverse.

In 1918, France defeated Germany in World War I and reclaimed Alsace. Everything German became French: textbooks, street signs, the lingua franca. Germans who had settled in Alsace were expelled, Alsatians in exile returned home. France enfolded her lost region (but delicately—the government declined to impose certain laws, notably the 1905 edict that separates church and state; even today there is no policy of *laïcité* in Alsace). The members of the cooking club were born during this period into a bilingual world: French at school, Alsatian at home. Until World War II.

175

La guerre. I mentioned the words, and everyone's eyes lowered a fraction. In 1940 the region switched *back* to German control when Hitler annexed Alsace. As girls, these women had seen German soldiers occupying their region, laying claim to their village, appropriating their crops, banishing French, forcibly conscripting their fathers and brothers to fight against France. The Alsatian soldiers were called the *"malgré-nous"*—against our will—and more than forty thousand of them died fighting on the Eastern Front.

"During the war we weren't allowed to speak a single word of French," said Georgette. "Not even behind closed doors. After the war I had to relearn everything."

After World War II ended, Alsace shifted *yet again*, back to France and her language. German and Alsatian were banned from schools and discouraged at home. "When I was a boy in the 1960s," René told me, "the teachers would punish you for speaking Alsatian. I still remember the slogans painted on the school walls: *'C'est chic de parler français.'*"

"What about today?" I asked.

"They teach Alsatian in school, but most young people don't speak it," René said. "My son doesn't."

"Ohhh, c'est français. Français, français!" the ladies chorused sorrowfully.

It seemed ironic that after surviving so many radical shifts in power—four in only seventy-five years—that the Alsatian language should begin to vanish now, swallowed up by the trappings and convenience of modern life.

"We're a mix of two cultures," Maria said to me.

The other ladies protested. "No, we're our *own* culture," said Yvette. "Not a mix of the two but something else, unique to us. It's kind of like . . ." She hesitated, her eyes scanning my face.

"Like me," I offered. "I'm ethnically Chinese, but I was born and raised in the States. And now I live in France." Even as I said it, I realized it was true. I'd lived in all three countries, and each had left its mark on me—America most widely and deeply, of course, but also France and China, too. I would always define myself as an American, and I would always fold dumplings at Chinese New Year, and I would always enjoy a bit of cheese between my main course and dessert. The home that Calvin and I shared was its own cultural island, not uniquely of the country we lived in or the country we came from but a third place with its own identity. Like Strasbourg, our home was nowhere—and everywhere—to me.

Before we could get too philosophical, the front door opened and René's son, Franck, appeared, a tall, thin young man with dark hair and a shy smile. A little frisson ran around the room as he stooped to greet each woman with two polite kisses.

"Are you hungry?" asked Anne-Marie, hovering by his side with grandmotherly concern.

"I'm starving. I just came from playing volleyball."

"How about some choucroute? There's tons left over."

He hesitated. "It's kind of late for a heavy meal. . . ."

Anne-Marie looked a little deflated.

"Bon, ben, vas-y . . ." he conceded. *"Pourquoi pas?"*

He went into the kitchen and came back holding a plate loaded with an enormous pile of choucroute and sausage. Everyone fell silent as he started to eat.

"C'est trop bon!" he exclaimed finally, his words muffled a little by the food. I felt the room exhale at his praise.

The Alsatian language may be disappearing, but love of Granny's choucroute is still alive and well, at least in one tiny village in far eastern France.

Choucroute sans Garniture

I wouldn't say it's impossible to make a traditional choucroute garnie without Alsatian charcuterie, but it would involve the difficult process of curing many cuts of pork yourself, a long and intense labor of love. Instead I'm offering you the recipe for slow-simmered choucroute, sans meaty garniture. You'll need raw sauerkraut (sometimes called "lacto-fermented" or "wild" sauerkraut), which can be found in the refrigerated section of your gourmet or health-food store. This is delicious paired with baked ham, grilled sausages (like andouillette, if you're brave), or poached salmon fillets, and boiled potatoes.

Serves 4

2 pounds raw fermented cabbage
1 onion, peeled and thinly sliced
1 tablespoon goose fat *or* any mild-flavored oil (goose fat is
    traditional)
1 bay leaf
5 juniper berries
1 whole clove
1 clove garlic, crushed and peeled
5 to 10 whole black peppercorns
3 coriander seeds
1 cup white wine (preferably Riesling)
Salt and pepper to taste

Rinse the fermented cabbage in cold water once or twice, depending on the season (the older the cabbage, the more rinsing it will need). Drain in a colander, squeezing out the excess water.

Heat a large pot over a medium flame and sauté the onion in the fat or oil until it has wilted. Add the cabbage and the bay leaf, juniper berries, clove, garlic, peppercorns, and coriander seeds. Moisten with the wine and add enough water to barely cover the cabbage. Lightly season with salt and pepper. Bring to a boil, lower the heat, and simmer gently, covered, for about 1 hour.

Stir the choucroute and check the liquid level. Some people like their choucroute crunchy and white; others prefer it soft and melting, lightly golden (I prefer the latter). Add up to a cup more water, depending on your taste. Cover and continue to simmer for another hour. The longer you cook choucroute, the more acidic it becomes, so start testing it for tenderness after 2 hours.

Before serving, remove as many of the whole spices as possible. Choucroute can be made in advance and reheated.

Chapter 8

Savoie & Haute-Savoie / Fondue

I t's hard to believe that I, a child of the 1970s, reached adulthood without tasting cheese fondue. But combine a father prone to high cholesterol with a mother who abstains from cheese and you can probably understand why I missed out on an entire cultural phenomenon.

Perhaps this explains why, on a limpid summer morning, I found myself in the French Alps at sixty-five hundred feet trying to discover the true story of fondue. Like all stories about food, it began with basic ingredients—in this case cheese: large wheels of aged cow's-milk Beaufort produced in distant meadows. I had rented a Smart car and urged it up a sinuous mountain road in search of cheese-making chalets and herds of cows grazing on the flowers, grass, and herbs of the Savoyard summer landscape. (Though fondue is eaten almost exclusively in the winter, I decided to visit the region in the summer because Beaufort is produced during the warmest months of the year.)

In the French Alps, elevation is everything. Numbers divide villages—Courchevel 1,300, Courchevel 1,650, Courchevel 1,850. They refer to meters above sea level, and the locals pronounce them with elegant languor—*Courchevel mille trois cents, Courchevel mille six cent cinquante, Courchevel mille huit cent cinquante*—a mouthful of words that's difficult to follow if, like me, you still have a little trouble counting in French. From the highway the signs read like a Jackie Collins novel with names like Megève, Chamonix, and Val

d'Isère evoking images of luxury hotels and après-ski furs. High in
the Alps, the atmosphere felt wintry even in full summer—not just
the temperatures, which were markedly cooler than in the valley below, or the air, which breathed thinner, but also the hot-chocolate-
colored chalets topped with sloping roofs, the empty ski lifts rising
above grass-covered slopes, and in the distance the famous bulk of
Mont Blanc capped, even in late August, with a ring of snow.

I crept around a hairpin turn, climbing from 1,300 to 1,650 and
downshifted when I felt the car's laptop-size engine strain. On my left
a Renault sedan passed me with barely a flick of the gas pedal, and I
eyed it with envy. Not for the first time, I cursed my inability to drive
a stick shift; it meant I always got stuck with the only automatic vehicles on offer at the rental agency, a series of ragtag, rattletrap jalopies.

At 1,850 meters the paved road ended and I veered onto a dirt
path, snaking across slopes that in the winter are part of some of the
world's most famous ski resorts. In my left hand, I clutched a vague
set of directions that I'd scribbled while on the phone with an
alpagiste, or local cheese maker. In less than half an hour, I was due
to meet him at his cheese-making hut. That is, if I could find it. The
notebook paper began to soften under the nervous sweat of my
palm, the words growing blurry: "Head toward the Belvédère restaurant." I scanned the distance. I saw dark groves of pine trees
above pale green grass, butterflies fluttering in fields of wildflowers,
saw-toothed mountains that appeared close enough to snap at the
hem of my summer dress. But I didn't see a sign.

With my mind on the clock, I bounced along the dirt track as
fast as I dared. At a fork in the road, I finally spotted a wooden
board that blended into the landscape—and through some panic-
fueled, superhuman effort I managed to make out BELVÉDÈRE, 5KM
inscribed in microfont upon it. I veered in the direction of the arrow,

feeling decidedly more cheerful. *See?* I thought. *You're a navigational genius! You'll be there with time to spare.*

But before I could scale the pinnacle of self-congratulation, a car appeared in front of me. It crept along with meticulous care, slowing nearly to a standstill at the barest hint of dust. Creep, creep, creep. Its wheels kicked up a tiny puff of dirt, and the brake lights illuminated. Inch, inch, inch. It was a silver VW convertible Bug, the modern kind, with a dirty back window and Swiss plates. A couple sat inside, a man and woman who, judging from the driver's fondness for the brake pedal, were either irrationally neurotic about their car's paint job or had been specially hired to drive me insane.

The seconds ticked by. I considered passing the Beetle, but the dirt track was too narrow. I could feel my punctuality leaking away. I was ten minutes late. Twenty minutes. Half an hour. I flexed my fingers and fantasized about reaching through the windshield and wringing the driver's neck.

Another vehicle appeared in the distance, moving toward us with a modest pace that, at our near standstill, seemed like breakneck speed. As it drew closer, it grew into a mud-spattered black truck. Now I could see a man at the wheel, a small boy bouncing at his side, and an industrial dairy container strapped into the flatbed. How many people on this remote patch of mountain would be driving around hauling milking equipment? Suddenly the truck was directly in front of me. I watched it perform a little jig with the Beetle—each vehicle inching backward and forward, pausing as they drew level to exchange a few words—before the Beetle finally putted ahead. I pulled up to the truck and rolled down my window.

"Bonjour!" I called, craning my neck to peer up at the driver.

A man with leathery skin and cheeks covered in stubble raised his hand in greeting. "Madame Mah?"

"Oui?" Uh-oh. How did he know my name?

"Je suis desolé, mais . . ."

It was the *alpagiste*. He'd been called down the mountain, he told me, to make an urgent delivery of cheese. Even in my disappointment, I wondered what constituted a cheese emergency.

"I was waiting for you," he said.

"Je sais . . . j'étais . . ." I began, and then stopped. I had no idea how to explain what had happened, not even in English.

He shrugged. "I'll be back in a few hours. Or you can talk to my wife. She's still up there." And with a quick wave, he took off down the hill. In my rearview mirror, I watched his truck as it rolled down the rutted track.

At the top of the mountain, I found a slope-roofed wooden building that housed a ski lift, dark and shuttered, with empty gondolas dangling inside. Next to it was the Belvédère restaurant, with dark wood panels and a sweeping balcony. In the parking lot, I spotted my nemesis, the VW Beetle, parked neatly in a space as if butter wouldn't melt in its mouth, its owners probably perusing the lunch menu on the restaurant's sunny *terrasse*.

A few yards away stood a small stone house, low and rectangular with a thick wooden door and no windows. Was this the summer cheese-making chalet? At the bottom of the driveway, a sign read VENTE DE FROMAGE—cheese for sale. When I got out of the car and approached the door, a wiry black sheepdog sprang to its feet and started barking. I took a few steps closer, and the dog barked harder, his cry deepening to a growl. I tried all the tricks I could muster, cooing in a friendly voice, searching in my purse for a treat, though I didn't think I could pass off a crumpled tissue as a ham bone. With his lowered tail and ears pinned flat, this was a working farm dog, loyal to his master and suspicious of strangers.

The dog paced a length in front of me. I took one step closer to the chalet, and he bared his teeth. One step back, and he stopped growling. Several steps back, and he lay down again in the shadow of a tractor, keeping his head raised so he could watch me.

I had come to learn about Beaufort cheese—the principal ingredient in fondue savoyarde—about the Alpine chalets that produce it and the meadows of sweet grass, herbs, and flowers that perfume it. Instead I found myself pinned to the side of my car. I gazed helplessly at a bank of purple wildflowers framed by soaring peaks and a radiant blue sky. But when a breeze whisked along the mountainside, it shook the grass with a rattle, leaving me chilled despite the sun soaking into my shoulders.

Eight months earlier, I'd eaten my first cheese fondue, gooey and melty, warmly insulating. It was January, one of those cold, damp Paris evenings, the kind that feel like the inside of an icebox. I had just returned from the balmy warmth of Southern California, where I'd spent the Christmas holidays with my parents. The December weather in Orange County had been just like my childhood—unvaryingly sunny—but for some reason wearing a sundress while trimming the Christmas tree felt unnatural. Maybe I'd spent too many winters away. More likely it was the cloud of displacement that hung over me, a gray, glum fog of missing Calvin that grew grayer as he and I opened our presents together over Skype and glummer as we sat down to separate holiday meals. At my parents' table, the turkey tasted a little drier, the stuffing a little blander without my husband, but I swallowed it as quickly as possible, before my mother could see the worry in my eyes and start worrying herself.

It was comforting to be back in my parents' home, to sleep in my childhood room, to be cocooned by my dad's spicy tofu and unlimited access to TV cooking shows, to have my parents' housekeeper take care of my laundry. But life there felt unreal, as if I'd slipped into an alternate universe where I was still a teenager with ironed T-shirts, a curfew, and very little privacy. By the New Year, I was ready to return to Paris, to pick up the reins of my routine, to come back to our apartment, which despite its drafty windows and leaky pipes still felt like home. Also, I missed Paris itself—even cold, dark, wintry Paris, where the sun, if there was any, shone for only a handful of hours a day. Being there in the dead of a Northern European winter felt like being part of a club—albeit a foolhardy, light-deprived, sniffling club with permanently cold feet and influenza-bright eyes.

One indisputable benefit of brisk winter temperatures, however, was winter food. Back in Paris I made soup from creamy parsnips and a knobby celeriac, bought a kilo of clementine oranges to brighten my palate and my kitchen counter. In the market I gazed at oysters plucked from icy ocean depths and scallops glistening in shells so delicately pink they could have hosted Botticelli's Venus. Melted snow created slushy rivers running along city gutters, and hearty fare like cassoulet, boeuf bourguignon, and choucroute garnie started to make even more sense.

One damp evening, when the sky had grown dark at four o'clock, leaving the cobblestone streets gleaming wetly in the yellow streetlamps, I headed to the home of Elena and her husband, Stéphane, who had invited some friends over for a fondue dinner. It was the kind of night that called for buttered toast and a mug of tomato soup eaten in front of the TV, but the promise of Stéphane's fondue lured me out of the house. As the party's resident Swiss, he busied himself in the kitchen, rubbing two stout cast-iron, enamel-glazed pots with a cut clove of garlic and then filling them with a mix of grated Swiss cheeses, a tablespoon of cornstarch, a slug of white wine, and a dash of kirsch.

"That's it?" I peered inside. "No secret ingredient?"

"That's it." He placed the pots on the stove and lowered the heat to a minuscule flame. "The secret is the cheese."

When the cheese had melted, Stéphane lit the Sterno flames under the metal grill of the fondue sets and the thin blue flames beckoned us to the table. We sat, fondue forks in hand, and he whisked the orange, round-handled *caquelon* pots from the kitchen to the dining room, the molten cheese bubbling slowly within. We plunged cubes of stale baguette into the mixture, swirling them round and round the circumference of the pot so that the thick liquid remained blended.

"Careful," said Elena, twirling her long-handled fork with a flourish. "If you lose your bread, you have to finish your glass."

I transferred a cheese-soaked cube of bread to my plate and took a cautious nibble. Through the lava-like heat, the melted cheese tasted soft and creamy, almost buttery, with a toasty, nutty flavor that gave way to a light, boozy finish. We dipped and swirled and sipped wine—a special Swiss white called Fendant—and small glasses of kirsch. Stéphane made sure to keep our glasses full.

"You must never, never, never drink water with fondue." His tone was very grave. "Only kirsch or Fendant wine. Or, for children, tisane. You know, herbal tea. Anything else and the cheese will form a giant ball in your stomach." I started to laugh, and he warned me, "Seriously, I tried it once, and I was *gravement malade*."

I took an extra sip of kirsch, just to be safe.

Though at first it had seemed impossible that six people could consume nearly five pounds of molten cheese, once we got caught up in swirling and chatting, laughing and eating, the thick, bubbling liquid disappeared. I passed the bread basket to Elena and waited for her to take a dip. Perhaps, more than any other meal, fondue relied on conviviality, a communal sharing.

At the bottom of the pot, a crust of cheese lingered, growing golden in the heat of the flame.

"La religieuse," Elena said, her tone reverent. "It's the best part." I had the feeling that had she not been bound by politesse, she would have scraped it off and happily consumed the entire thing herself. But being a good hostess, she painstakingly divided the wafer-thin shards of crisp cheese among her guests. The bits dissolved in my mouth with a brittle crunch.

In case you're wondering, in Swiss homes—and probably in French ones, too—chocolate fondue does not follow cheese fondue, no matter that the long forks are already on the table and the Sterno burners are already lit. In fact, if you mention the idea, even jokingly, you might receive a revelatory, so-*that's*-why-so-many-Americans-are-obese type of look from your lean, rock-climbing host. Instead we ended the meal with sliced pineapple, a bright, tropical counterpoint to all the dairy fat we'd just consumed.

"They say pineapple helps digest the cheese," Elena said.

The French, I was discovering, had an obsession with digestion that I'd only ever encountered before in China. They avoided anything that could hamper the delicate process, reviling cold drinks and ice cubes and embracing hot tisanes and fizzy water. In some families children weren't allowed to drink water during dinner for fear they would ingest too much *air* while gulping it down. Though none of us at the table were French, digestion was such a local mania that anyone living in France became familiar with the established beliefs and superstitions. I myself had received several dire warnings, mostly from older women, about my insouciant consumption of ice.

Later that evening I wrapped myself in a long scarf and a lumpy down jacket and left the yellow glow of Elena and Stéphane's apartment to find the métro home. Outside, the winter air stung my cheeks, but burrowed deep inside my multiple layers, I felt warm, invincibly so, as if all the melted cheese were glowing within me.

A few weeks later, I had the chance to consider sustenance, both emotional and nutritional, when I invited some friends over to make dumplings in celebration of the Chinese New Year. Friends? Actually, I wasn't quite sure how to describe them.

I hadn't met many new people since Calvin's departure ten months earlier. This was partly due to my inherent shyness and partly because I felt a little guilty about having fun while he was serving in a war zone. Don't get me wrong—I wasn't a hermit— Elena and I met regularly for lunch, my library colleagues and I shared an occasional postwork *verre*, and Didier and Alain always had a warm welcome and a demitasse of coffee waiting for me at Le Mistral. Still, if I was being completely honest with myself, I had to admit, I was often lonely.

Whereas once I longed for a weekend to recover from my week-end's social engagements, now the days of solitude stretched in front of me. I spent Sunday afternoons alone at the movies, rushing into the theater after the previews had started, squeezing into the last empty seat in the middle of a row. I explored the flea market at Saint-Ouen, gazing at the antique cookware—burnished copper kettles, thick-walled mustard pots, battered wooden boards—with only my camera to keep me company. The vendors huddled next to their stalls on camp chairs, bundled up and smoking, and sometimes I asked them questions just so I could practice my French. I sought out pretty new pastry shops, buying a single éclair au chocolat or one shell-shaped madeleine, which I'd bring home and split over two days. And as I walked and wandered, I tried to absorb Paris— for myself, because I wouldn't live there forever, but also for Calvin.

I tried to save the funny conversations and quirky moments for him, to brighten his days, and also, I hoped, so I could share my new discoveries with him when he returned. Unfortunately, thinking about him only made me more lonely.

On the métro I watched a young woman sending text messages, laughing as she typed, and I felt a pang for my pals in New York, for our frequent, quick, funny exchanges. I missed my assortment of friends there and in Beijing, the deep well of people who came from different parts of my life. My wish for female friendship, I eventually realized, went beyond Calvin's absence. Even if he'd been by my side, I would have felt the lack—though I probably would have ignored it, tamped it down, booked a table for two at a new restaurant.

But Calvin wasn't here. And as the prospect of another quiet weekend stretched in front of me, I decided I needed to stop being patient, or passive, or secluded. I decided to *do* something.

But what? How did people make friends in this town? I'd heard that Parisians were cold, that they formed their social groups at school and remained within them for life, and maybe it was true. But I was even beyond hoping for a French friend. At this point I'd settle for an extroverted American or an enthusiastic Australian or, really, anyone who shared a common language and maybe an interest in food.

Of course, as it turned out, the answer was food.

I haven't mentioned it before, but this whole time I had been writing a food blog about my life in Paris. I enjoyed having an excuse to eat, explore, and take photos, and so I continued even though, truthfully, no one read the blog except Calvin and (occasionally) my father. If a blog has an audience of two—and both of them are family members—does it make a sound . . . ?

One day I wrote a post about Krishna Bhavan, a tiny Indian vegetarian restaurant near the Gare du Nord that served dosa crêpes stuffed with curried potatoes, paired with an unapologetically spicy lentil sambar sauce. I didn't know it then, but blog posts about ethnic-food discoveries in Paris were like catnip for expats. By the end of the day, someone named Colette had left a comment thanking me for the recommendation. A stranger had read my blog!

Colette, as I soon discovered from reading *her* blog, was American, a pastry chef who lived in Paris with her husband. She liked regional French cuisine and craft beer and whipping up dinner from her CSA basket, all of which I found mildly interesting, but it was her ode to xiaolongbao soup dumplings that made me sit up and bookmark her site. I loved soup dumplings, those little round purses filled with ground pork and a secret slurp of broth, and after four years in China I missed them. Now I had found someone who not only *knew* about soup dumplings—a rarity in France—she had actually *made them herself.*

Before I could consider the wisdom of the idea, I had sent Colette an e-mail:

"Would you and Nate"—Nate was Colette's husband, I knew from reading her blog—*"like to come over on Saturday night to make soup dumplings?"*

After I hit SEND, the doubts started to creep in. Had I really just invited two complete strangers over to my home on a Saturday night? What if they were murderers? What if they were grifters who lured in lonely young women by pretending to like soup dumplings? What if they didn't know how to use chopsticks?

A few hours later, Colette had responded. *"Sounds great!"* she wrote. *"What can I bring? How about some broth made from a pig's hoof? We can use it in the soup dumpling filling."*

I wasn't just hosting two possible ax murderers for dinner. I was hosting two possible ax murderers and my very last meal on earth was going to be broth made from a pig's foot. This was going to be either a disaster or the best Chinese meal I'd had since moving to Paris.

The second time I ate cheese fondue was during a raging August heat wave. I had traveled to Annecy, the capital of the Haute-Savoie region, to do more fondue research. Such was my dedication to my subject that record-breaking temperatures couldn't stop me from ordering a big pot of melted cheese and eating until the grease came out of my pores. Not the sticky swath of humidity that lay draped over the city. Not the amazed incredulity of my B&B owner when I asked her for a fondue-restaurant recommendation.

To combat the heat, the restaurant, Le Fréti, had moved all the tables and chairs outside onto an adjacent square. I joined the throng of tourists—because let's face it, only tourists would eat fondue in a month without an *r*—and breathed in the lightly toxic scent of Sterno. When the orange *caquelon* pot of bubbling cheese arrived, I speared a cube of bread and took a lazy dip. The fondue hit my palate with a creamy punch and tiptoed away in a breathy hint of wine. But after a few turns around the pot, I couldn't continue. A light sheen of sweat covered my forehead, and my stomach curled into a rapidly tightening knot. No, I hadn't taken a single sip of water during the meal (I'm not crazy). It simply turns out that ninety-degree heat actually repels one's hunger for gently bubbling, melted cheese.

The next day I asked Daniel Monbeillard if he'd ever eaten fondue in a heat wave. He is head of the Petit Mont Blanc, a group of villagers who have banded together to raise a modest herd of Tarentaise cows and make Beaufort cheese.

"Jamais," he replied, giving me the type of look you might receive before being bundled into a straitjacket.

We were sitting on Monbeillard's patio, outside his home in Saint-Bon Courchevel. Geraniums spilled from window boxes, bright splashes of color against the honey-colored wood of his chalet. In the small garden, a condominium of cages housed a family of gray rabbits that were making a steady, quiet crunching sound (yes, he eats them). Oversize honeybees tumbled in and out of drooping roses, and the last of the season's blackberries hung from a thorny bush. It was the type of gingerbread home kept by energetic grandparents, the kind who produce pots of homemade jam and are good at handyman projects. As Monbeillard and I discussed the particulars of Beaufort cheese, we could hear the wails of his small granddaughter resisting her afternoon nap inside the house.

The Petit Mont Blanc, the collective of Saint-Bon villagers led by Monbeillard, employs a small team of *alpagistes* to tend their herd of cows. During the summer months, the *alpagistes* lead the cows to herb-flecked Alpine pastures, climbing from 1,150 meters to 2,160 to 2,500. The commune owns a chalet at each elevation, where twice a day the *alpagistes* make cheese from the fresh milk.

This process of summer Alpine grazing and cheese production is called *alpage*, and it's a tradition that dates to the Middle Ages. Cistercian monks from nearby mountain abbeys—most notably the Abbaye de Tamié near Albertville—introduced the process. They cleared the land of coniferous trees and bushes of juniper, rhododendron, and blueberry, creating high pastures for grazing cattle; later they planted fields of wheat and rye. A few centuries later, in the 1930s, the area filled with another lucrative crop: skiers drawn to the generous sweep of treeless slopes.

"The region is poor gastronomically but rich because of tourism," said Monbeillard.

The cheese produced from these Alpine pastures was a way to

preserve milk from one summer to the next, a form of dietary insurance against starvation in a region where long winters prevented bountiful cereal crops. The monks made a type of cheese called vachelin, but by the early seventeenth century locals had imported cheese-making techniques from neighboring Gruyère, in Switzerland. The resulting large wheels—called *grovire* in the local dialect—traveled well and stayed fresh over long periods of time, making them prime candidates for export. Cheese became the backbone of the local economy, reserved for export, with montagnards enjoying the fruits of their labor only on special occasions. By 1865 *grovire* had been renamed Beaufort after the Beaufortain, one of the three Savoyard valleys that produces the cheese.

Fondue is considered a *plat du pauvre*, a way of using up bits of hard, cracked, or unattractive cheese. In fact, most of the Savoyard region's dishes involve some sort of melted cheese, whether it's tartiflette (sliced potatoes layered with morsels of bacon, cream, and melted Reblochon) or raclette (melted cheese with potato slices). Of course, the quality of your fondue depends on the quality of your cheese. If you're a Savoyard like Daniel Monbeillard, you use only Savoyard cheese. Swiss fondue uses only Swiss cheese, fondue comtoise only Comté cheese, fondue Wisconsin would use only cheese from the Badger State, and so on.

In the 1950s, after centuries of production and export, Beaufort cheese production declined. The work of an *alpagiste*—spending half the year in primitive mountain huts, rising every day at 3:00 A.M. to perform the morning milking—began to attract fewer young people. *Alpage* herds dwindled, and the cheese almost disappeared. In 1961 a group of locals joined together to form a cheese cooperative. They gathered milk from several *alpage* herds, combining it to produce a quantity sufficient for commercial production of cheese. The prestigious AOC label *(appellation d'origine contrôlée)* followed in 1968. Today seven cooperatives in the region produce more than five thousand tons of Beaufort each year. The "prince of Gruyères," as the eighteenth-century French gastronomic philosopher Jean-Anthelme Brillat-Savarin called it, has reclaimed its place in the world.

France has long been protective of her food and drink. The origins of AOC date to 1411, when Charles VI decreed that Roquefort cheese could be ripened only in the caves of the Roquefort region. Today the Institut National de l'Origine et de la Qualité, a branch of the French Ministry of Agriculture, oversees the label and enforces the regulations, guaranteeing that a specific product was made in a specific *terroir* under specific traditional, time-honored guidelines.

The Syndicat de Défense du Beaufort regulates Beaufort cheese from its headquarters on the edge of Albertville, a three-story office building with a chalet roof and a life-size cow statue in the parking lot. Inside his (disappointingly cheese-free) office Maxime Mathelin, the Syndicat's publicity director, described the *cahier des charges,* or guidelines, for producing Beaufort cheese, as "the most *exigeant* of any *appellation*," he said.

To understand the regulations, he explained, I had to first know the different types of cheese protected by the Syndicat: Beaufort d'Été and Beaufort d'Alpage. (He didn't mention a third variety, Beaufort d'Hiver, pale and bland, which is made from the milk of wintering cows fed on hay and is disdained by serious cheese connoisseurs.)

Seven cooperatives in the region produce Beaufort d'Été. It's a large, heavy, semi-industrial cheese, one that may be fabricated only from the milk of Tarentaise or Abondance cows that have grazed in summer Alpine pastures. Like all Beaufort cheeses, it curves inward with a signature, concave dip, caused by the tight circular mold used to shape the wheel. Beaufort d'Été has a creamy, supple texture and flavor reminiscent of toasted hazelnuts. But it's not the prince of Gruyères. That title is reserved for Beaufort d'Alpage, a cheese made under the strictest of regulations.

Here are four things I learned about Beaufort d'Alpage:

1. *It's made only at high altitudes.*

During the summer, from June to October, the cows must graze in pastures above fifteen hundred feet. The resulting cheese must be made on location, immediately after milking, in special chalets at the same altitude. As the herd finishes the grass in one area, it climbs higher and higher, finding different chalets at each level.

2. *Each cheese is made from the milk of a single herd.*

The cows stick together, grazing on the same free-range buffet of wild pastures, which perfumes their milk. As a result, every *alpagiste*'s cheese has a distinct flavor.

3. *The cheese-making techniques are laborious and old-fashioned.*

Copper scalding vats, wooden hoop molds, and cheese-cloth made of pure linen are among the tools of the trade. The *alpagistes* scald and coagulate, separate and press the cheese curds, all by hand, using the same method that's been used for two hundred years.

4. *The Syndicat demands respect.*

It may be a self-policing agency, funded by dues from the *alpagistes,* but the Syndicat is like the Godfather. You don't want to mess with it. A team of experts drives between cheese-making chalets all summer long, enforcing the *cahier des charges* regulations and collecting milk samples for testing in the Maison de Beaufort's laboratory. If it sounds serious, that's because it is—a single misstep and a small cheese producer could lose the right to label his cheese AOC.

It occurs more often than you might think. For example, remember the impenetrable cheese-making chalet? The one guarded by the possessive sheepdog? Well, it turns out the *alpagiste* had recently lost his AOC status, as I eventually discovered during the course of my visit to the region. I never found out why. Maybe it was something as simple as the Syndicat's having caught him using a cotton-blend cheesecloth instead of pure linen. Or maybe he got so fed up with the appellation rules that he chose instead to rebuff the AOC and make cheese on his own terms. The Beaufort experts spoke of him in hushed tones, and I wondered if there had been a scandal. Perhaps that explained why he'd canceled our interview at the last minute and rushed down the mountain, leaving his dog behind to ward off any curious visitors.

D-Day—that is, Dumpling Day—was approaching, and I still hadn't figured out if my guests were serial killers.

"I'm sure they're normal," Calvin said when we talked over Skype. I breathed a sigh of relief until he continued, "Just make sure to send me an e-mail when it's over to let me know you're still alive."

I contemplated canceling, but then I felt silly. I didn't want Colette and Nate to think I was crazy, even if I was convinced they were.

Finally I called Elena. "Do you guys have plans on Saturday night?" I tried to keep my voice calm as I told her how I'd invited two strangers over for dinner. "Would you like to come over to make pork dumplings? I mean, I know you're a vegetarian, but . . ." I was pretty sure Elena ranked pork dumplings right behind offal.

"I love pork dumplings! That's the only thing I make an exception for."

"Really? You don't eat any meat *except* for pork dumplings?" I wasn't going to argue but still, her logic baffled me a little bit.

"What can I say?" She laughed. "I'm a Jewish girl from the Upper West Side. I love dumplings. Count me in."

I knew we were friends for a reason.

On Friday afternoon Elena and I trekked to the thirteenth arrondissement, where boxy, Soviet-style buildings mingled with Haussmann confections, where roast ducks hung in shop windows and the cafés dispensed bubble tea and bánh mi sandwiches. The guidebooks call this neighborhood Paris's Chinatown, but it seemed more diverse to me, with a cacophony of languages that I didn't quite recognize and rows of restaurants serving food from across Southeast Asia.

Down a narrow driveway, next to a parking garage, stood our destination: the Asian supermarket Tang Frères. We pushed through the strips of clear plastic in the doorway and entered into a warren of grocery aisles packed with Asian grannies every bit as aggressive as their French counterparts. They nudged my heels with their shopping carts, elbowed me away from the best mangoes, edged in front of me at the butcher counter. I loaded up my basket with dark soy sauce, dried shiitake mushrooms, frozen dumpling wrappers, fresh ginger, scallions, tofu—ingredients impossible to find in my staid Rive Gauche neighborhood. Elena and I wandered the produce section, inspecting bumpy-skinned bitter melons, jade green bunches of leafy Chinese vegetables, pale celadon eggplants as tiny as gumballs. The store reminded me of the Vietnamese supermarkets of my childhood, with the familiar ingredients stacked right next to the exotic. But the space was tighter here, the narrow aisles marked with signs in French and prices in euros.

After we paid, Elena and I surveyed our heavy bags of groceries with dismay. The plastic sacks cut into my hands as we walked several blocks to the métro, up and down flights of stairs, onto one train and then another. When I got home, I was tempted to drop the bags next to the front door and leave them there until the next day. Instead I forced myself to unpack them, stowing the tofu and vegetables in the fridge and setting the heavy bottles of Asian sauces on my kitchen counter. Then I collapsed onto the couch, almost too tired to worry about what tomorrow would bring.

The next evening Elena arrived a full forty-five minutes before Colette and Nate, just as we'd planned. "Stéphane said he'd stop by later," she told me, and Lifetime-movie scenarios again began running through my head. We got to work shredding carrots and plumping dried mushrooms for the vegetarian dumpling filling, and then the doorbell rang. Elena and I looked at each other. It rang again.

"Do you want me to get it?" She wiped her hands on a dish towel.

"No, no. It's okay." I put my knife down and went to open the door. There stood Colette, looking just like the photo on her blog, and next to her a young guy with thinning hair and a plaid shirt. They smiled awkwardly and looked so American.

"Are you Ann?" said Colette, running a hand through her short brown hair.

"Hi! Come in! Can I get you a beer?"

"We brought the pig's-foot broth!" She held up a plastic container filled with a solid mass that jiggled slightly.

In the kitchen I introduced Elena (who blanched slightly when she saw the tub of jellied stock), and we divided up the cooking tasks. Colette began kneading dough for the soup dumpling wrappers, while Nate minced ginger and garlic for the ground-pork filling. Meanwhile, Elena started folding vegetarian dumplings and I bounced among all of them, helping them find kitchen utensils and ingredients. Colette and Nate didn't seem like psychopaths, I thought, but then again we hadn't talked much yet.

But soon everyone had drunk a few beers, and we commenced a lively debate over how much jellied stock we should mix into the seasoned ground pork. We rigged up a makeshift steamer using a large sauté pan and the lid of a jam jar and then finally sat down at the table and ate our first basket of dumplings—and agreed they needed more soup. We adjusted the filling, steamed, and ate more dumplings, and then more, and more, and then we all sort of slid back in our seats and I almost forgot that Colette and Nate were strangers. We swapped tales of French administrative woe, stories we could share only with other expats, because when you live in Paris, everyone back home assumes your life is magical and turns an unsympathetic ear upon your problems. We talked about the places we wanted to visit before we left Europe—Colette and Nate were also here temporarily, thanks to Nate's job as a research scientist—throwing out names like San Sebastian, Biarritz, and Siena.

When the doorbell rang again, we all jumped, and then Elena said, "Oh, right, *Stéphane!*" and went to let him in. Colette and Nate stood up to introduce themselves, and something about the set of their shoulders, their suddenly stiff smiles as they greeted Stéphane, made me realize that they had been a little nervous when they'd first arrived, a vulnerability that I found reassuring. Being an expat, I thought, was hard even when your partner was right beside you. Tonight, for the first time in a long time, I felt like I belonged to something, this small group of people bumbling along trying to create a new life in a new place, and I was grateful. All it had taken was a little openness, a little courage—a little foolhardiness, perhaps— for us to connect. And pork dumplings, of course.

After everyone left, I washed the dishes and went to bed, hopeful that the night had left me too tired and content for insomnia. Though that wasn't the case, maybe the evening had brought a new flush of confidence. For the very next day, I finally contacted a friend of a friend, Olga, a Russian graphic designer, and met her for an impromptu Sunday movie matinee and hot chocolate. A few weeks after that, I e-mailed another friend of a friend, Elizabeth, a fresh-faced, freckled American from Illinois who spoke impeccable French and introduced me to Pierre Hermé macarons. Judith, the mother of our friend Adam, told me about famous French gardens as we ate delicious lamb curry and spiced pilau rice prepared by her Indian housekeeper. Colette, Elena, and I met at a tea salon, where we shared a bevy of beautiful pastries and planned a picnic in the Champ de Mars for when summer finally arrived. And at a Web site launch party, I met Katia, an Australian who warmed me with her sunny accent and enthusiasm for salsa verde enchiladas, Indonesian laksa, and wonton soup.

Sometimes I met these new friends for dinner, and when we did meet, we usually skipped French bistros for more exotic fare: Indian dosas, or Persian lamb kebabs accompanied by fragrant piles of basmati rice, or plastic plates of tacos al pastor splashed with fresh lime juice, or deep bowls of udon noodles adorned with shrimp tempura. And sometimes when we gathered together, I was reminded of the Savoyards and how they warded off the bleak loneliness by convening around a fondue pot—the heavy, satisfying dish was traditional Alpine insulation against the dark bite of winter. Of course, so, too, was friendship. We weren't that different from them, I thought. The Savoyards might have bonded over fondue, but expats in Paris, we found comfort in ethnic food.

Fondue à la Maison

I adapted this recipe from one given to me by Pierre Gay, a *fromager* in Annecy. "People ask me where to eat the best fondue," he said. "I always tell them it's at home. *Chez vous*. Just make sure you use good cheese." His recipe combines cheeses from Jura and Savoy in France and Gruyère from Switzerland. Drink dry white wine (Gay would pour Apremont, from Savoy), herbal tea, or a smoky black tea like Lapsang souchong, and sip cold water at your own risk.

Serves 4

2 baguettes, slightly stale
1 pound Comté
¾ pound Gruyère, such as L'Étivaz
¼ pound Beaufort d'Alpage *or* Beaufort d'Été
1 clove garlic, peeled and cut in half
½ tablespoon cornstarch
½ bottle dry white wine
Dash of kirsch (optional)
Special equipment: fondue set, including a *caquelon*, an
    enamel-coated cast-iron pot (Le Creuset is popular)

Cut the bread into bite-size cubes.

Grate the cheese or cut it into a very small dice. Rub a *caquelon* pot with the cut side of the garlic. Add the grated cheeses to the pot, along with the cornstarch, wine, and kirsch, if desired. Combine thoroughly.

Place the pot over low heat and stir continuously, until the cheese is completely melted. Light the Sterno under the fondue set at the table, set the *caquelon* over the flame, and eat immediately.

Chapter 9

Burgundy / Boeuf Bourguignon

The first time I set out to find it, I missed it. I'd scrawled the address on a scrap of paper and walked along the rue de l'Université with it in my pocket. When I found the number, I crossed the street and knelt on the ground to capture the building's entire height in my camera lens. But when I got home and looked for the photo, it had vanished. Perhaps I confused the memory with a dream. Eventually I realized I didn't have the right address at all.

A few weeks later, I made a second attempt, and this time I was more deliberate, plotting my course in advance. That day I did find the apartment building at 81 rue de l'Université, a modest four-story, nineteenth-century limestone structure with tall, slender windows and a pair of solid, dark blue wooden doors. The building's windows overlooked a little *place*, a small, cement-paved triangle lined with motor scooters. Next door stood a café with smoke-stained walls and a zinc bar that could have been preserved in amber. There was no plaque to indicate that she had lived there, but I could imagine her all the same, charging back from the market, a wicker basket of vegetables heavy on her arm, eager to dive into the kitchen and start cooking. The apartment was still indisputably chez Julia Child.

I had been thinking about Julia recently because I'd been considering boeuf bourguignon, the dish that helped make her famous. It was early March, and the weather was as blustery and fierce as the proverbial lion. But I had seen the determined buds of forsythia in the planters that ran along the center of my street, and finally I had tangible evidence that spring—and, with it, Calvin's return from Iraq—was on its way, our year apart almost finished. I anticipated our reunion with uncomplicated happiness. But first we had a few more months to get through.

Several weeks earlier, I had received an assignment from the *New York Times*—the *New York Times*! My forehead broke out in beads of nervous sweat every time I even thought about it—for a travel article retracing Thomas Jefferson's 1787 journey through the vineyards of Burgundy. The focus would be wine, but as I packed my bags for the Côte d'Or, the narrow territory that produces the region's renowned vintages, my mind kept turning to boeuf bourguignon. The wine-rich beef stew was one of the first dishes Julia Child had ever cooked on television, the one she chose to launch her show *The French Chef.*

For Julia, boeuf bourguignon offered many teachable French cooking techniques: how to brown and braise meat, how to sauté mushrooms and make a fine sauce. But in recent years the dish had acquired a rare patina, transforming from a humble beef stew into, for many Americans, the symbol of French cuisine. And yet what did we know about its origins? Now I had the opportunity to visit Burgundy and discover the true story of boeuf bourguignon. And though I was traveling alone, I thought I could imagine twin voices on either side of me—Julia's and Jefferson's—two Americans separated by centuries but united by their admiration of the region.

The drive from Paris to Beaune, the wine capital of Burgundy, takes about four hours, a steady southwesterly slog along the A6 national highway. Even if I hadn't been following the GPS as if it were the Messiah, I would have known I'd arrived in the Côte d'Or by the gentle, vine-covered slopes rising up on either side of the road. Though the region of Burgundy is large, its wine territory is focused mainly on this small strip of terrain, an almost mythical chain of microclimates, mildly pitched hills, and rocky, rust-colored, mineral-rich soil. When the French speak of *terroir*—a word that literally means "earth"—they're referring to a special confluence of climate, soil, geography, plant species, and farming techniques. But if I had to pick one place in the world to illustrate the term, it would be here in the Côte d'Or, which packs more than a hundred *appellations* into a space half the size of New York City, where the same grape varietals have been cultivated into wine for almost a thousand years.

Legend has it that monks established the Burgundy winemaking tradition in the eleventh century, clearing the land, testing grape varietals, and perfecting viticulture techniques. They divided the Côte d'Or into the Côte de Nuits and the Côte de Beaune (*côte* means "hill") and traveled between the slopes, mixing the soil with water to taste the differences in *terroir*. They were the first to realize that neighboring plots of land could produce wines with wildly different flavors, mapping these designations into *appellations*, many of which are still used today.

The monks came from two very different orders: the permissive Benedictines and the rigid Cistercians. The Benedictines had an abbey farther south, at Cluny. The Cistercians, whose headquarters were at Cîteaux, nearer to the Côte d'Or, were, ironically, ascetics, forbidden to eat meat, eggs, fish, or dairy or to drink anything but water (though they permitted themselves to sample the wine they produced). For the Cistercians wine was purely a commercial endeavor, sold to support their monasteries or offered as gifts in return for political favors.

During the Middle Ages, Burgundy was not part of France but a powerful and independent duchy with borders that stretched to Flanders and the Netherlands, governed by a series of dukes with names that sound like superheroes': Philippe le Hardi (the Bold), Jean sans Peur (the Fearless), Philippe le Bon (the Good), Charles le Téméraire (the Reckless). The first, Philippe le Hardi, could also have been named Philippe the Wine Lover. A dedicated oenophile, he forever defined Burgundy wine when he commanded the removal of all Gamay grapes (he described them as "disloyal"), ordering instead Pinot Noir to be planted in the region, an edict that remains unchanged since he issued it in 1395. Today only two varietals are grown on the Côte d'Or: Pinot Noir for red wine, Chardonnay for white.

I noticed these very grapevines climbing up the hillsides, attached to wood-and-wire trellises. In the chill damp of early spring, the landscape was bare, the region's famous reddish soil clearly visible beneath the orderly rows of short, twisting, black stumps. And yet even in their denuded, hibernating state, the vinestock appeared well tended, neatly clipped and trimmed, waiting patiently for the warmer weather to coax out leaves, flowers, and fruit.

The lines of vines stretching up the hill appeared—to my untrained eye—like a single, vast vineyard. In reality, however, my gaze was sweeping across tens, if not hundreds, of different properties, unmarked by walls or fences as tradition dictates. Until the French Revolution, a few wealthy landowners held the majority of Burgundy's vineyards, the largest being the Catholic Church. That changed in 1790, when the Church's land was sold as national property and its huge swaths of vineyards were carved into small plots. Today Burgundy remains a region of modest vineyards—some as tiny as a garden patch—with many owned by independent producers instead of large conglomerates.

In Beaune I admired the town's prosperous shine, the buffed

stone *hôtels particuliers* opening to well-preserved courtyards, the roofs tiled in colorful geometric patterns, the medieval ramparts edging manicured streets lined with gleaming wine shops and *fromageries*. Foreigners flock here in all seasons, a steady stream of tourists that have left the locals a bit blasé in their welcome. I sat in one café and watched a group of British tourists keen to partake in a glass of local refreshment. The waiter rattled off the wines by the glass—Gevrey-Chambertin, Meursault, Nuits-Saint-Georges—and their jaws dropped. Mine did, too, a little, hearing all those famous names offered so casually. It felt like a celebrity sighting.

Later I had a chance to taste some wine with Thibaut Marian, a young winemaker and owner of Domaine Seguin-Manuel, a winery in Beaune. Thibaut's family has been making wine since 1750, but he acquired his own establishment more recently, in 2004. We sat in his office separated by a long row of bottles—about half of the twenty *appellations* that the domaine produces—and Thibaut started pouring. First the whites, golden, crisp, flowery, minerally. He described each one with a father's tender pride. We swirled, sipped, sucked air into our cheeks, swished, as if cleansing the entire mouth with wine—actually, Thibaut did all these things, and I copied him, always half a beat behind—and then we spit. I had expected the expectoration, but even so it wrenched me to lean over the terracotta pitcher. Could one even properly taste wine without swallowing? I considered my car, parked a few blocks away, and tipped the rest of my glass into the *crachoir*. Thibaut promptly poured from another bottle.

Thibaut's winery is small and artisanal. He produces about seventy thousand bottles a year, and his production is linked, like that of many independent producers in the region, to organic farming and a lunar bottling cycle, which gives the wine "more purity, more freshness and lightness, and better aging capacity," he said. We finished tasting the whites and moved on to the reds. Until this point we'd been using the same glass to taste all the wines, but now Thibaut noticed a bit of sediment at the bottom of mine.

"Let me find you a new glass," he said.

"No, don't worry, we can just rinse it out with a little water."

"Water?" A look of horror crossed his patrician features. "*Non, non,* we will use wine." He reached for one of the bottles of white and poured a slug, thoroughly rinsed the glass, and drained it into the *crachoir.*

That was when I knew I was in Burgundy, where wine replaced water.

In March 1787, Thomas Jefferson set out from Paris on a three-month tour of France. The purpose of the voyage, he claimed, was to heal a broken wrist by taking the mineral waters at Aix-en-Provence. On the way he planned to fulfill his obligations as America's top envoy, researching French agriculture, architectural, and engineering projects. But when he chose to begin the trip in the vineyards of Burgundy, his daughter Martha became suspicious.

"I am inclined to think this voyage is rather for your pleasure than your health," she teased him in a letter.

In fact, Jefferson's five-day visit to Burgundy was not accidental. After spending two years establishing diplomatic relations in the court of Louis XVI, he had tasted his fair share of fine vintages. Now he was keen to explore the Côte d'Or's cellars and vineyards, to discover the art of viticulture with the hope of transporting it back to Virginia, to taste the wines of a region famous—even in the late eighteenth century—for its *terroir.*

Thomas Jefferson had first arrived in France three years earlier, a handsome forty-one-year-old widower with two young daughters. He had been sent by Congress to join John Adams and Benjamin Franklin, succeeding the latter as minister plenipotentiary. For Jefferson, whose wife had died two years prior, the appointment fulfilled a childhood dream of living in Europe. He found housing in a series of grand *hôtels particuliers* with his daughter Martha and a slave, James Hemings (his younger daughter, Maria, joined him in 1787, accompanied by another slave, Sally Hemings), and he began to circulate among a swirl of artists and intellectuals. Among them he met Maria Cosway, an artist born in Italy to English parents, and her husband, Richard Cosway, a renowned miniaturist and portraitist.

A friendship (or was it a romance?) between Jefferson and Maria blossomed over six weeks, as the two met often on a series of group sightseeing excursions to places like Versailles, Saint-Germain-en-Laye, and Marly-le-Roi. During this period Jefferson dislocated his right wrist while attempting to jump a fence at the Cours-la-Reine park—some have speculated that he was trying to impress Maria—an injury that would trouble him for the rest of his life.

Jefferson's injured wrist confined him to home for a month, forced him to correspond through his secretary, and—most tragically—cut short his time with Maria. Less than a month after the accident, she departed France with her husband, leaving Jefferson in a gloomy state. "I am indeed the most wretched of all earthly beings," he wrote in a letter to her. "Overwhelmed with grief, every fibre of my frame distended beyond its natural powers to bear, I would willingly meet whatever catastrophe should leave me no more to feel or to fear."

Titled "Dialogue Between My Head and My Heart," the letter portrays a lively debate between Jefferson's tender emotions—"I am rent into fragments by the force of my grief!"—and his cooler sense of logic, which tempered his affection for a beautiful married woman (albeit one whose husband was a notorious philanderer). A facsimile of the document shows his handwriting cramped and crooked—he was forced to use his left hand—but the sentiments rocket off the page. It constitutes the only existing love letter that Jefferson ever wrote.

By March 1787, Jefferson's wrist had sufficiently healed for him to travel, but his mood remained pensive throughout his solitary journey. Could the three-month trip have been an elaborate distraction from a broken heart? "One travels more usefully when they travel alone, because they reflect more," he wrote in a letter. But when he reached Beaune, he sought guidance, hiring a wine adviser, Étienne Parent. Like many men of the era, Parent dabbled in viticulture and barrel making, but his main income came from acting as a *négociant*, or wine merchant, blending wines from various producers to create and sell a sufficient commercial quantity. He led Jefferson on a brisk tour of the Côte d'Or, whisking him in and out of cellars from Nuys to Pommard to Meursault, and introducing him to the wines that would become his favorites.

As I toured vineyards and visited vaulted cellars, I tried to see the region through Jefferson's eyes. The funny thing was, although more than two centuries separated our journeys, it wasn't that hard to imagine him there. For one thing the landscape still resembled his description, with "the côte in vines. Some forest wood here and there, broom, whins and holly, and a few inclosures of quick hedge." The famous soil was still "a good red loam and sand, mixed with more or less grit, small stone, and sometimes rock." The people still appeared "well fed." Or at least they bloomed with the aura of well-fed confidence that comes from centuries of prosperity.

Also, I had found a wine adviser, Anne Parent, a direct descendant of Étienne who owned Domaine Parent, a winery in Pommard. She led me through her *cave,* a dimly lit space sharp with the sour tang of vinegar, pausing before various casks and drawing out drafts for us to swill, savor, and spit (directly onto the gravel floor).

Though Jefferson's diaries offered meticulous travel notes, they revealed no clues to his emotional state. Like him, I traveled alone and, like him, I discovered that the solitude offered lots of opportunity for reflection. Were his thoughts, too, filled with someone who was far away? I imagined him wandering through vineyards with Étienne Parent, quiet as they sipped different vintages, seduced by the magic of the *terroir,* marveling at the good fortune that allowed him to admire firsthand the beauty and history of Burgundy and the skill of its *vignerons.* I imagined him feeling all these things and yet all the while being wistful for Maria. When you love someone, you want to share with that person the things you enjoy most in the world.

I had come to Burgundy with two goals: to taste the region's wine and sample its food. I had drunk the wine. But when it came to the pleasures of the table, Jefferson was a terrible guide.

Aside from a few potatoes in Dijon—"the best round potatoes here I ever saw"—his diaries don't mention food at all. Where were the descriptions of beef braised in a wine-dark sauce? The tales of snails roasted in garlicky butter and pried from their burning shells with the help of a special clamp? The stories of jambon persillade— pink Easter ham coated with verdant chopped parsley and slipped into a jellied case? Didn't he eat any gougères—those cheesy puffs that are so delicious with white wine—or sample the local cheeses, either the soft, creamy fromage de Cîteaux (made by Cistercian monks) or the decadent, sloppy Époisses?

He did not. Or if he did, he didn't write about them. Perhaps Jefferson—a semivegetarian—didn't consider matters of the stomach worthy of his diary. This was one of the many major differences between us. His travel diaries neglect food. Mine talk about nothing else.

No, if I wanted to explore Burgundy's storied cuisine, I would need another guide. Someone who had sampled the region's rich and classic dishes and knew how to cook them. Someone who shared my omnivorous approach and American sensibilities. Someone like Julia Child.

In her classic cookbook *Mastering the Art of French Cooking*, Julia describes boeuf bourguignon as "one of the most delicious beef dishes concocted by man." She provides a meticulously detailed three-page recipe but also offers a disclaimer: "As is the case with most famous dishes," she writes, "there are more ways than one to arrive at a good boeuf bourguignon."

That, I soon discovered, was a gross understatement. Over plates of wine-braised beef, Burgundy's professional and home cooks offered me a wealth of contradictory advice, dispensed in hushed voices or with defensive shrugs. *You should use only Burgundy wine. You can use any good-quality wine. Add a dash of vinegar to the marinade. Pfff . . . He uses a marinade? Bacon adds a wonderful smoky flavor. The one thing I never use is bacon. My mother makes the best boeuf bourguignon. My grandmother's is the best. Mine is the best.* Julia Child would be happy to know that Burgundy's debate over boeuf bourguignon is alive and well.

Whatever their particularities, however, most people acknowledged that the dish is a rustic one, a ragout with humble beginnings (or at least as humble as a plate of meat can be considered). Meat was precious back then, more precious even than wine, which in the days before the phylloxera blight was produced in every region of France, with vines growing right up to the gates of Paris. Thrifty cooks endeavoring to use every scrap of an animal soon realized that tough cuts like *paleron*, or chuck roast, became tender when slow-cooked in wine.

As I left the grape-centric hills of the Côte d'Or and drove south into the wide, flat plains of the Charolais, the origins of boeuf bourguignon became even clearer. There, dotting the green pastures in groups of two or three, I spotted Burgundy's *other* famous product: Charolais cattle.

According to local legend, Crusaders brought the snow-white livestock back from their overseas travels and used a rudimentary form of animal husbandry to breed them into powerful, utilitarian farm animals. In 1747 word of their meaty flanks began to spread when an enterprising cattle farmer marched his herd to the market at Poissy, outside Paris, a folkloric journey that took only seventeen days. By 1770 herds of Charolais dotted the route from Burgundy to Paris. "You found them all along the Loire, passing through Nevers, and Orléans," said Frédéric Bouchot, director of the Maison du Charolais, a museum in the town of Charolles that is devoted to the breed. By the late nineteenth century, Charolais cattle had spread throughout France. Today they're found around the world—notably in the United States, Canada, and Australia—in either single-race herds or crossed with other breeds.

In 2010, boeuf de Charolles—that is, beef from Charolais cattle, produced in the Charolais region—was awarded the title *appellation d'origine contrôlée*. According to the *cahier des charges*, the animals must graze on the region's rich grass from March to November and move indoors during the winter months. They're slaughtered at six years instead of the usual five, which allows them more time to grow. The result is generous cuts of beef, prized by connoisseurs for their light marbling and high flavor.

From the roof deck of the Maison du Charolais, Bouchot and I surveyed the lush pastures of the region, divided by hedgerows and dotted with white cows. The animals dominated the landscape in the same way that vines characterized the Côte d'Or.

"Does meat represent Burgundy?" I asked Bouchot as we gazed at the view.

He hesitated. "Wine is more attractive."

In her memoir, *My Life in France*, Julia talks about a trip she and her husband, Paul Child, made to Burgundy in 1949, lingering in "valley towns whose names sounded like a carillon: Montrachet, Pommard, Vougeot, Volnay, Meursault, Nuits-Saint-Georges, Beaune." She doesn't mention boeuf bourguignon, but I thought of her as I ate it there, admiring the tender melt of the beef, the tang of its sauce, making a few mental notes to my own recipe as I wiped my plate clean with a piece of bread.

I had known about Julia's recipe for boeuf bourguignon ever since I was a little girl, when my dad used to cook it for parties. I used to sit on the kitchen counter and watch him wield his Chinese cleaver, shouting "Bang the garlic, Daddy!" when he brought the side of his blade down on an unpeeled clove. Over the years he melded Julia's recipe with one for Provençal daube from *Sunset* magazine—adding black olives and orange peel to the wine and beef—but her fleur-de-lis-covered book was still the one he consulted for questions on French technique. It maintained a place of honor on our kitchen bookshelf, an authority on timing and temperature, on the right kind of cooking equipment to buy, on the best way to trim an artichoke or line a charlotte mold with ladyfingers.

I wasn't really allowed to watch TV, but cooking shows were different, educational. My dad and I sometimes watched Julia together, each of us inspired by her confident, clear instructions. One Friday night when I was about thirteen, my parents had some friends over for dinner, and my father and I decided to make a Grand Marnier soufflé for dessert. I prepared the base before everyone arrived, whisking the flour into warmed milk, dropping egg yolks into the liquid and watching it thicken over the heat. I rubbed sugar cubes over a "bright-skinned orange"—as Julia specified—and released a faint mist of citrusy oil that clung to my fingers. Midway through the meal, my dad nudged me and we slipped to the kitchen to whip the egg whites and fold them into the base. The electric beaters whined over the conversation in the dining room, but though I whisked and whisked, the egg whites refused to form stiff peaks. The plastic bowl probably hadn't been squeaky-clean enough.

"What would Julia do?" my dad asked me.

"Start over?"

"She's not a perfectionist."

"She would use them anyway," I said reluctantly. And so we folded the drooping clouds of white into the warmed bouillie sauce, turned the mixture into our sugared mold, and placed it in the oven. The word *souffle* means "breath" in French. Did they name the dish soufflé because you hold your breath for the entire twenty minutes that it bakes? When the timer rang, we rushed to the oven. The soufflé's golden surface had risen just above the rim of the dish, but it was a shaky puff, nervous and unsure. When we removed the dish from the heat, the soufflé started to slump like a sulky teenager. "Serve it!" my dad urged. "Hurry!"

We rushed the dish to the dining table and scooped portions onto every plate. The texture was all wrong—like a spongy flan edged with grainy sugar rather than an airy cloud—but the orange flavor was bright and sweet, almost flowery, darkened by the boozy edge of Grand Marnier. "Mmmm!" exclaimed Mrs. Chang, the ninety-three-year-old mother-in-law of my mom's friend Janet. Thus far she had picked her way through the Chinese dinner my father had made—when you're ninety-three, you don't have much appetite, I suppose—but now she gobbled up her dessert.

"You like it? Ann made it," my dad told her. She smiled, but I wasn't sure if she'd understood him. Mrs. Chang was as sharp as a mandoline, but she didn't speak much English and my dad spoke no Mandarin.

When we had finished eating, I rose to clear the dessert plates, reaching past Mrs. Chang's unnaturally jet-black head to move the soufflé dish. I felt her hand grasp my arm, stilling me with a surprisingly firm grip. A voice said something in Chinese. "She wants you to leave it," said my mom. "Leave the dish."

I placed the dish in front her, and all of us at the table watched as Mrs. Chang took her spoon and scraped out every last morsel of imperfect soufflé. In my head I heard Julia's high-pitched, slightly madcap, swooping voice: *Never apologize.*

That was the first time Julia had inspired me—as the careful, methodical teacher who broke down recipes step by step, illustrating that even the most complicated were possible as long as you were thorough. And if something went wrong, as things inevitably did, she simply patched up her mistake and ate the dish anyway without apology or embarrassment.

The second time came a few years later, during a cold, damp winter, my first on the East Coast. I had just graduated from college in California and moved to Boston to work as an assistant at a book-publishing company. I lived in a lightly heated apartment, with roommates I'd met through an ad in the *Boston Globe,* made $18,500 a year, and subsisted on rice and beans. For entertainment I relied heavily on the public library, which is where I found Noël Riley Fitch's biography of Julia Child, *Appetite for Life.*

On the book's original dust jacket, Julia's face appeared younger and moodier than her television persona. I kept glancing back at the photograph as I read, absorbed by a tale that has by now become the stuff of legend: the awkward girlhood in California, the string of unsuccessful careers, the classified job in the Office of Strategic Services (the precursor to the CIA), the post in China during World War II, her romance with Paul Child, their assignment in Paris, her gastronomic blossoming, her astonishing late-in-life success.

I loved Julia's story of reinvention and determination. But I was twenty-three and still in the middle of my own invention. It would be years before I felt the resonance of Julia's tale, before I experienced just how profoundly a change in circumstances could alter a course, or provoke a transformation.

For Julia that change was her husband. Her life blossomed after their marriage, shifting from one of secretarial work and badly cooked meals to passion and glorious food. He was the great love of her life, the reason she came to France, the inspiration behind her cooking. "I would have never have had my career without Paul Child," she wrote in *My Life in France.*

Before our move to China, my friend Erin, the wife of one of Calvin's foreign-service colleagues, warned me about life at post. "Prepare yourself for the 1950s," she'd said. I nodded even though I had no idea what she was talking about. But once in Beijing, I quickly found out. I found out at the embassy orientation, where my name tag was preprinted with my husband's last name. I found out at the coffee mornings that gathered accompanying spouses—

almost all women, almost all unemployed—for a few hours of light gossip followed by lunch and shopping. I found out every time my hostess introduced me—not as Ann but as Calvin-from-the-political-section's-wife. I found out when people asked me at parties, "What do you do?" and I could only mumble about a job I used to have.

Even though I loved being married to Calvin, even as I relished our cozy, exclusive domesticity, the weekday hours stretched before me long and purposeless. Oh, I had plenty to do—cooking, cleaning, sightseeing, lunching—but even as I went through the motions, I felt drowned by this new life, one that defined me by my husband's job, not my own. It was, I knew, hopelessly American to link my identity and self-worth to a career. But I *was* American, the product of an immigrant mother who went back to her job as a doctor a few weeks after I was born. The idea of spending the rest of my life without a career made me feel as if I'd amputated a limb.

And yet my husband was a *diplomat*—the very word was synonymous with frequent overseas transfers. And anyone who has ever accompanied a partner on an overseas transfer knows that nothing slows your own career more quickly. For a while I wallowed in Kafkaesque existentialism. At least I wasn't alone in my predicament. Diplomacy has been called the world's second-oldest profession, and ever since the sixteenth century—and maybe even before—other wives of diplomats have endured similar existential crises, fading into obscurity while their husbands' achievements were recorded in history. Perhaps, then, that is why I turned to Julia for inspiration for a third time, not just because she loved food, and had also lived in China, and was also a trailing spouse, just like me—but because I was looking for proof that professional success and marriage to a diplomat were not mutually exclusive.

It was Paul's work as a diplomat that took the couple to Paris in 1948, an assignment that would surround Julia with some of the best food in the world and launch her on the path to a legendary career. She didn't know that then, though. As she toiled away in a basement classroom at the Cordon Bleu, perfecting the fundamental mother sauces and pâte brisée, she had no idea that one day she would demonstrate those same techniques on American television to audiences of millions. No, she practiced them because they lay at the root of traditional French cuisine and because she was committed—deeply, seriously committed—to learning to cook it.

Julia fell in love with Paris—"I shall never find anyplace more to my tastes," she wrote—reveling in its markets and cafés, the way a famous monument like Notre Dame could loom suddenly out of the misty distance. She started teaching cooking classes and collaborating with two Frenchwomen, Simone Beck and Louisette Bertholle, on the book that would become *Mastering the Art of French Cooking*, a massive project that consumed her for almost a decade. But foreign-service posts last only a few years. In 1953 the Childs moved to Marseille, and then Bonn; Washington, D.C.; Oslo; and Cambridge, Massachusetts—six moves in just thirteen years. And with each move came a new house, new friends, a new community, a new life.

Julia had a project and a path, but reading her letters I thought I could sense her anxiety—"From the point of view of cooking career, [it's] a real blow"—she wrote to her friend and literary mentor, Avis DeVoto, about the move to Marseille. Or, "We are both just sick about this move," as she and Paul packed for Bonn. Or, "You can prepare yourself to enter a new culture, but the reality always takes some getting used to," as they arrived in Oslo.

I recognized her apprehension from my own, the same atomic cloud of unease that mushroomed over me every time Calvin and I discussed our next move, studying the list of open assignments and trying to find the perfect place that offered interesting work for both of us, despite our wildly disparate fields. I felt lucky to have found a path of my own to nurture and climb, one strewn with small triumphs and messy disappointments. I knew I *was* lucky to have a portable job that I loved, one enlivened by our itinerant lifestyle, one made possible by Calvin's emotional and breadwinning support. And yet each move was a stark reminder of the things that couldn't be packed into boxes and sent on a transport ship: contacts, friends, inspiration, the daily routine that was my life.

Sometimes it felt like an opportunity; sometimes it felt like an injunction. Sometimes I felt like chattel, a numbered item on my husband's official orders; sometimes I felt we were a team, more powerful together than alone. Always I tried to remind myself of Julia, remembering her staccato, self-mocking tone when she became a little maudlin. "Too bad." *"C'est la vie."* "WOE."

Julia and Paul left France in 1954, a departure that she described in her memoir as "painful" (though, in classic Julia fashion, she enthused over "an honest-to-goodness American steak" in the very next breath). I understood her sorrow, because I felt it myself. I had been dreading leaving my beloved, beautiful France ever since the day I found out we were moving there. When Calvin returned from Baghdad, we would have two years in Paris before we moved somewhere else. And then we'd do it again, and again, and again, every two, or three, or four years until he retired.

"This is Paul's career, and if he wants to stay in it, we've just got to resign ourselves to abrupt changes," wrote Julia to her friend Avis. "Trouble is, neither of us likes to move around at all. We dig in with our paints and pots, as though it were for a century." I wondered if Julia ever dreamed of a house, a place that didn't get packed and unpacked every thirty-six months, a place where she knew every creak of the floorboards, where she could reach for the kettle and make a cup of tea without turning on the kitchen lights, where the children she never had left small, muddy footprints in the hallway, a place drifting with the happy ghosts of countless meals cooked by her own hands. A permanent place. A home.

There was a poem, "The Blue House" by Tomas Tranströmer, that I thought about sometimes when the gnaw for permanence became ferocious. In it the narrator contemplates the life that might have been.

> It's always so early in here, before the crossroads, before the irrevocable choices. Thank you for this life! Still I miss the alternatives.

I missed them, too. A house I'd never seen, its entry hall papered in mad toile prints. A kitchen hung with copper saucepans. The hairdresser who knew my daughter's favorite ice-cream flavor. Friends who dropped by and stayed for dinner. Business cards that I could print in batches of ten thousand. Colleagues who surprised me with carrot cupcakes on my birthday. And, probably, a career in an office, and not as a writer. Long weekends in Florida, not Luang Prabang. Perhaps no books published, no second, or third, languages spoken. Quite possibly no Calvin.

Nine years earlier I met Calvin and made a choice to live a peripatetic life instead of a more permanent one. I had made my decision, and knee-deep in the glorious, messy minutiae of our daily existence I didn't regret it. Still, when things got challenging—when the idea of moving to another foreign country and learning another foreign language exhausted instead of excited me, when the loneliness of being new again clawed at me, when Calvin and I fought about our choices instead of compromising—it was easy to dream about that other, steadfast world, where things rarely changed. It seemed so wide open, so rich with the possibility of deep friendships, with attics that I could fill to overflowing, with career opportunities that could grow out of running into someone every morning at the coffee shop.

But when my perspective shifted back to reality, I knew there couldn't be a world wider than mine, ringed with adventure yet anchored with love's safe harbor. It was love for Calvin, and his love for me, that made me choose this vagabond life. It was love that made us support each other, and it was love that made us listen to each other, and it was because of love that we agreed to compromises—like going to Baghdad for a year—that didn't feel good but maybe, possibly, turned out to be the best decisions after all. Calvin and I didn't have a permanent address to call our own, but instead we had made the world our home. We'd left pieces of ourselves behind in each place we lived, and perhaps we were stronger together—and stronger individuals—because of it.

Of course, it still sailed next to me, that parallel life—it would always sail next to me—as full of joy and challenge as the one I was living. I thought of it sometimes, pale and chilled—lit by a satellite moon, not the sun of reality—a ghostly ship charting a route to what might have been, while I remained on the course of what was.

The Château du Clos de Vougeot is the kind of haughty building that couldn't be anything *but* a château, an immense stone structure looming over a sea of well-tended Côte de Nuits vines. Founded in the eleventh century by the thin hands of Cistercian monks, the vineyard had produced fifty thousand bottles a year in its heyday, a veritable ocean of wine for the period. In 1787, Thomas Jefferson stopped there on his journey to observe the monks' prodigious winemaking process with an eye toward importing it to the United States. Over the years he would ask his wine adviser, Étienne Parent, to include Burgundy vine clippings with his shipments of wine, in the hope of cultivating them in Virginia soil.

Today the château houses a museum and a conference center, as well as the headquarters of the Confrérie des Chevaliers du Tastevin, a prestigious wine club. But the monks' industry is still evident in the enormous fifteenth-century grape presses on view in the covered courtyard, the cavernous fermentation vats that stand in the *cuverie*, and the sweeping ground-floor cellar, built to store two thousand casks.

In 1790, only a few years after Jefferson's visit, the French Revolution removed the monks from the château and confiscated the property from the Church. Several families owned the estate until 1889, when the 124 acres of vineyards were separated from the buildings, divided, and sold to several producers. The land is currently split among more than eighty owners. The monks have long disappeared. The *cuverie* and *caves* where they toiled have been dry for centuries. Two hundred twenty-five years, a vine-ravaging epidemic, and several wars separate us from Jefferson's visit. And yet the Château du Clos de Vougeot remains a symbol of the Côte d'Or. Today it is a veritable embassy of Burgundy wine, represented by the twelve thousand members of the Confrérie des Chevaliers du Tastevin.

One afternoon I visited the château and met with its director, Richard Fussner, and head chef, Olivier Walch. As we sat in one of the Renaissance-era meeting rooms, a Confrérie delegation milled around in the gravel courtyard, occasionally breaking into loud refrains of the "Ban de Bourgogne," the semimusical Burgundian battle cry, which is accompanied by choreographed clapping and hand gestures.

"The Confrérie's mission is to promote Burgundy's products, protect its viticulture, and, also, to promote a certain *art de vivre*," said Fussner as a tuneless chorus drifted in through the window. "Being a member is like being an ambassador for Burgundy's wine, culture, and cuisine."

When the Great Depression caused Burgundy's wine trade to stagnate in the 1930s, two enterprising Côte de Nuits winemakers had the bright idea of starting a wine club inspired by the Bacchic societies of the seventeenth and eighteenth centuries. They founded the Confrérie in 1934, adopting a motto—"*Jamais en vain, toujours en vin*" (Never in vain, always in wine)—and shared their finest vintages with friends and strangers, hoping to spread the word about Burgundy and thus encourage international wine sales.

In 1944 the Confrérie established the Château du Clos de Vougeot as their headquarters, restoring it and in fact improving upon its former austerity, creating luxurious banquet rooms where monks had once lived in spartan simplicity. (In the monks' former dining room, re-created as part of the château's museum, long wooden tables, benches, and a pulpit hinted at their austere lifestyle; one brother would read passages from the Bible as the others ate gruel in enforced silence.) Today the Confrérie is an international organization, with chapters on five continents. Members gather at the château sixteen times a year for *chapitre* banquets. Dress is usually black tie, and around their necks members wear a small, shallow silver cup dangling from a wide striped ribbon. This is the *tastevin* (pronounced "tat-van"), which, as its name implies, was once used to sample wine.

Burgundy wine and diplomacy share a long history, dating at least to the fourteenth century when the duc de Bourgogne (and Pinot Noir fanatic) Philippe le Hardi carried casks of the wine in all his convoys throughout France and Flanders, using it to spread festive cheer at banquets and smooth his path at the negotiating table. Burgundy wine was also used to curry favor (or to bribe), as with Jean de Bussières, the abbot of the Abbaye de Cîteaux, who in 1359 sent thirty barrels of Clos de Vougeot to Pope Gregory XI. Four years later de Bussières was ordained a cardinal.

Thomas Jefferson, too, knew the political significance of wine. Though he had enjoyed the occasional tipple of Madeira or port as a young man, he gave up the two when he renounced British colonial rule, rejecting the Englishman's culture of fortified wines and long-winded toasts. "The taste of this country [was] artificially created by our long restraint under the English government to the strong wines of Portugal and Spain," he wrote. For the rest of his life, he sipped and served the lighter wines of France and Italy and hoped his fellow Americans would follow suit.

By now Chef Walch had launched into a discussion of boeuf bourguignon, musing over its global appeal. Perhaps the dish could be considered another ambassador, made with the two products that best illustrate Burgundy: wine and beef.

"I make mine with beef cheeks," he said, adding with a spark of defiance, as only a classically trained French chef could, "The recipe has to live! It's a form of globalization on the plate."

I considered his words later that evening, as I sat down in a lively Beaune bistro, to a menu bourguignon. The dishes sounded classic, but they were modern interpretations, simplified and fresh. Instead of snails nestled into crocks of garlic butter, there was a garlicky green parsley soup garnished with escargots curled like seared shrimp. Instead of mini-gougères on a plate, there was a puffed gougère soufflé, a crisp-shelled marvel that shattered to reveal steamy, cheese-scented layers. Instead of boeuf bourguignon fortified with bacon and mushrooms, there was a fine stew sparked with the tang of ginger and orange peel, its meat shredding under the gentle pressure of my fork, its sauce a marriage of bright wine and deep, beefy redolence.

I used every scrap of bread and mashed potato to sponge up the sauce. I licked my knife to capture every last vestige of that sauce. If I'd been alone, I might have licked my plate. It haunted me, the sauce, with something richer and more profound than its dark depths. If wine is a Burgundian diplomat, I thought, perhaps boeuf bourguignon is like a diplomatic marriage, two successful, independent entities joined together, more powerful united than apart, at its base a simple, rustic recipe—and yet one that is constantly adapting, modernizing, and being reinterpreted.

Boeuf à la Bourguignonne

Olivier Walch, the head chef at the Château du Clos de Vougeot, gave me rough instructions for his boeuf bourguignon, and I turned them into the recipe below. Rather than boeuf bourguignon, this is beef cooked in the Burgundian style—because I believe you should be able to use any kind of red wine.

Serves 4

2 to 2½ pounds beef cheeks *or* chuck roast, trimmed of fat
    and cut into 2½- to 3-inch chunks
1 onion, peeled and chopped into 1-inch pieces
2 carrots, peeled and chopped into 1-inch pieces
1 leek, trimmed and chopped into 1-inch pieces
1 sprig thyme
2 bay leaves
3 or 4 juniper berries
2 whole cloves
2 or 3 whole black peppercorns
One 750-milliliter bottle full-bodied wine, such as a sturdy
    Pinot Noir, Côtes du Rhône, *or* similar
3 to 4 tablespoons neutral-flavored vegetable oil
Salt and freshly ground pepper to taste
1 quart meat stock (*or* water)
2 tablespoons Cognac *or* brandy
2 tablespoons all-purpose flour
2 cloves garlic, peeled and crushed

Garniture

¼ pound bacon, cut into ¼-inch matchsticks, *or* lardons
1 pound fresh button mushrooms
18 to 24 pearl onions
Salt and freshly ground pepper to taste
1 tablespoon vegetable oil

Marinating the meat

In a large bowl, combine the beef, onion, carrots, and leek. Add the thyme, bay leaves, juniper berries, cloves, and black peppercorns. Pour over the red wine, making sure everything is submerged. Cover and refrigerate overnight, or for at least 3 hours.

Browning and stewing the meat

Remove the beef and vegetables from the marinade. Reserve the liquid. Heat 1 tablespoon of the oil in a large frying pan over moderate heat. Meanwhile, dry the beef thoroughly with paper towels and season it with salt and freshly ground pepper. When the oil shimmers, arrange the beef chunks in the pan in a single layer, taking care not to overcrowd the pan (you will probably need to do this in two batches). Brown the chunks, turning them so that they are golden and crusted on all sides, adding another tablespoon of oil if necessary. Remove them from the pan and place them directly into a wide-mouthed 6-quart casserole or Dutch oven. When all the beef chunks are browned, heat another tablespoon of oil and sauté the vegetables until softened, wilted, and almost golden, about 10 minutes. Remove them to the casserole with the beef. Deglaze the frying pan with 1 cup or so of the stock or use water, scraping up the browned bits.

Over moderate heat, sprinkle the Cognac over the meat and vegetables, and set it aflame with a match, gently shaking the casserole until the alcohol burns off. Stir in the flour and toss lightly so that it coats everything. Stir in the deglazing liquid, the wine from the marinade, the garlic, and enough stock or water to barely cover the meat. Bring to a simmer and cook, partially covered, until a fork easily pierces the meat, 2½ to 3 hours.

Finishing the sauce

When the meat is done, remove the casserole from the stove top. With tongs or a slotted spoon, remove the beef chunks. Strain the remaining liquid through a sieve set over a bowl, pressing on the vegetables to collect all the juices. Return the liquid to the casserole. Discard the vegetables. If the sauce appears too thin, boil it rapidly until it reduces slightly, about 10 minutes.

Preparing the garniture

In a saucepan, blanch the matchsticks or lardons of bacon (this makes them less greasy). Clean and quarter the mushrooms. Blanch and peel the onions. In a frying pan over medium heat, brown the lardons until they are lightly golden (but not crisp) and the fat has rendered. Remove them from the pan and, in the remaining bacon fat, sauté the mushrooms until they begin to release their juices; season with salt and freshly ground pepper and remove from the pan. Heat the tablespoon of oil and sauté the onions, turning them so that they brown on as many sides as possible. Add ½ cup of stock or water, season again, bring to a boil, cover, and cook until the onions are tender, about 10 minutes.

Return the meat to the casserole and stir in the bacon-mushroom-onion garniture. Bring the stew to a quiet simmer. Taste the sauce and adjust the seasonings. Serve with buttered noodles or small boiled potatoes.

Chapter 10

Aveyron / Aligot

The thing about time is that it trickles by if you're watching it, each second as slow and wearing as the drip from a tap. I had kept a vigilant eye on the clock for nearly twelve months, and now that it was almost over, I hoped it would pick up speed, succumb to gravity. But time being time, it continued at its own stately pace while I counted, with increasing impatience, the remaining weeks, days, and minutes until May 1, when my husband would come home.

"Only two weeks left? That went by so *fast*!" said an acquaintance when I ran into her in the embassy's mail room. I smiled and nodded, because for her the time probably *had* gone quickly, enrobed as she was in her own routine of *métro-boulot-dodo*. My year, however, had been counted out in Calvin's morning e-mails and our evening Skype sessions, in giant pots of soup portioned into weeknight meals, in the books I read while eating dinner, in walks taken on Sunday afternoons. It had been a productive, carefully structured, often solitary year, a year that had allowed me to create something unexpected: *my* Paris—not Calvin's Paris or our Paris but mine, one of new friends and cobblestoned street shortcuts and pastry-shop discoveries of my very own, one for me to share with my husband once he returned. For the rest of my life, I would, I knew, remember my experiences in Paris, drawing upon them like a long, cool drink of water, as we moved through our other posts.

But a fast year? No, it had not been fast.

It is perhaps the fate of those left behind, this slow seep of time. Penelope knew it as she waited twenty years for Odysseus to return, weaving his shroud by day and unraveling it by night in order to foil her would-be suitors.

The spouses of thousands of deployed soldiers endure it, single-handedly juggling jobs and family, all the while keeping one wary ear cocked for the ring of the phone, praying it won't be that call bringing unbearable news.

Other diplomats' wives experienced it, like Abigail Adams, who spent most of her married life separated from her "dearest friend," as she and her husband, John Adams, addressed each other in their letters. While he traveled as a circuit judge, served as a delegate to the Continental Congress, and lived overseas as an envoy to England, France, and the Netherlands, she toiled in colonial New England with little hired help, planting and harvesting the crops, managing her husband's finances, raising their four children. She spent months without hearing from her distant husband, the silence as much a product of his self-indulgence as of the unreliable mail service and his fear that spies would intercept his messages. And when John did write, he scolded his fretful wife for her complaints: "For God's sake never reproach me again with not writing. . . . You know not—you feel not—the dangers that surround me, nor those that may be brought upon our Country." And yet can you blame Abigail for worrying? Given the disease and danger that haunted the era, she probably feared that the silence meant he was dead.

Abigail spent most of her life dreaming about a stable family existence, hoping that every time John ended a post, his return home would be permanent. But as one more appointment turned into another, then another, then another, it became obvious that John was unable to deny the call to public service. Abigail feared that they had spent the best years of their lives miserably separated. "Who shall give me back Time? Who shall compensate to me those years I cannot recall?" she wrote in a letter to him. "How dearly have I paid for a titled Husband; should I wish you less wise that I might enjoy more happiness?"

In 1784, her children mostly grown and her father recently deceased, Abigail overcame her dread of ocean travel and joined John in Europe, where he was serving as an envoy. After thirteen years of "widowhood"—as Abigail referred to John's long absences—the couple finally reunited, moving from Paris to London to the Hague as John fulfilled his diplomatic duties. They returned to the United States in 1788, installing themselves in their new farm, Peacefield, in Quincy, Massachusetts. Abigail hoped, of course, it would be their final move. She was wrong. It would be more than twelve years before they returned home permanently—and only after John had served two terms as vice president and one as president of the United States.

Abigail had sacrificed decades of family life—a sacrifice she believed was her patriotic duty, her personal offering to a country she loved—but she had not surrendered the years willingly. In her letters to John, her resentment toward his ambition glows like a searing cattle brand. "Do you not sometimes sigh for such a Seclusion—publick peace and domestick happiness?" she wrote to him in 1781. "I know the voice of Fame to be a mere weathercock, unstable as Water and fleeting as a Shadow." Abigail's domestic happiness didn't arrive until 1802, when she was fifty-eight and it lasted only sixteen years, until her death in 1818. John's career—more illustrious than either of them could have imagined when they married—had offered Abigail an uncommon, well-traveled, often lonely life, a life colored by her husband's absences and her resulting strength and ingenuity, a life enriched by an economic and intellectual independence unheard of for most women of the era. Even so, you get the feeling she would have traded it all for a few acres of rural farmland and a pot of Yankee beans, had it meant spending more time with her husband. But for better or for worse, that was not her choice to make.

On April 29, I flew to Washington, D.C., to give a bookstore talk about my novel, which had been published a few months earlier. Afterward some friends and I ate dan dan noodles and fish poached in spiced oil at a Sichuan restaurant on K Street, and then we went home and I lay on their pullout couch, wide awake the entire night.

Early the next morning, I took a taxi to the airport, watching from the backseat as the sky slowly brightened from dawn into daylight. I checked in for my flight and waited in line for security, tapping my left foot, trying to peer around the crowd to see *what* was taking so *long*?! Couldn't that businessman start taking off his shoes sooner? *Why* hadn't that college student unwrapped her laptop before sending it through the X-ray machine? And how on earth could that woman forget to empty her pockets before passing through the metal detector?

Once clear of security, I re-dressed, reshod, and repacked before taking off through the terminal. I began to count the gate numbers, pausing to consult the boarding pass clutched in my hand—27, 28 . . . 29. I turned off the path and into the waiting area, which at seven o'clock was already full of business travelers, their faces lit by the cold glow of their cell-phone screens. Was he there? I quickly scanned the crowd. No, no, no. I took a step back. His trajectory had been complicated—Baghdad, Amman, Frankfurt, D.C.—

there had been a lot of variables. Maybe he had missed one flight and, as a result, all the rest.

And then, in the corner, I saw him. His back was toward me, but I knew him from the shape of his head, the color of his hair, like chestnut honey. I ran over to him, and my bag dropped at his feet, and he sprang up when he saw me, and suddenly we were hugging before we'd even had a chance to say hello. I pressed my face into his chest, and his shirt smelled faintly soapy, even after so many hours of travel, and when we kissed, his cheeks felt scratchy and familiar, and as we hugged, I felt droopy with relief, and love, and gratitude. We were together, and the glow of fluorescent lights had never been so beautiful, the crackly boarding announcements had never sounded more musical, the aroma of stale coffee had never smelled sweeter. His assignment in Iraq was over.

A few minutes later, we flew to New York, rented a car, and drove to the Hudson River Valley. There, in a strident burst of spring, we celebrated the wedding of two beloved friends amid more friends, a heartfelt weekend strewn with tears that had as much to do with our collective joy as it did with the high pollen count. We drank sparkling wine and ate carrot wedding cake, and Calvin chatted with the bride's new in-laws, and I joined the bride herself on the dance floor, and . . . well, life pretty much went on again as ordinary. Except not quite. Because after a year apart, being together would never truly feel ordinary again.

Back in Paris, we settled into our apartment, together *enfin*. Calvin started working again at the embassy, and I continued working at the American Library and writing my new novel. I bought a voluminous straw shopping basket, one that I could fill with vegetables from the outdoor market across the street. We watched Ernst Lubitsch films at the art-house cinema on Sunday afternoons and ate chic artichoke pizzas on Thursday evenings (well, I ate artichoke; Calvin ate ham and mushroom) and split raspberry financier cakes down the middle after dinner. We made lists of places to visit before we left Europe, and sometimes this led to talking about life after Paris, which always made us both a little blue.

"It's going to be so hard to leave," I said one afternoon as the golden late-summer sunshine played upon the marble mantelpiece of our apartment.

"I know," Calvin agreed. I thought he'd change the subject or encourage me not to think about it, but instead he said, "We'll come back one day."

"When you retire?"

"Or sooner?"

"Well . . ." I took a deep breath and launched into the idea I'd been thinking about for a few weeks. "We've been saving money for a long time. Maybe we could buy a place here. Something small, where we could come on vacations. A pied-à-terre?"

"A foot on the ground." Calvin smiled.

"Huh?"

"That's the direct translation, right? *Pied-à-terre*. A foot on the ground."

I started to smile, too. A foot on the ground, a permanent place—in Paris—was more than I ever could have dreamed of.

"Do you think . . . ?" Now it was Calvin's turn to take a deep breath. "It could have two bedrooms? Just in case?"

"In case we have a baby?" I said slowly. And then I found myself nodding. "Good idea." For a second we gazed at each other in a mix of excitement and terror, the kind that only the idea of parenthood could bring.

"When you're ready," Calvin said, smoothing my hair.

Cocooned in our domestic idyll, time did a flip turn and began to flit, then flee. And yet, even though my husband was home— even though we'd cooked the spaghetti and meatballs to prove it— something felt incomplete. Had we skipped a rite of passage, a ritual offering to the household gods? I puzzled over it for several weeks, but when at last I figured it out, the answer was obvious. We needed to go back to the beginning. We needed to visit the friends who had become our French family. We needed to see Didier and Alain.

Calvin called the brothers, and when he finally tracked them down, he discovered they were not in Paris at Le Mistral but down south, at their home in Aveyron. *"Venez!"* they urged. "Come down! Stay with us! We'll pick you up at the train station."

Aveyron is a *département*—akin to an American state—located in south-central France, 350 miles from Paris. With its lack of high-speed TGV or direct train service, the region remains relatively inaccessible. For most travelers, including Calvin and me, the journey from Paris takes a full day, starting with a train to Clermont-Ferrand, followed by a 125-mile drive south into a pocket of *la France profonde*, deep France, lost in time.

Calvin first visited Aveyron more than twenty years ago when he was an exchange student in Paris, taking Russian classes, and sharing an apartment in the twentieth arrondissement, one that featured views of the Eiffel Tower (if you climbed onto the roof via the fire escape and leaned over the side of the building) and a healthy cockroach population. One long weekend he joined Didier, Alain, and some other friends and drove down to Didier's country house, a drafty half ruin perched on a bluff overlooking a wild ravine. It was midwinter, cold and damp, and the house had only an ancient fireplace to warm it. That night Calvin slept next to the hearth, fully clothed and still completely frozen.

In an effort to ward off the chill, the group drank the region's coarse wine and ate its hearty fare—dishes like truffade, a golden cake of crushed potatoes studded with bacon and cheese; farçous, fried pancakes laced with spinach, herbs, and pork fat; local cured sausages and hams; and aligot, a fine potato puree beaten with melted cheese until it resembled molten lava. At the farmhouse table of Didier and Alain's aunt, Louise, they debated French politics, history, and philosophy. It was while seated in her rustic kitchen that Calvin truly learned to speak French, to express his ideas with eloquence. When the freezing rain slowed, he discovered the region's rough landscape, a juxtaposition of mountains and pastures, interlaced with river valleys dotted by stone villages.

That trip was the first of many that Calvin has made during his twenty-year friendship with Didier and Alain. When he and I got married, I joined him, to stroll along fields speckled with grazing cows and sheep, admire the elegant Romanesque church at Conques, sip wine at a café shadowed by the ramparts of an ancient château. During our visits we purchased folding pocketknives at the famous forge in Laguiole (pronounced "lye-ole"), viewed a Neolithic menhir standing stone that Didier had found and donated to the village museum, and one golden afternoon in late summer we lunched in the luminous calm of Michel et Sébastien Bras, the region's celebrated Michelin three-star restaurant.

On the phone Calvin settled on a date for us to *descend* to visit Didier and Alain, a weekend they'd both be in Aveyron and not in Paris swapping shifts at Le Mistral. Later, when I scribbled it into my calendar, I realized it was the fourth weekend in November: Thanksgiving. How, I wondered, would we celebrate in deepest, darkest rural France? The germ of an idea began to take root. I wanted to cook for everyone.

Aligot is not a dish you'd find in a Julia Child cookbook. Unlike boeuf bourguignon, it is not cooked in home kitchens from Chicago to Melbourne. Unlike cassoulet, it is not worshipped by Brooklyn food bloggers doubling as homegrown *charcutiers*. Unlike andouill-ette, it is not divisive; it does not provoke impassioned disgust or de-light. Unlike fondue, it is not synonymous with bell-bottom trousers; its equipment cannot be found stacked knee-deep at garage sales.

Aligot is none of these things because . . . well, almost no one outside France has ever heard of it. Even *in* France it's hardly a household word.

All this makes little sense to me, because the first time I tasted aligot, at a restaurant in Laguiole, I fell in love. Our waitress deliv-ered the family-style platter of whipped potatoes beaten with melted cheese and actually climbed onto a chair to tame the stretching, gooey mass, swirling scoops of it around two spoons so she could dollop it onto our plates. As I ate, I felt lost in a rapture of springy fresh cheese dissolving into silken puree, the tang of crème fraîche softened by sweet milkiness. When I finished the last bite, my heart gave a slight twinge of sadness (though it could also have been indi-gestion).

Aligot is a relatively simple dish, made with only a few ingredi-ents, though these must be of pristine quality and freshness. The potatoes should be Bintje—a Dutch variety halfway between waxy and floury—and the cheese, called tome fraîche, must be less than three days old. The cheese is aligot's not-so-secret ingredient, the key to its supple elasticity, and probably the reason it hasn't traveled around the world.

Tome fraîche is simply a wedge of pressed cheese curds, similar to fresh mozzarella. It's white and clean, speckled with tiny holes like a new sponge, and it squeaks between the teeth. The flavor, though bland—it's completely unsalted—gleams with the pearly essence of fresh milk. As tome ages, it quickly loses elasticity; an aligot made with stale cheese lacks the dish's characteristic ooziness.

If tome fraîche is allowed to ferment and mature, it becomes fromage de Laguiole, Aveyron's renowned hard-textured cheese, dense and creamy, with a sharp, tangy bite reminiscent of aged cheddar. Awarded an AOC mark of *appellation d'origine contrôlée* in 1976, it is distinguished by its special scent of wild herbs and flowers, the result of summer grazing in high-altitude pastures.

According to local legend, aligot was first made in the twelfth century by monks at the Abbey of Aubrac, on a volcanic plateau in northern Aveyron. They mixed stale chunks of bread with water and tome fraîche, stirring everything together into a nourishing porridge, which they fed to pilgrims and other travelers who passed through their doors. Could their accompanying calls of *"Allé cuit"*—something to eat—have eventually turned into the word "aligot"? Another theory claims that the word comes from the Latin *aliquid*, which means "something." Still another alleges that it comes from the old French verb *alicoter*, meaning "to cut."

By the nineteenth century, potatoes had finally arrived from the New World to replace the bread, and the dish had spread to the *burons*, the steep-roofed stone huts that dot the mountainous Aubrac landscape. Cowherds, or *buronniers*, lived in these primitive structures during the summer months, climbing up in late May and descending in mid-October, an annual tradition called the transhumance that enabled their herds to graze on the surrounding high pastures. Traditionally the *burons* had only three rooms: one for sleeping, one for making cheese, and one for aging it. In the 1930s there were more than three hundred of these stone structures. Now only a handful remain, some renovated into summer holiday cottages, some turned into restaurants catering to tourists, others derelict. Not a single one houses herders or produces cheese. Instead fromage de Laguiole and its tome are produced at the Coopérative Fromagère Jeune Montagne, a gleaming, modern facility established in 1960, when the last *buronniers* began to retire and disappear. What it lacks in old-fashioned charm, the Coopérative makes up for in year-round production, hygiene, and efficiency, as I discovered when I visited the factory floor. It is the region's best hope of sustaining its cheese-making tradition.

Though the *burons* have all but disappeared and the abbey, destroyed during the French Revolution, now lies in rubble, a few elements of the Middle Ages still remain on the high Aubrac plain. The landscape is still sweepingly beautiful, a series of elevated pastures undulating beneath an expanse of open sky. The locals still cook aligot, beating it in huge kettles with flat wooden spoons the size of rowboat oars, offering it to travelers and eating it on festive occasions. And pilgrims still journey through the region, tracing the ancient spiritual route of Saint-Jacques de Compostelle.

Travelers have walked the Chemin de Saint-Jacques (in Spanish called the Camino de Santiago), for more than a thousand years, joining the network of paths at various points throughout Europe— including England, Italy, Poland, and even Scandinavia—and ending at the town of Santiago de Compostela in northwestern Spain. In the ninth century, the body of Saint James the Apostle was purportedly discovered there in a Roman-era tomb, and the devout soon followed. During the Middle Ages, a pilgrimage took months, if not years, but the successful were rewarded by the *compostellana*, a certificate granting remission from purgatory.

All these pilgrims—and in the Chemin's heyday, there were thousands—required basic services: shelter and sustenance, both physical and spiritual. Special churches were designated at five key points along the path, and the truly pious endeavored to make a tour of them all, to visit the saints' bodies housed within. The five stops included the towns of Tours, Limoges, Toulouse, and Santiago de Compostela itself, as well as Conques, a small village laid out in the shape of a scallop shell—the symbol of the Chemin de Saint-Jacques—located in Aveyron.

The abbey at Conques honors Sainte-Foy, a young girl from Agen in Aquitaine who in the fourth century was tortured to death with a blazing-hot brazier because of her *foi*, or faith. In the eighth century, her remains were brought to Conques, abducted by a local monk—he allegedly spent ten years at a monastery in Agen gaining the trust of his superiors in order to kidnap the relic—and soon after, the abbey became a part of the Saint-Jacques circuit. Pilgrims flooded Conques, bringing different languages, cultures, and religious traditions. These early tourists took shelter at hostels marked with a scallop shell, they ate aligot, prayed before the gold reliquary of Sainte-Foy with its Roman head dating to the fifth century, and continued on their journey.

Today the Romanesque abbey, which along with the Chemin de Saint-Jacques is a UNESCO World Heritage Site, welcomes a small but steady stream of visitors. They are but mere specks amid the gaping space of the building's enormous transepts, which were constructed in the eleventh century to house floods of worshippers. And yet, on the winding country roads of Aveyron, it's not unusual to catch sight of a pair of modern pilgrims, recognizable by their scruffy clothes, walking sticks, and heavy backpacks. They lodge for a small fee at homes or hostels marked with a scallop shell, eat aligot, and chat with the locals who treat them with a gentle, almost protective kindness. And then, refreshed, they proceed with their journey, some to hike a small portion of the Chemin, others to continue on the path of nearly 720 miles that remain to Santiago de Compostela.

As I packed my bags to go down to Aveyron, it occurred to me that we, too, were pilgrims of another, ecumenical sort, Calvin and I—we were strangers in a strange land, bearing gifts that I hoped to cook: sweet potatoes, fresh cranberries, cans of pumpkin. And if we were the pilgrims, I guess that made Didier, Alain, and our other Aveyronnais friends the Indians, the natives who would gather to share a Thanksgiving feast with us (minus the smallpox blankets).

We arrived in Aveyron late in the night, after taking an after-work train to Clermont-Ferrand and meeting Didier there for the two-hour car ride south. Driving with Didier was like being strapped onto a luge against your will and sent down the side of a mountain. At his house, I crept into bed, feeling lime green around the edges. But lulled by the deep country silence, I fell asleep and woke refreshed to a frosty morning filled with the sounds of mooing cows, a fly buzzing fiercely at the window, and the clicking jingle made by Apache, the wirehaired dachshund of Didier's wife, Chantal, as he scuttled down the stairs.

"Where are we going?" I whispered to Calvin when we had all gathered in the living room. Didier opened and closed every drawer in the house in search of Apache's leash.

He shrugged. There was always a significant relinquishment of control that came with hanging out with Didier. We tended to spend a lot of time driving around in his car, stopping at quaint villages, throwing back a coffee at the bar of the local café, then getting into the car again. I never had any idea *where* we were stopping or, when we did stop, *why*—a state of oblivion that I used to blame on my inability to speak French, until I learned how and realized that *no one* knew the plan, perhaps not even Didier himself.

"Voilà!" With a spectacular crash, Didier pulled a leash from the junk drawer. Apache spotted it and ran to the door. We followed them to the car, buckled ourselves in, and plunged through space for a few terrifying minutes, eventually shuddering to a halt in Espalion, a neighboring town. We entered the café a few steps behind Didier. Everyone greeted him with a handshake or *des bises*—cheek kisses—and then turned to us with an outstretched hand, warmly welcoming yet also openly curious about these foreign FOD (Friends of Didier). We clambered into a booth, and Didier ordered a café serré—a coffee screwed into hypercaffeinated viscosity—and a tartine, which he proceeded to feed to Apache, who perched on his knees so as not to miss a single buttery crumb. Eventually Didier's friend Jérôme showed up. Then his brother, Alain. And more friends, Jean-Louis and Michel. The five of them gathered at the café most mornings to drink a few serrés and shoot the breeze—their very own coffee klatch.

One minute everyone was talking loudly and drinking coffee and the next they were suddenly pushing their chairs back from the table and fishing coins out of their pockets. We strapped ourselves back into Didier's bobsled and hurtled away. In the backseat I fixed my eyes on the horizon as we whizzed by herds of caramel-colored cows and the occasional stocky bull, a hefty, broad-shouldered, pin-legged creature who bore an undeniable resemblance to Didier. The landscape was as empty and sweeping as any I'd seen in France, a lonely expanse of prairie isolated by the surrounding Massif Central plateau, a country more populated by cattle than by people.

For generations of Aveyronnais, this region was the beginning, the place they had left to make their fortune. The Aveyronnais helped create modern Paris with their cafés. For me at least, it was impossible to picture the city without their zinc bars and chalkboard menus, the bentwood chairs at marble-topped tables, the small cups of coffee garnished with a paper-wrapped sugar cube, the names like La Butte Aveyronnaise, Le Charbonnier, L'Auvergnate. I couldn't pass any of them without imagining the homesick Avey-ronnais who had first opened it. Yes, Aveyron had left its mark on Paris. But, I realized now, Paris had also left a mark on Aveyron, in the sprawling new holiday homes built by returning sons and daugh-ters, in the friendships cemented over long hours of toil in Paris ca-fés, in the siblings whose lives were dictated by tradition—the oldest son who stayed behind to run the farm, the younger who went up to Paris to run the café. This land had inspired a million nostalgic daydreams of broad pastures, herds of running cows, grapevines that climbed the hillside under the nourishing glare of sun.

It's surprising how hungry you can get careening around the countryside. By one o'clock I was starving, and I was pretty sure it wasn't just out of relief that I was still alive. Didier stopped the car and announced, *"On va déjeuner aux Bessades, chez Cathy!"* Seconds later we were walking through a graveled yard and into an ancient farmhouse, sitting down around the long wooden table that filled the room.

Cathy and her husband, Jean-Louis, ran a table d'hôte, a kind of small restaurant operated from their family home that, I had the feeling, they tended more as a hobby than out of actual necessity. Eating here was like dining in a farmwife's kitchen of half a century ago, with strangers and friends sitting on benches, the fireplace smoking, and a litter of kittens sleeping in a basket near the hearth. Cathy had inherited the business from her mother, who took over from her mother before her, and meals here have remained gently unchanged for a couple of generations. We started with la grande soupe, a rich, porky broth bobbing with cabbage and chunks of bread, self-served from a lion-headed tureen. Next came an oval platter of ham and sausage, made from Cathy's own pigs, and then a flurry of her farçous, in this case savory, parsley-flecked fritters, eaten with spoonfuls of homemade red currant jam. A roast chicken followed, and then cheese: a wedge of moist, speckled Roquefort and one of fromage de Laguiole, golden and sharp. Except for the cheese and the sun-warmed wine we'd drunk to wash it all down, which had come from the local cooperative, everything had been produced on the farm by Cathy and Jean-Louis.

The three *mecs* in workman's overalls were the first to get up from the table, heading outside to smoke before returning to their construction site. We'd see them later when we went to visit the eighteenth-century château that Cathy and Jean-Louis were re-building from a pile of rubble. Next to leave was a frail, white-haired couple who everyone had *vouvoyé*-ed throughout the whole meal. Jean-Louis got up to clear the table, and then there were just me and Calvin, Didier, and Cathy, the four of us sipping coffee from the same small glasses we'd used to drink water and wine.

This was my moment of opportunity, and I knew it. Calvin knew it, too. I could sense him looking for an opening in the conversation so he could help me chisel my way inside. Tomorrow we would gather here at Les Bessades for dinner, Calvin and me and a crowd of Aveyronnais, joined together to celebrate our American holiday Thanksgiving. The menu would be almost identical to the one we'd just eaten, with roast turkey replacing chicken, but I hoped to contribute to the meal—a spot of cranberry sauce, a dab of sweet potatoes, perhaps a pumpkin pie or two. I wanted to give the feast an authentic touch, and—I admit—I also wanted to show off in front of Calvin, to demonstrate how much my French had improved and how comfortable I felt here. I'd imported the ingredients from Paris just in case Cathy agreed. And that was why I was so nervous: I had to ask her if I could cook with her in her kitchen.

Now, let me clarify something. Cathy is not an intimidating person. She has a soft voice, two bright teenage kids, and blond hair cut into a long shag, reminiscent of the Monkees'. But she is also French, and I had noticed that the kitchen was sensitive territory in France. Though my French friends loved food, loved to eat, loved to cook and talk about cooking, their kitchens remained private, not, as in America, a place to gather and socialize but a room hidden behind closed doors. Cathy and I had met a few times, but we were more acquaintances than friends. Asking to join her in the kitchen was like asking if I could help her clean out her closet.

Cathy and Didier had been discussing the recent grape harvest, but now their conversation had quieted. Calvin caught my eye and raised his eyebrows.

"Is the . . . uh, turkey ready for tomorrow?" The last word stuck in my throat a little bit.

Cathy nodded. *"On l'a tuée ce matin!"* The turkey had been raised on their farm, of course, nurtured by Cathy since chickhood and killed by Jean-Louis. "It didn't get pardoned by Obama like the one I saw on television," she added, and everyone laughed.

I swallowed hard. "Can I do anything to help?"

"*C'est très gentil.* But just come at seven, with everyone else."

"No, I mean, I'd love to help you cook . . . *si c'est possible.*"

"Oh!" She let out a little laugh, as if she hoped I was joking.

"I could make a pumpkin pie—*une tarte à la citrouille.* Cranberry sauce . . . *sauce aux airelles.* Sweet potatoes . . . *patates douces.* I brought the ingredients with me."

"*J'sais pas . . .*" She bit her lip.

"Ann *est très douée dans la cuisine.*" Didier gazed into his glass, but his tone was persuasive.

My suggestion hung so heavily in the air I almost wished I could retract it. But as the silence grew, I realized how true it was. I wanted to be in the kitchen, to trade my American recipes for her French ones, to share not just the celebration of eating the feast but also the communal act of cooking it.

"*Laissez-moi réfléchir un peu, d'accord?*" Cathy said eventually. I understood her hesitation—she had her rhythm, after all, an intricate kitchen choreography perfected while preparing thousands of meals. But I couldn't deny that I was a little disappointed.

"She didn't say no," Calvin reminded me as we walked back to the car. "She said she'd think about it."

It was, we both knew, a polite, French way of saying no. Still, before we got into the car, we searched for a can of pumpkin that had shaken loose from its bag of groceries during one of our wild descents. Calvin eventually dislodged it from underneath the front seat. I slipped it into my purse, just in case I needed it the next day.

The turnoff is so discreet you would miss it if you didn't know it was there, a small, subtle sign indicating a narrow, tree-lined road. But the next day we did find it, venturing through the trees and up the hill, where we saw a low-slung, sharp-edged glass house floating on the horizon, an unexpected outcrop of modern architecture emerging like a *buron* from the grassy Aubrac mountainside. This was one of France's finest temples of gastronomy, the Michelin three-star restaurant of Michel et Sebastien Bras.

Calvin and I had eaten lunch there with Didier, Chantal, and Chantal's daughter, Anne, a few years ago on a bright, late-summer day. It was a near-perfect meal, not just because of the food, which had been exquisite, but also because of the restaurant's loving interpretation of place and culture and cuisine. Perhaps I was lightly tipsy on ambience and Champagne, but I thought I could read a story in some of the dishes. The gargouillou was like a warmweather idyll of bright colors, summer vegetables, herbs, and wildflowers; a childhood sweetheart salad, tender and playful, drizzled with a delicate, chicken-scented sauce that hovered close to the safety of Mama's hearth. In the slow-braised onion—cooked for seven hours—I saw the bitter, unyielding cold of an Aubrac winter, warmed by wood fires, and a protective robe of bread and truffle crumbs. The aligot told the history of a family, an unbroken line of generations surviving on the rough plain, passing down traditions from mother to son to daughter; in fact, our waiter told us, it was *"une recette de Mamie"*—Grandmother's recipe—and until recently Michel Bras's mother had made it herself.

It had been an unforgettable lunch, a love letter to Aveyron, and my memories of it—of the sun-scattered dining room, the smoothmoving wagon of a cheese cart, the parade of desserts marching past in a sweet blur—had stayed with me, would *always* stay with me, as one of my happiest, most heartfelt food souvenirs. But that was then, in the summer. Now it was November, and the restaurant was closed for the winter, its windows shuttered. Didier and Calvin dropped me off near the main entrance, and I scrambled down the hill to the back door. In the thin, late-autumn sunlight, the land appeared washed out, the fields dry and brown.

I had come to talk to Sébastien Bras, the son of Michel, who became his father's partner at the restaurant. He waited for me in his office, a tanned man dressed in jeans and a sweater, with the lean build of a runner. (Indeed he had just run the New York City Marathon, he told me.) Like most Aveyronnais I'd met—like most *French* people I'd met—he waxed lyrical about his region.

"It's a little crazy—here we are, lost in the middle of the Aubrac," he said. "But we are very attached to this territory, and when people dine here, we invite them to share our history."

That history is partly relayed through herbs—Bras's "palette of expression"—some collected from the wild, others cultivated by a local *maraîcher,* still others nurtured in the restaurant's garden. The gargouillou alone, a dish inspired by the summer countryside, gathers several handfuls of aromatic leaves, seeds, herbs, fruits, flowers, and nuts that change according to the season or to the chef's whim. Even the restaurant's logo is an herb, a delicate fernlike sprig of *cistre,* a type of wild fennel that grows only at high altitudes like the Aubrac plateau.

Aligot depicts another chapter of the region's history, a peasant dish originating squarely from the Aubrac. "Farther south in the region, like Millau, it doesn't even exist," Sébastien told me. The restaurant still makes it in the traditional way, using a family recipe. "Aligot is not our signature dish, but it is part of our *patrimoine*"— their heritage—he added.

At this moment I sensed movement by the door, and then a slight, tidy figure entered the room, as if drawn in by the word *patrimoine*. It was Michel Bras. I swallowed a gulp of air. One of France's most revered chefs was standing before me, and then

Sébastien was introducing me and inviting him to join us, and now he was sitting and listening to my awkward, accented French, waiting for me to ask him intelligent questions. My palms started to sweat. Michel Bras has been described as famously reserved, monkish, elusive, a purist. His father was a blacksmith, his mother was the chef at a family-run hotel restaurant in Laguiole. As a child he began to cook at her stove, bypassing the traditional French system of kitchen apprenticeships for a self-taught, scientific approach. He rarely leaves the Aubrac and has notoriously declined to open a restaurant in Paris, though he does have an offshoot in Hokkaido, "lost in the Japanese countryside."

"I am a native son," he told me. "This is a rustic region. When we ate, we were dying of hunger. But this region allows an opening of the spirit, it permits us to open the eyes in a different manner."

In the long silences that punctuated our conversation, I strove to connect the reticent, introverted man before me with the food I had eaten on that summer day, with the unfolding emotions of joy, whimsy, nostalgia, and resolve that I'd tasted on the plate. Perhaps, I decided, he was more comfortable expressing himself with food than with words.

Our discussion wound down, and I got up to leave. We stood for a few minutes making polite small talk. Sébastien asked me where I was staying, and I told them about Didier and Alain, about the dinner we had planned for the next evening.

"Do you know about our American holiday, Thanksgiving? We all get together—and eat!" I laughed a little self-consciously.

And Michel said quietly, "You know, that is really the true definition of gourmandise. Gathering around the table, with friends and family."

At that moment their next appointment arrived—a Japanese

camera crew filming a documentary—and in the ensuing flurry of activity I slipped away. But I thought about those words for the rest of the day and have considered them again and again ever since. There is no exact English equivalent for the word "gourmandise." Gluttony? Greed? Yes, but it is also the enjoyment of a good meal, the art of fine dining, and something more—the cultivation of an educated palate, perhaps. It's a quintessentially French term, developed most notably in a book of gastronomic essays, *The Physiology of Taste*, by Jean-Anthelme Brillat-Savarin, born in 1755, who was not a professional chef or writer but a magistrate in a provincial French town, an enthusiastic eater, a hobbyhorse philosopher who believed that the pleasure found at the table was one of the truest, strongest bonds of society.

At the root of *la gourmandise*—and the heart of Brillat-Savarin's book—lies another word: "taste." It is the development of this sense, he argued—the "act of judgment by which we give preference to things which are agreeable to our taste over those which are not"—that separates animals, who feed, from man, who eats. The link is not strong in English, but translate "taste" into French and you see it immediately—the nucleus of *goût* and its offspring "gourmandise."

The word *goût* comes from the Latin *gustus,* or taste. Curiously, the English word "taste" has a completely different Latin root: *tangere,* which means "touch." And yet in English we have our own derivative of *gustus*—the word "gusto"—that is, "zest." Appreciation. Appetite. Enjoyment. Enthusiasm. Perhaps, then, this etymology proves that Brillat-Savarin was right: The deepest essence of our humanness is the gusto—the taste—we bring with us to the table. And the joy we find there with each other—the gourmandise—is the true luxury of life.

* * *

The baby veal was only three days old. She stood on shaky legs, her floppy ears spread like bats' wings, her brown-and-white coat rumpled and downy. She was so sweet I wanted to kidnap her from the dairy farm and take her back to Paris. But Benoît, Didier's cousin and the owner of the farm, assured me that she would enjoy a long and happy life as a milk cow, unlike her male counterparts, who were slaughtered and sold as . . . well, veal. He had just started to tell me how he and his daughter had found the calf—by chance, in a field—when Didier's phone rang. He stepped out of the barn, away from the barking dogs and lowing cows, and returned a few minutes later. *"On y va!"* he called out, and Calvin and I followed him to the car. Soon we were zooming again through the countryside to yet another unspecified destination, which turned out to be Cathy's house.

"Voilà! Les Bessades!" Didier parked the car. "I'm going to take the dog for a walk. *Tu veux te promener, doudou?"* he asked Apache. The dog shot out of the car, Didier close behind.

I stared at the pair of them—one broad-shouldered and tall, the other short-legged and long, each head topped with a curly, gray-streaked mop—as they wandered down the road, pausing to investigate the edge of a field. "What's going on? Should we wait for them in the car?"

"I think"—Calvin turned around in the front seat—"you're supposed to go inside and start cooking."

Cathy's kitchen smelled exactly like every other kitchen in America did on this fourth Thursday in November, wafting with the cozy, toothsome scent of roasting turkey. We kissed each other hello, and she gave me an impromptu tour, whisking the lid off a cavernous stockpot to show me her pumpkin soup, opening the fridge to reveal a vat of batter for the farçous, pulling down the oven door to rotate the gently sizzling turkey. In contrast with the rustic dining room, the kitchen gleamed with modern stainless-steel counters, fluorescent lights, and a small professional dishwasher.

I retrieved my groceries from the car and displayed them a little shyly, showing her the sack of fresh cranberries, the cans of pumpkin, the heavy bag of sweet potatoes, hoping she wouldn't ask just how much I'd spent at La Grande Épicerie. I explained the recipes, circling verbosely around a few French cooking terms that I didn't know. Calvin was next door in the dining room, reading his book at the table and ready to translate, but in the end I didn't need his help.

I had brought along a cookbook, but it turns out that Thanksgiving recipes are pretty intuitive, for the experienced French cook anyway. Cathy had never tasted cranberry sauce, but she knew how to make a quick confiture, just as she knew how to puree the sweet potatoes—adding a dash of nutmeg—and whip up a custard for the pumpkin pie. She handed me the bumpy-shelled eggs laid by her own hens, and as I beat them together with milk, sugar, and spices, she made some pâte brisée right on the counter—no food processor for her—eyeballing the amounts of flour, butter, and water and rubbing them together with a practiced hand. She divided and rolled out the dough, pressed it into three tart tins, popped open a can of applesauce, and spread the contents on one of the shells. With quick confidence she peeled, cored, and sliced a pound of apples into slender, perfectly even slivers and fanned them into an elegant overlapping pattern. Meanwhile, I had barely managed to scrape the pumpkin out of its can.

We juggled for space in the oven, sweating lightly as we shifted the turkey from one scorching rack to another, maneuvering the uncooked pies above and below it. On the stove the cranberries popped, and steam from the puréed sweet potatoes fogged the windows. I thought about my parents, halfway across the world in California, my American friends in all the cities where I had lived, each preparing this meal, not an exact replica but sketched in the same broad strokes. I missed them, and I would continue to miss them for most of the Thanksgivings of my life. But there would be different meals together, feasts cooked to celebrate other holidays or the occasion of being with one another again.

By the time the pumpkin pies emerged from the oven—perfectly jiggly—the first guests had arrived. They sat in the dining room and sipped cloudy glasses of pastis as the room filled with more and more people and kids and dogs until it felt hot and sweaty and festive. I wondered how we'd all manage to eat dinner—standing up?—but the mystery was solved when Didier announced *"À table!"* and everyone headed through a door that I hadn't noticed before, into another, larger room lined with long tables set for twenty, or perhaps more.

Everyone was turning to watch us as we entered the room, and I smiled to hide my embarrassment, not understanding why. But then Calvin squeezed my hand and I saw it—an enormous banner spanning the back wall:

THANKSGIVING EN AVEYRON
WELCOME CALVIN AND ANN-MARIE

A huge image of Les Bessades dominated the banner's background, a cartoon turkey superimposed upon it; two smaller photos framed the text, one of the Capitol Building, the other of the Eiffel Tower—the United States and France. Our two homes, past and present.

I sat next to Sylvie, the wife of Jérôme, who owned a print shop and had made the banner, and Fred, a Belgian émigré. The chestnut-stuffed turkey was a triumph, moister and more tender than any newfangled brine-soaked, tented, high-heat/low-heat roasting could produce. Everyone agreed that the cranberry sauce was the perfect counterpoint to the meat, but I sensed less enthusiasm for the sweet potatoes. "My cows eat those," I thought I heard someone say, though I might have misheard him.

Next to me Sylvie and Fred were discussing the finer points of rabbit breeding. Me: "Do you raise them for *eating*?" Sylvie: "Well, yes"—and with her words, I felt a pang, sharp and piercing, for our life in France. We still had two years left in Paris, but already I felt the looming shadow of our departure, and already I missed France. I couldn't slow time down, but, I told myself, I could savor it, like the first spring strawberries eaten over the kitchen sink, or the gentle quiver of a soufflé au Roquefort as it traveled from oven to table, or the smear of sharp mustard daubed on a simple café croque-monsieur. I had fallen in love with the connection between food and history and place in France, and I would be a very poor Francophile indeed if I didn't *profité* from life's happiest moments and enjoy them one bite at a time.

Across the table Calvin was talking to Didier and Alain about his next assignment. "Maybe Washington, D.C. Maybe Beijing. *Qui sait?*" I heard him say. His career would continue to move us around the world in increments of two or three or four years, and our home would continue to be transient, the place in the world where we lived together. But after our year of being apart, the idea of a more permanent place had also taken root, a sunny spot we could dream about together from smog-choked Beijing or during blowhard bureaucrat dinner parties or the other unbeautiful moments of life. We had started looking for an apartment to buy in Paris, and though our budget limited us to a shoe box, we hoped to find a shoe box large enough for a table for two and, maybe one day, three.

The pumpkin pie was, I'm sorry to say, not a success. After a polite bite or two, the slices went ignored in favor of the apple tart. I feared I had made a mistake with the recipe—confused salt with sugar, for example—but it turns out I had underestimated the visceral French hatred of cinnamon. To me the pumpkin pie tasted cold and creamy, sweet and spicy, just like the pies of my childhood. I thought it was delicious, which proves that, even culinarily, some things can get lost in translation.

At some point the dessert plates were cleared, more wine was poured, and an accordion appeared in Cathy's hands. She played a few jaunty bars in invitation, and then people were moving the tables, opening up the floor, and joining hands in pairs to bound across the room. I watched them advance and retreat, circle and release, and I imagined, a little romantically, all the Aveyronnais before us who had danced these same steps after a good dinner. And I knew I would dream of this meal forever, just as I dreamed of the spicy punch of my dad's mapo tofu, or the doughy chew of a bowl of Beijing noodles, or the bright tang of cassis sorbet eaten in the brilliant light of a Paris summer evening—all the food memories dancing their own country jig, advancing and receding to make way for the next one.

Aligot

The key to aligot is tome fraîche, a semisoft fresh cheese that is, un-fortunately, not available in the United States. Purists would say that it's impossible to make aligot with any other cheese, but like Julia Child, I don't believe in dogmatism. In the recipe below, I have used mozzarella, which is another fresh cheese (albeit a salted one). But any fresh, uncured, preferably unsalted cheese or cheese curds would be a good substitute, the fresher the better. (Aged cheeses, however, should never be used.) It's not quite the same as *le véritable aligot,* but it would comfort a homesick Aveyronnais in a pinch.

Serves 4

2½ pounds nonstarchy potatoes, such as Bintje *or* Yukon
 Gold
¾ cup crème fraîche *or* sour cream
1 clove garlic
Salt and pepper to taste
14 ounces fresh mozzarella, cut into ¼-inch dice

Peel the potatoes and cut them into 1- to 1½-inch chunks. Place them in a large saucepan and just barely cover them with cold water. Bring to a boil and cook for 15 to 20 minutes, until a fork pierces them easily. Drain thoroughly and pass them through a food mill or ricer to obtain a fine puree. Try to keep the puree as hot as possible.

Return the potato puree to the saucepan. Stir in the crème fraîche and the whole garlic clove. Season with salt and pepper (remember, the mozzarella is salted as well).

Place the saucepan over low heat and stir the cheese into the pu-ree. With a large wooden spoon, beat the mixture for at least 15 minutes, making a figure-eight pattern within the saucepan. The aligot is ready when it begins to pull away from the sides of the pan. Remove the clove of garlic. Lift the spoon. If the mixture flows in ribbonlike strands, serve it immediately, piping hot, preferably with a rare steak.

Epilogue

Rue de Loo

It was January, the darkest period of a Parisian winter, and our apartment search felt as cold as the weather. As we trooped up endless flights of stairs to converted *chambres de bonne*, the gloom seemed to send us back in time, to the days when maids inhabited the attics, without heat or running water. One apartment had a spectacular view of Montmartre rooftops and a bedroom in a crawl space, accessible only by a pull-down ladder. Another had slanted wood-beamed ceilings, creaking floors, and an air so desolate I felt ghosts swirling above our heads. Several places had never seen direct sunshine, though the agents tried to convince us that "lots of light reflected off the buildings opposite."

At first Calvin called the real-estate agents—mainly because his French was better—but it soon became clear that apartment hunting was a full-time job, not something to be squeezed in during your lunch break. "I don't have any other time," he said. I believed him, but I also felt our months in Paris dwindling—we had about a year and a half left. And so I found myself doing something unexpected: I volunteered to take over the project.

On my first phone call, I responded to an apartment advertised as *"vente en viager."*

"Do you know what that means?" the agent asked me. It was, he informed me, a special agreement that meant the elderly seller could spend the rest of her days in the flat in exchange for a lowered price.

"How old is she?" I asked.

"Sixty-five. But you never know what might happen!"

Non, merci.

My second call I got flustered and *tutoyé*-ed the agent, who frostily informed me that the apartment had already sold.

On my third call, I managed to set up an appointment. I felt triumphant until a few hours later when I saw the place. It had sloping floors and cracks running down the outer walls. It appeared to tremble when the wind gusted.

January turned into February, which turned into March. I thought I knew Paris before I started hunting, but now I *really* knew Paris—the soft edges where trendy neighborhoods met the up-and-coming, the packed métro lines that passed nowhere near the city's historic center, the distinguished but dull *quartiers* that emptied during the school holidays. I became an expert at deciphering real-estate code: *"à rafraîchir"* (to refresh) hinted that the place hadn't been touched since 1959, *"plein de charme"* (full of charm) indicated a toilet shared with all the other apartments on the floor, *"travaux à faire"* (work to do) meant avoid at all costs.

One sunny day in April, I called about a new listing. "It's bathed in light," the agent told me. "Magnificent parquet, crown moldings, two bedrooms, an elevator . . ." It sounded lovely, but then again they all sounded lovely until you saw them. I agreed to meet her at four o'clock and scribbled down the address. "Rue de l'Université," she said.

I gripped the phone a little tighter. "Rue de l'Université?"

"Oui. Vous la connaissez?"

Did I know it? I almost laughed. How many times had I walked down rue de l'Université, pausing in front of number 81—Paul and Julia Child's former flat—which they had dubbed "rue de Loo"?

"Oui, bien sûr," I assured her. "I'll see you there."

In the three years I'd lived in Paris, Julia had never been far from my thoughts. I looked for her in all the usual places—outside her old apartment, her haunts like the cookware shop E. Dehillerin, or the Les Halles bistro Au Pied de Cochon (I felt sure the latter two must have been more honest and appealing in her time). Lesser-known spots, too, like the Hôtel de Talleyrand, home of the Marshall Plan and postwar diplomatic cocktail soirees, or the place de la Concorde, where our husbands worked at the embassy, albeit separated by sixty years. Now there was an apartment for sale on her street? It seemed too good to be true. Or maybe it was fate.

Outside the apartment the hallway was dim, but when the double doors opened, the light dazzled me. I blinked and saw a salon flooded with sunshine, a small kitchen adorned in lime green tiles, two modest bedrooms facing a flowered courtyard. The apartment was tiny, with yellowed walls that hadn't seen a lick of paint in thirty years, but the light and tall windows made it feel spacious and airy. I could picture myself making a morning cup of tea in the kitchen, sunlight spilling across the counters.

"Do you like it?" the agent asked, and I tried to frown.

"I'll have to show my husband." I strove to inject a note of doubt into my voice.

"How about tomorrow?" she said. "I already have a lot of interest."

"Are you sure this is the one?" Calvin asked me. "Even though it only has one bathroom?"

"And the kitchen is this terrible color . . . the electricity needs rewiring. And it's smaller than we wanted." Later that evening I had started to have doubts.

But the next day I watched Calvin's face as he walked through the rooms. Perhaps it was just the reflection of afternoon sunshine, but he seemed to glow with appreciation. We both struggled to maintain our poker faces until back on the street, when the words burst from him. "You're right. It's the one. You found it."

"Are you sure? The kitchen . . . ?"

"All it needs is a little love."

We stood on the street corner smiling at each other. I started to say something about how nervous I was about spending our entire life savings, but when I glanced at Calvin again, I stopped. Because I felt sure that his expression reflected my own—and what I saw there was peace.

Five minutes later we called the agent to make our offer. And after a few months—and a lot of administrative angst—we gathered in the hushed conference room of a *notaire*'s office and signed the deed.

"Bienvenue à Paris," the agent said as the ink dried on the contracts. *"Bienvenue chez vous."*

One of the first things I bought for our new apartment was the photo. It was a picture of Julia Child in *her* Paris kitchen, and I wanted to hang it in my own. When we moved into our new home, on a cloudy June afternoon—almost a year after we had purchased it—I immediately hung it on the kitchen wall.

Two years had passed since Calvin's return from Baghdad. In the blink of an eye—a gold-tipped, market-stall-striped, gleaming-cobblestoned blink—it was time for us to move on and discover another city, in this case Washington, D.C. A day earlier the movers had swept through our rambling apartment on boulevard Raspail, leaving the rooms empty and scuffed and so vulnerable. I could scarcely bear to say good-bye to the place that had seen me through some of the happiest and hardest moments of my life. But I grasped Calvin's hand, and he helped me into a taxi and into rue de Loo, into our next adventure.

And yet Paris. It captured me still, with its weekly open markets, and Frenchwomen with voices like songbirds, and Frenchmen adorned in pastel sweaters thrown across their shoulders. There was no experience, I thought, quite as wonderful as being an American in Paris. But part of the romance was the heartache. Vacations ended, visas expired, and, in the end, most of us were obligated to return home. As I unpacked a stack of blue-and-white flea market dishes in our new kitchen, I felt a rush of relief and gratitude that we had found this tiny haven, a place for us to nurture and love and dream about during life's difficult moments.

In 1952, Paul Child's assignment at the American embassy in France ended, and he and Julia never again lived permanently in Paris. (Though they kept a small stone house in Provence, they used it only for vacations.) If I were being honest with myself, I had to admit that I, too, would probably never again live permanently in Paris—a hard truth that made my heart seize up.

But thinking of Julia reminded me of the important things in life: the essential humanness of sharing good food with the people you love, even when you may be in a place you don't love very much. Somehow everything tastes better eaten with your favorite dining companion. I looked up at Julia in her kitchen on rue de Loo. I hoped she would keep an eye on things until I returned.

FIN

Index

Académie Universelle du Cassoulet, 149

Adams, Abigail, 232–34

Adams, John, 209, 232–34

Aigle, L', 172

aligot, 231–59
    recipe, 258–59

alpagistes, 182, 184, 193–94, 197

Alsace, 161, 171–72
    choucroute from, 157–79

Alsatian dialect, 164–65, 174–75, 176, 177

American Foreign Service Association, 48

American Library in Paris, 78–82, 130, 235

andouille, 38

andouillette, 29–53

andouillette à la sauce Maury (recipe), 52–53

AOC (*appellation d'origine contrôlée*), 195, 197, 240

Appetite for Life (Fitch), 217

Association Amicale des Amateurs d'Andouillette Authentique (AAAAA), 36–37, 41–42, 43

Association de Défense des Bouchons, 89

Association la Boule Dorée, 114

Au Boeuf Couronné, 2

Aubrac, 249–51

Au Jardin Gourmand, 44

Au Pied de Cochon, 263

Auvergnate, L', 245

Au Vieux Quimper, 60

Aux Fins Gourmets, 134–35, 151

Aveyron, 15, 19, 20, 23, 237–38, 240, 242–45, 247, 249, 250
    aligot from, 231–59

Aveyronnais, L', 19

bacon, salade lyonnaise, 97–98

Baeckeoffe, 165

basil, 111
    soupe au pistou, 125–27

bavette aux échalotes (recipe), 26–27

beans:
    cassoulet de Castelnaudary, 153–55
    soupe au pistou, 125–27

Beaufort cheese, 185, 192–97
    d'Alpage, 196–97
    d'Été, 196

Beaune, 204, 206–7, 210, 225

Beck, Simone, 219

beef, 214
    boeuf à la bourguignonne, 227–30

Belvédere restaurant, 182, 184

Benedictine monks, 205
Benoît, Bruno, 93–94
Bernet, William, 12, 13–15, 26
Bertholle, Louisette, 219
Bessades, Les, 246, 253, 255
blé noir, 69, 70
"Blue House, The" (Tranströmer), 221
Blum, Léon, 105–6
boeuf à la bourguignonne (recipe), 227–30
boeuf bourguignon, 203–30
Bonnieux, 106, 111, 113, 114, 118
Boucheries Nivernaises, 13
bouchons, 83–84, 86, 87–88, 90–91, 92, 93
Bouchot, Frédéric, 213–14
Bourgogne, Philippe le Hardi, duc de, 206, 225
Bras, Michel, 249–51
Bras, Sébastien, 250–51
Brasserie Lipp, 20
Breizh Café, 55
Bretagne, Anne, Duchess of, 70
Brillat-Savarin, Jean-Anthelme, vii, 195, 252
Brittany, 58, 70, 72
    crêpes from, 55–74
buckwheat crêpes, *see* galettes
buckwheat flour, galettes de blé noir, 72–74
buckwheat tea, 57–58
Burgundy, 204–6, 212, 223–24
    boeuf bourguignon from, 203–30
burons, 240–41, 249
Bussieres, Jean de, 225
Butte Aveyronnaise, La, 245

cabbage, 161–63
    choucroute sans garniture, 178–79
Café de Flore, 20
Café des Fédérations (La Fédé), 89, 90
cafés, 11–12, 19–20, 21, 245
canuts, 85, 92–94
caramel au beurre salé, 60, 61, 68–69
Carcassonne, 14, 137, 148–50
    cassoulet from, 129–52
carrots, boeuf à la bourguignonne, 227–30
casse-croûte, 20–21
cassole, 139, 146, 147, 150
cassoulet, 129–55
cassoulet de Castelnaudary (recipe), 153–55
Castelnaudary, 137, 138, 144–46, 147–48, 150
    cassoulet from, 129–55
Cathars, 148–49
Catherine de Medicis, queen of France, 143–44
cattle, 213–14
Charbon, Le, 19
Charbonnier, Le, 245
Charcuterie Muller, 164
Charles VI, king of France, 195
Charolais, 213
Charolles, 213
Château du Clos de Vougeot, 222–24, 225, 227
Château Saint-Martin, 149
cheese, 239
    aligot, 258–59
    andouillette à la sauce Maury, 52–53

Beaufort, *see* Beaufort cheese
fondue, *see* fondue
fondue à la maison, 202
from Laguiole, 241, 246
Roquefort, 195
Savoyard, 194
soupe au pistou, 125–27
vachelin, 194
cheese production, 193–95
Chemin de Saint-Jacques, 241–43
Chez Georges, 85
Chez Hugon, 91
Child, Julia, vii, 3–4, 5, 37, 203, 204,
212, 214–15, 217, 218–19, 220,
239, 262–63, 264, 265
Child, Paul, 3, 214, 217, 219, 220,
262, 265
China, 1, 29, 107, 217–18
choucroute, 157–79
choucroute sans garniture (recipe),
178–79
Cistercian monks, 205, 222
Cîteaux, 205
Code du Travail, 82
Colombier, Le, 138–39
Columbus, Christopher, 144
Compagnons de la Gastronomie
Porcine, 43
Confrérie des Chevaliers du
Tastevin, 223–24
Confrérie des Francs-Machôns, 84,
85, 89, 91
congés payés, 105
Coopérative Fromagère Jeune
Montagne, 241
Cordon Bleu, 3, 219
Cosway, Maria, 209, 211

Cosway, Richard, 209
Côte d'Or, 204–5, 208, 210, 213–14,
223
Coupole, La, 20
Courtine, Robert (La Reyniere), 42
cranberry beans, soupe au pistou,
125–27
crème fraîche, aligot, 258–59
crêperies, 55, 59, 60, 63, 66, 68, 70
crêpes, 55–74
buckwheat, *see* galettes
Curnonsky, 87

dandelion leaves, 87–88
Dell, Martin, 162
Deux Magots, Les, 20
DeVoto, Avis, 219, 220
"Dialogue Between My Head and
My Heart" (Jefferson), 209–10
Domaine Parent, 211
Domaine Seguin-Manuel, 207
Dossier, Le: Casse-croûte, 94
duck, cassoulet de castelnaudary,
153–55
Dunod, Philippe, 147

Eclogues (Virgil), 117
E. Dehillerin, 263
eggs, salade lyonnaise, 97–98
épiceries, 105, 113, 132, 154, 160
Espalion, 244

Fables de la Fontaine, Les, 49
Fabrique Délices, 52
Fendant wine, 187
Ferme de Kerheü, 64–65
Ferme de Kerveguen, 69

Festin Occitan, Le (Montagné), 137

Finistère, 59–60, 67

Fitch, Noël Riley, 217

flammeküeche, 172

Floch'lay, Hervé, 62, 66–68, 72

fondue, 181–202

fondue à la maison (recipe), 202

formation civique, 159, 166–70

Franco-Prussian War (1870), 175

Franklin, Benjamin, 209

French Alps, 181–82

French Chef, The (Child), 204

French Ministry of Agriculture, 195

French Revolution, 206, 223

Fréti, Le, 192

Freud, Sigmund, 107

Fussner, Richard, 223–24

galettes, 56–57

galettes de blé noir (recipe), 72–74

garlic:
    cassoulet de Castelnaudary, 153–55
    salade lyonnaise, 97–98
    soupe au pistou, 125–27

garlic sausage, cassoulet de Castelnaudary, 153–55

Gaul, 86, 138

Gay, Pierre, 202

Gérard Joulie, 22–23

Germany, 175–76

Gesten, Louise, 61–62, 64, 69

Gnafron, 84, 90

gourmandise, 251–52

Grande Confrérie du Cassoulet de Castelnaudary, La, 145–46, 147, 149

Grande Épicerie, La, 132, 254

Great Depression, 224

green beans, soupe au pistou, 125–27

Gregory XI, Pope, 225

gros lait, 63, 66

Guillermou, Stéphane, 65–66

Guillermou, Valérie, 64–66

haricot beans, 144

Haussmann, Baron, 175

Haute-Savoie, 192
    fondue from, 181–202

Hemings, James, 209

Hemings, Sally, 209

Henri II, king of France, 143

Hitler, Adolf, 176

Hoelt, René, 162

Hôtel de Talleyrand, 263

Hundred Years' War, 144–45

Innocent III, Pope, 148–49

Institut National de l'Origine et de la Qualité, 195

Jefferson, Maria, 209

Jefferson, Martha, 208, 210

Jefferson, Thomas, 204, 208–11, 212, 223, 225

kig ha farz, 71

kirsch, 187

Krautergersheim, 162–64

Krishna Bhavan, 190–91

Lacoste, Alain, 138–39

Laguiole, 239–41, 246, 251

laïcité, 158, 159, 175

lait ribot, 63, 66
Languedoc, 137, 144, 145, 148
Languedoc-Roussillon, 137
lararium, 139
Lar Familiaris, 139–41, 152
Larousse Gastronomique (Montagné),
 137
Léa, Madame, 87–88
Lebois, Jacques, 45–46
leeks, boeuf à la bourguignonne,
 227–30
Le Floch, Sophie, 59, 62
Le Gall, Youenn, 69
Lemelle, Benoît, 41
Lemelle, Dominique, 41–42, 43–44
Lemelle andouillette factory, 41
Louis II, king of France, 40
Louis XIV, king of France, 40
Louis XVI, king of France, 208
Lugdunum, 86
Lyon, 83–89, 91–92
 salade lyonnaise from, 75–98
 silk production in, 85, 92–93

macaroni, soupe au pistou, 125–27
mâchon, 84, 89, 91–94
Maison du Charolais, 213–14
Male, Jean-Louis, 145–46, 147–48
Marian, Thibaut, 207
"Marseillaise, La," 175
Marseille, 107, 109, 118
Mastering the Art of French Cooking
 (Child, Bertholle, and Beck), 3,
 212, 219
Mathelin, Maxime, 195
Matignon Agreements (1936), 105
Maury, Patrick, 38–40, 42–43, 52

Mère Brazier, 87
Mères Lyonnaises, 86
Meyer, Jean-Luc, 163–64
Meyer Wagner, 163
Michel et Sébastien Bras, 238, 249
Miquel, Alain, 15, 16, 17–21, 23–25,
 189, 237–38, 243, 244, 251,
 256
Miquel, Didier, 15, 19, 20, 23, 24, 25,
 36, 64, 189, 237–38, 243–48,
 249, 251, 253, 255, 256
Mistral, Le, 15–16, 19, 21, 23–24,
 189, 237, 238
Monbeillard, Daniel, 192–93, 194
Montagné, Prosper, 137, 138, 150
mustard:
 andouillette à la sauce Maury, 52–
 53
 vinaigrette, 98
My Life in France (Child), vii, 214,
 217

Napoleon I, emperor of France, 12,
 165
New York Times, 204
Not, Jean-Pierre, 147

Office Français de l'Immigration et
 de l'Intégration, 157
onion:
 boeuf à la bourguignonne, 227–30
 choucroute sans garniture, 178–79

PACS, 169
Pagnol, Marcel, 109, 111
Parent, Anne, 210–11
Parent, Étienne, 210–11, 223

Paris, 1, 2–3, 8, 9–10, 11, 34–35, 47, 51, 79–80, 94, 101, 108, 111, 129, 171, 186, 198, 231, 235–36, 245, 261–65
  steak frites in, 7–27
Penates, 139–41, 147, 152
pesto, *see* pistou
Petit Bougnat, Le, 19
Petite France, La, 165
Petit Mont Blanc, 192, 193
Peyre de Fabrègues, Emmanuel, 84–86, 89, 91
Physiology of Taste, The (Brillat-Savarin), vii, 252
pistou, 116, 117, 119
  soupe au pistou, 125–27
Poilâne, Apollonia, 133
Poilâne, Lionel, 133
Poilâne, Pierre, 133
Poilâne bakery, 132–34
Popular Front, 105
pork:
  cassoulet de Castelnaudary, 153–55
  tripe sausage, *see* andouillette
potatoes:
  aligot, 258–59
  Bintje, 239
  soupe au pistou, 125–27
Poterie Not Frères, 146
Procope, Le, 19
Procopio dei Coltelli, Francesco, 19
Proton, Christian, 84–85, 86, 89, 91
Provence, 103–4, 106, 109, 111, 113, 118, 120, 122, 125
  soup au pistou from, 99–127

Quimper, 59–60, 62–63, 67, 69
Quintal d'Alsace, 162

Rabatel, Philippe, 87–88
raclette, 194
Renaissance, 138
rentrée, 129
Rivoiron, Yves, 89–90
Rodriguez, Jean-Claude, 149–50
Roman Empire, 86, 118
Roquefort cheese, 195
Rosheim, 164
Roth, Lydia, 172

Sainte-Foy, 242
salade composée, 82
salade lyonnaise, 75–98
  recipe, 97–98
Santiago de Compostela, 243
sarrasin, 69–71
sauerkraut, choucroute sans garniture, 178–79
Savoie, fondue from, 181–202
Savoring the Past (Wheaton), 144
Savoyard cheese, 194
Severo, Le, 12, 13, 26
shallots:
  andouillette à la sauce Maury, 52–53
  bavette aux échalotes, 26–27
silk production, 85, 92–93
Simenon, Georges, 17
Société des Amis de Lyon et de Guignol, 91
soufflé, 215–16
soupe au pistou, 99–127
  recipe, 125–27

sour cream, aligot, 258–59
steak, bavette aux échalotes, 26–27
steak frites, 7–27
    see also bavette aux échalotes
Stein, Gertrude, 78
Strasbourg, 165–66, 177
Syndicat de Défense du Beaufort,
    195–97

tartiflette, 194
tea, buckwheat, 57–58
tickets-restaurants, 82
toast, 131–32
tomatoes, soupe au pistou, 125–27
tome fraîche, 240
Toulouse, 136–37, 138, 139, 144, 150
    cassoulet from, 129–52
Trachet, Gérard, 91–93
Tranströmer, Tomas, 221
Trenet, Charles, 1, 106
tripe, 38–39, 41, 44, 85
tripe sausage, *see* andouillette

Troyes, 38, 40, 41, 43, 44, 86
    andouillette in, 29–53
Truchtersheim, 172–73
Tschumi, Bernard, 22

UNESCO World Heritage, 242

vachelin cheese, 194
Villette, La, 21–22
vinaigrette, salade lyonnaise, 97–98
Voûte Chez Léa, La, 87

Walch, Olivier, 223, 225, 227
Wheaton, Barbara Ketcham, 144
white beans, soupe au pistou, 125–27
wine, 205–8, 210–11
wine production, 205, 207–8, 223
Winstub, 171, 173
World War, I, 86, 175
World War II, 146, 175–76, 217

zucchini, soupe au pistou, 125–27